The Power
to *Thrive!*

Building the Foundations of a
THRIVING Career & Life

Randy Kay

The Power to Thrive: Building the Foundations of a Thriving Career & Life
by Randy Kay
Copyright © 2017 by Randy Kay

Published in the United States of America

ISBN-10: 0985458992
ISBN-13: 9780985458997
LCCN: 2017915887

Previously Titled *PACESETTERS: Start Moving Yourself in the Direction Other Want to Follow*

Book cover design and cover layout: Beverly Haney

Editor: Rob Bignell

Interior format and design chief: Ellie Searl, Publishista®

Research firm: TenorCorp @ http://www.tenorcorp.com

Technical advisor: Ryan Kay

www.pacesetters.training

UpWord Media
7894 Estrella De Mar, Suite 3C
Carlsbad, CA 92009

To all the PACEsetters in the world—you help others thrive as well!!

CONTENTS

CONTENTS

Contents

CONTENTS

CONTENTS

THE POWER TO THRIVE represents a multidisciplinary study including decades of research into the mindset and practices of people who thrive. The formula for thriving in your career and life has been discovered and detailed in this book, along with the corresponding skills required to thrive.

The human development firm, PACEsetters, has also developed a transformational program that teaches individuals and organizations how to thrive in their career and life. This includes a corresponding course, workbooks, and a *self-assessment which allows participants to determine whether they are currently surviving, striving, or thriving.*

If you would like to order any of these complementary materials in addition to this book, please visit our website at www.pacesetters.training to order your copies. You may also schedule an e-learning course, webcast training, or onsite training course for your organization through this site. Or, you can call us at 760-814-2988.

By reading this transformational book, you are embarking on a journey to thrive in all aspects of your life. Continue the journey with us as together we venture toward your best life.

The following books are the correlative assessments and workbook materials available to you:

SELF-SCORING THRIVING INDICTORS TEST

PACESETTERS
THE POWER TO THRIVE
WORKBOOKS

Workbook 1 – PLAN WITH PURPOSE
Workbook 2 – GROW A THRIVING ATTITUDE
Workbook 3 – LEARN TO CONNECT WITH PEOPLE
Workbook 4 – FREE THE ENERGY TO THRIVE

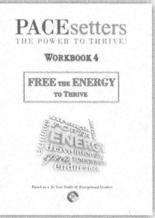

INTRODUCTION

THE HEALTHY LIFE GROWS AND regrows. Instead of viewing our best in the elusive future, or in the past, we would do well to instead focus on improvement. Our best is good. Getting better is best. With each new experience we gain insight. The healthy individual continuously develops. Getting better means that we can do more, be more, and achieve something greater than before. We can pursue our personal best, however, the journey in going after it will be far richer if done with a perspective of opportunity. If we ever get to the point where we think that we have arrived at our best, we stop achieving.

Even great performers who achieve gold medals or establish thriving entities never can finish their pursuits. Great achievers always strive for the next big impact. When they do fail, they always fail forward, by learning and gaining from their mistakes, and believing that their best awaits. They celebrate their accomplishments without being mired in the past, with honed purpose, and a keen focus on the goal. They live in the present, cherry pick the past, and look toward the future from a 10,000-foot level. They analyze systems instead of parts to develop solutions in place of simply trying to fix the minutia. PACEsetters consistently learn, continuously improve, and dream big.

They also fail. Some of the most prolific achievers fail big time. They fail in business; they fail with people, and some of them even end-up losing everything. I've known great achievers who lost everything but their faith and their hope. Bankrupted and alone, these achievers found their mojo, because their drivers were intrinsic and not extrinsic. Something deep inside spoke the new. And through perseverance, each one of these found something better.

Failure is in our future, it's inevitable—so you need to stop worrying about it. Investing all of our efforts to try to eliminate or minimize failure will not contribute one ounce to your success. That's because success changes with different expectations, and the possibility for failure accompanies each one. So now, where you're at, you first need to dispel the myth that success should be your target.

Most of the time, we base success on what it can give us, whether that's status, material things, or a lifestyle. When external influences serve as our motivation to succeed, we can be left feeling empty. When our motivating force comes from within ourselves, intrinsically we feel more secure, more capable. So focusing on what imbues within us joy, confidence, and hope will help us get to the place where we want to be now—not just in the future.

You need to remain center-focused in the present so that you're not continually seeking after something that may never come to pass. Once you get there, you need to stop worrying about what you can't do and start establishing confidence in what you are now, in this moment, prepared and able to do. Doubting yourself is a useless feeling that prevents you from taking action. Thinking about what's possible instills in you a positive self-image that, of course, you will make mistakes, but you will not allow the downside of trying something to keep you from taking action right now.

Success is a very subjective and variable goal. Working toward what is possible and within your control is a very attainable and strengthening exercise—that should be your goal. The outcome of getting better and reaching new heights of performance probably will lead to your also obtaining some of your external desires.

So how do you build a better you with the intention of making something happen? Forget what others expect of you and just do what you feel driven to do. Many of the expectations we perceive are simply made-up expectations of what we believe others expect of us. So use your own strengths and values to make decisions without the constraints of wondering how it will turn out. Your success is not what others think or how it looks. It's what you believe.

This approach will create within you a greater perspective on what's possible. Some call this wisdom. Wisdom is understanding forged through trials. It is one of the most important ingredients of purposeful achievement. Wisdom says, "I am getting better, stronger, and more capable because of what I've learned through even the darkest of times." It never quits. It stays appreciative of the past, focused on the present, and prepared for the future. No one can achieve anything of merit without first gaining wisdom—and finding purpose.

Purpose fuels our engine for moving forward. That blood-fueling passion for someone or something compels us to give without reservation. It's the energy to find a solution. It stokes the fire of invention or the desperate need to improve another's life. Without purpose, we succumb to the competing demands of this world. The person who lives out their purpose thrives with vigor to do that which is greater than before. Purpose births within us the reason to excel—and it also leads to an attitude of renewal.

If we can't renew ourselves daily, we might as well stay in bed. People who renew themselves practice their faith as overcomers. They do so with gratitude and a welcoming approach to challenges and opportunities. We can only renew our mind by letting go of the past. Starting fresh means seeing the unseen, inventing it, reframing problems in order to jumpstart our forward progress. We invent something new each time we consider the possible over the probable. It starts with a dream and works backwards from there. A renewed mind remains grateful for opportunities and wonders what lies ahead. It sets the pace to new frontiers.

These are some of the ideas with which my team and I at TenorCorp designed the "PACE Formula" for achievement with satisfaction, merit, and social benefit. PACE is an acronym for moving forward with: **P**urpose, **A**ttitude, **C**onnection, and **E**nergy. These cornerstones stand as the four pillars of peerless achievement with purpose and aplomb!

Achieving something grand begins with answering the "billion dollar" question as to our purpose, based on some techniques I'll explain later. It starts much farther than the conventional idea for simply producing a "to-do list." We used the acronym P.L.A.N. to explain how to live out your purpose with intention and that "wow factor" that keeps us all motivated. It stands for: **P**lan, **L**earn, **A**nalyze, and **N**eed-Satisfy. Living out our purpose intentionally doesn't always have to produce exacting plans. But a purpose must be enacted with a plan that answers the questions of the who/what/why/when and how to make it happen. A purpose provides direction and begins with defining the plan for making concept a reality, and the motivating factors to bring it to fruition. A fulfilled purpose must answer key questions:

- What have we learned, and what can we do differently to achieve significance?

- How can we apply what we've learned to make things better?

- How can we analyze our plan to objectively determine what's most effective in achieving our purpose?

- What is the need-satisfaction that tells us when our purpose is complete?

The second foundation for setting the PACE toward achievement is Attitude. Our attitude is entirely dependent on our commitment to G.R.O.W. with **G**ratitude, **R**enewal, **O**vercoming, and **W**isdom.

Developing gratitude is much easier said than done—an attitude of gratitude takes a series of psychological triggers to instill a consistent (rather than occasional) attitude of gratitude. This necessitates a renewal of our mind, not just a reworking of our thoughts.

Renewal begins by reframing the past and continues with an ever-present inner spark that keeps us going at full speed, through proven techniques I explain in this book. A healthy attitude triumphs despite the inevitable trials of life. Which means that we must perfect the art of overcoming. If we can't overcome our challenges, we will succumb to them, and that's not an option for PACEsetters. Overcoming our trials requires that we face opportunity and challenge with equal thankfulness. Through the hard knocks of life, wisdom is developed. And once wisdom has arrived, so do we.

Communication lies at the center of our ability to overcome roadblocks in reaching new heights of connection. If we communicate effectively, the world eagerly accepts us. If not, we can turn into an afterthought, or worse. Healthy connections happen when we follow the L.E.A.R.N. model: **L**isten, **E**mpathize, **A**dapt, **R**elate, and **N**egotiate. Despite countless courses on how to listen, very few really listen well. Listening occurs with an others' focus, which runs counter-intuitively against the typical egocentric way of thinking.

We can genuinely start understanding others by empathizing with them. Without the ability to step into another person's "skin," we view people as separate—we cannot truly connect. By adapting our behaviors to what works best in a relationship, we bridge that divide to establish connection. We can then relate to another more effectively. Then we enter into the most achievement-based form of connection that creates a harmonious relationship. These graduated degrees of connection are the essentials for effective relationship.

When true connectedness occurs, a fire is lit that causes joy—but we must continually feed the fire. To stay motivated and engaged, the final and most vitalizing factor in the PACE formula is Energy. Life exists with energy, and without it, life withers. This goes for people as well as purpose. Knowing how to maintain that energy sets us free to achieve our goals. The final step of PACE explains how we can be F.R.E.E. through: **F**aith, **R**est, **E**xercise, and **E**ating right. A deficiency in any one of these areas saps the life out of our ability to achieve something of significance. Faith gives us hope. Rest gives us direction (but the productive form of rest also allows us to achieve more by doing less). Exercise gives us vigor. And Eating gives us life.

Through some extensive research at my strategic development firm, TenorCorp, we determined that the most satisfied achievers who perform with the utmost integrity in advancing themselves and others practice the skills and foundations revealed in the PACE formula. The PACE foundations are absolutely paramount to a thriving life. We called these high achievers with a purpose, the right attitude, and stellar character, *PACEsetters*. These are the people who live lives of significance. Many are the people we admire. My goal in writing the book *PACEsetters* is to help you realize your purpose as a PACEsetter, so that you can be that person others (and you) admire. I believe our best always lies before us. May this book provide you with the map to something greater than you've ever experienced before!

CHAPTER 1: THE PACE FORMULA

I HAD JUST MINUTES AT the airport to discover Joni's amazing secret. A long day at Baylor Hospital in Dallas left us both tired, but especially Joni, who as a quadriplegic often struggled to breathe with only about 50% of her lung capacity. She'd been visiting physically challenged patients at the hospital, praying, for example, with a seven-year-old girl who had meningitis. *God, I hope Joni doesn't come down with the disease, I thought—she can't afford to lose any more of her health—it would probably kill her.* But here Joni sat in her wheelchair, waiting for her flight to Los Angeles, as cheerful as ever.

For those that don't know, Joni Eareckson Tada has written dozens of bestselling books, paints award-winning artwork with her mouth, leads disability camps for thousands all over the country, supplies tens of thousands of free wheelchairs internationally to those who cannot afford them, and has spoken to packed out stadiums and other venues all over the world—all with a positive, can-do attitude despite unfathomable hardships.

She's done this and more without the benefit of her limbs while battling breast cancer, consistent pain, skin and pressure sores, neurological damage, muscle spasms, poor blood circulation, respiratory disease, coronary complications, and bladder dysfunction.

She is one of the most accomplished, and at the time of this writing, the longest surviving quadriplegic on record at 63 (she was paralyzed at 17 because of a diving accident in a lake).

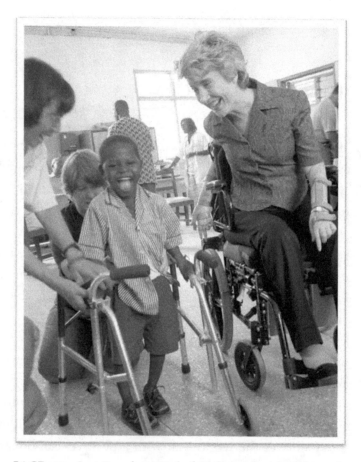

PACEsetter Joni Eareckson Tada (right) supplies disability aid to thousands around the world, as she is doing for this delighted boy who can now walk.

Joni is an encourager and contributor to suffering people throughout the world, and I wanted to know her secret: What makes Joni so invincible and extraordinarily effective against all odds? Her faith in God, she said, and something else, something very powerful! I wanted to be able to replicate this powerful success formula so that others could thrive as well or better.

"We will now be boarding flight 1782 to Los Angeles," came the announcement near our gate. We continued to talk, and in the process, I discovered some of the answers as to why Joni is what I now call, a *PACEsetter*. A PACEsetter doesn't wait for something to happen. She moves forward with purpose and unyielding determination to not only succeed but to help others win as well. Joni sets the pace for achievement wherever she travels, in whatever she does, because she lives with purpose, maintains a positive and grateful attitude, communicates with harmonious grace to all she knows, and exhibits an energy that most able bodied persons would be unable to sustain.

Sometimes a PACEsetter sets the pace at the beginning of an event in order to help another person succeed, just as Joni sets the pace for people with disabilities to overcome their own challenges. Joni is what we call a servant leader, in that she leads with a perspective of helping others.

My conversation with the guileless Joni motivated me to learn more. It began my career-long project of helping others replicate the formula for thriving in life. A thriving life doesn't have to be all about hard work, driving ambition, and exacting plans. Being a PACEsetter is about purpose, character and significance. PACEsetters thrive with an attitude of gratitude and a view toward the possibility in every situation. They communicate with people at the highest level of connection. And they plug into a source of energy that keeps them perpetually motivated while driving forward.

What keeps them moving forward is *not*, surprisingly, the drive toward success. They understand that success is a moving target, often evaluated by others, and therefore outside of the bounds within their control. Besides, PACEsetters that we studied do not seek the adulation of others—they are amazingly humble. They are way past trying to seek the approval of people and instead focus on their own development and in satisfying the needs of others as their primary focus. They're not entirely altruistic, but they have found a way to sublimate their ego toward more lofty goals that are mostly within their sphere of control.

As I finished my conversation with Joni, one thing became very apparent. She wasn't just about herself. Joni was primarily about others. Her assistant wheeled Joni to board the plane, and I remember looking at her smile, thinking how she lived in two worlds—the broken world of her body—and the transcendent world of fulfilling her magnificent purpose. She lived, I deduced, mostly in the world of her purpose. And as her paralyzed body could only look forward, she viewed life in a perpetual state of "What's next?" Joni has achieved incredible wonders and none higher than the next one.

Results of Our Research about PACEsetters

Here's what we discovered after "tons" of research with people like Joni: By definition, PACEsetters are high achievers but not necessarily on the world's stage (although some PACEsetters are famous). PACEsetters make a *big impact* for themselves and those they can affect. They can be found as leaders of colossal organizations as well as single contributors making a difference. They *thrive* in the most important areas of their life despite challenges. Their relationships are typically strong, however, when these relationships are challenged, they possess the tools to correct any imbalances. And they *help others* achieve their own purpose.

In short, PACEsetters are high achievers, satisfied with life, and they help others (see Figure 1.1).

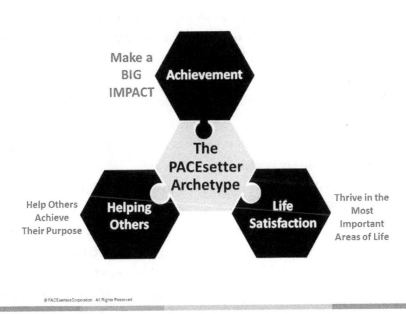

(Figure 1.1 - The PACEsetter Archetype)

The most significant contributors in our society—those we admire for who they are and what they do—display a surprisingly consistent modus operandi. PACEsetters like Joni are leaders when appropriate, and followers, too—when needed. That's different from the classic definition of leadership, which states that leaders are always ahead of the pack. PACEsetters display some of the typical characteristics of leaders, but they know when to step back and let others take charge. In fact, that's their primary goal as a leader. They enable other PACEsetters. That takes empathy, wisdom and an overriding desire to see others succeed irrespective of personal pride—

and we typically admire these people. In the book, *THE ART OF WAR*, the best leaders are described as having teams who say, "We did it ourselves." This collective expression heralds effective teams that tend to also hold their leader in high regard.

We know what types of people are most admired because people we surveyed to uncover the formula for PACEsetters were asked *why* they admired someone. Most noted integrity as one the most important foundations, while some used analogous descriptors like "honest," "trustworthy," "strong character," "respectable," "steadfast," etc. When we further qualified respondent's definition of integrity, they referenced qualities that demonstrate sound moral and ethical principles. Honesty and trust were central hallmarks of integrity referenced by those surveyed.

As long as the respondents were assured that the PACEsetter behaved in honorable ways even when no one is watching—even in the most trivial of matters, they believed in that person's integrity; like something as trivial as someone replacing the toilet paper in a stall instead of leaving the roll empty for the next person, taking responsibility for missed deadlines instead of blaming others or circumstances, and not gossiping. People notice these little acts of integrity, even when the person doing them has no idea he or she is being watched.

Although an almost universally admired quality, integrity did not typically explain someone who was recognized as a *high achiever.* When respondents were asked to describe what qualities those they admired as high achievers displayed, they rarely noted the word, "integrity." Initially we thought that integrity was just assumed, but upon further investigation, that wasn't true. That's because people often identify high achievement as making a significant contribution irrespective of personal qualities. We think of high achievers as great inventors, executives, top performers, highly educated, master artists, and winners in a competition. They achieve their goals with a motivation to succeed, and typically they go beyond expectations on a consistent basis, without needing any direction to do so.

Defining the PACEsetter

In defining the PACEsetter through studying those we generally admire, and the characteristics and skills required to be like them, we established integrity and achievement as the two foundational requirements most frequently identified through our research. Another defining characteristic of PACEsetters was that they exhibit a high internal locus of control, which is directly reflected in their positive attitude; whereas underachievers with an external locus of control tend to be more negative about the world and their standing in it. Those with an internal locus of control believe that they are essentially responsible for the outcomes in their lives. They display the characteristic of self-reliance and believe that few external influences can prevent their achievement—only they can do that.

Research reveals that people with an internal locus of control tend to be more successful because they remain committed to a goal while earnestly believing that they will attain it. These are the people often referred to as steadfast and optimistic. On the flip side, those with an external locus of control believe that influences outside of themselves invariably affect their ability to achieve something of significance—a quality we tend *not* to admire. These are the people often accused of making excuses.

When completing our surveys, people were generally clear as to what high achievement looks like and the descriptors for achievers. However, when we asked people what qualities best described a high achiever *with* high integrity and a healthy attitude, they noted an entirely different set of conditions or requirements. They noted altruistic qualities like self-sacrifice, honesty and generosity in addition to high achievement traits. Most organizations we interviewed consider integrity as a threshold characteristic for employment—if someone doesn't have it, "They cannot be a member." So it's generally implied.

But when consciously coupling the typical definitions of integrity and healthy attitudes (e.g., life satisfaction) with the qualities of achievement, the definition of a successful person takes on a wholly different interpretation that is more socially conscious and altruistically based. High achievement, high integrity, and a good attitude best described the qualities others "admire." Over 94% of surveyed respondents listed integrity (and its related characteristics), achievement and a positive attitude in the individuals they most admire when given numerous qualities from which to choose. Hence, we used these three characteristics as the qualifiers for the PACEsetter, and that's why PACEsetters are able to achieve great works while serving the best interests of others with steadfast purpose.

The "Over-Ego" PACEsetter

Here's the catch, though: Considering others' well-being as vitally important to our own well-being runs counter intuitively to our ego or even our super ego (our self-critical conscience). The person who practices integrity *and* achieves something of significance with a confident attitude can override their ego, or selfishness, while maintaining their own interests as well, often as a byproduct of helping others.

PACEsetters control their ego and find their singular purpose through intense personal integrity and steadfastness of purpose, *by considering themselves as the person they wish to become*, through *pacing.* Pacing is a "neuro programming" form of self-communication that views possibilities as fact and is often used by the PACEsetter to turn expectations into reality, thus resulting in a type of self-fulfilling prophecy. So instead of only dreaming of their ideal, PACEsetters actually consider their ideal as an expectation.

They do this through reasoning together self-regarding or egoistic reasons, and other-regarding or altruistic reasons. When morality and self-interest come into head-to-head conflict, PACEsetters do not view either as being mutually exclusive. They view situations through the prism of achieving the best of both worlds. Thus freed of any preconceived restrictions, PACEsetters do not compromise either their own interests or the interests of others. That's because PACEsetters focus on doing the *right things,* whereas conventional achievers focus on doing things *right.* In other words, PACEsetters override their ego to achieve something greater than themselves.

They also keep the following question at the forefront of their conscious or subconscious thinking in order to do so: "What would I attempt to do if I knew I could not fail?" The answer serves as their guiding purpose.

PACEsetter Characteristics

Several characteristics describe the PACEsetter. They live with intention. They feel comfortable in their own skin. They overcome trials masterfully. They are change-makers. They love life and embrace hope. They are genuinely positive. They give priceless treasures to others while growing their own lasting wealth. They plan well, grow continuously, learn voraciously, and enjoy the freedom to motivate themselves and others through constant renewal. They lead a life of benevolence, leaving behind them positive legacies—and they master their well-being.

So, for the confident PACEsetter, the question is not just about being someone others can admire. Rather, it's about being the person *they* can admire. PACEsetters feel confident because they see themselves through the perspective of trying to do what is right for others as well as themselves. They feel good about their abilities and their overall personhood without appearing cocky, because by maintaining a commitment to continuous improvement they're never fully complete with their mission in life.

PACEsetters display strong character traits like courage, steadfastness, openness and loving-kindness.

By inculcating all of the qualities of a PACEsetter, the personal statement for these people we admire could be summed up like this: "We" becomes less about "me" and more about *"all"* of "us." In the process of determining the PACEsetter's actions, the question for them always becomes not about "How can I merit the admiration of others" but "How can I be the person *I* would admire as a collective human being?"

The PACEsetter Leader

Ironically, people whose primary intent is to be admired typically do not fit the PACEsetter model, and yet the PACEsetter leader always finds himself or herself admired by others. This happens because at the core of the PACEsetter's fabric is a desire to serve the whole of her organization before serving herself. This runs counter to the norm in most organizations, where executives *reward themselves* for sacrificing (e.g., laying off) *employees*, whereas the PACEsetter leader willingly *sacrifices herself* for *rewarding her employees*. As did Lola Gonzalez, owner of Background Check in Ocala, Florida, who said that she could not bear to fire employees who had worked there for years despite losing one of the company's major clients, so she stopped paying herself a six-figure salary and got a job for less than half the pay as a social worker.

The result? A reinvigorated organization reversed the downward trend into a 20% profit, thanks in large part to more motivated and dedicated employees due to PACEsetter Gonzalez's generosity.

CEO Lola Gonzalez opted to stop paying herself a six-figure salary and got a job for less than half the pay in order to save the jobs of her employees.

Over and over, we found that these kinds of PACEsetter leaders benefitted from a more committed, enthused and motivated base of workers. Like former Japanese airline president and CEO Haruka Nishimatsu, who gained the admiration of his workforce during the downturn in the airline industry by slashing his own pay three straight years to a $90,000 salary—less than what his pilots earned—to save company costs and improve revenue, and keep people employed. Compare that to the 380:1-spread between the CEO and average worker pay among the S&P 500 (according to the 2011 research conducted by Executive PayWatch).

We noticed over the course of identifying leaders others admire that the heads of organizations who sacrificed their fortunes, in more instances than not, were deliverers of success later on. Leaders such as FedEx CEO, Fred Smith, and Motorola's co-CEOs Sanjay Jha and Greg Brown who willfully reduced their wages by 20%. Or, Dee Hock, the founder of Visa, who made the ultimate sacrifice by resigning at age 55 in order to prove that organizations should be "management proof."

Six years later, in an acceptance speech as a laureate of the Business Hall of Fame, Hock put it this way: "Through the years, I have greatly feared and sought to keep at bay the four beasts that inevitably devour their keeper—Ego, Envy, Avarice, and Ambition. In 1984, I severed all connections with business for a life of isolation and anonymity, convinced I was making a great bargain by trading money for time, position for liberty, and ego for contentment—that the beasts were securely caged."

All reaped benefits for their organizations and themselves in making personal sacrifices, demonstrating that self-sacrifice often precedes reward while benefitting others. Indeed, leaders engaging in self-sacrificial behavior are considered more charismatic, effective and legitimate by their followers than self-benefiting leaders (Choi & Mai-Dalton, 1999; De Cremer & Van Knippenberg, 2004; Van Knippenberg & Van Knippenberg, 2005; Yorges, Weiss, & Strickland, 1999). Consequently, self-sacrificial leaders elicit more positive affect, trust, cooperation and improved performance among their followers (De Cremer, 2006; Van Knippenberg & Van Knippenberg, 2005). And the sacrifice has an elevating effect, so after giving up personal value, as when CEOs sacrificed their salary to help save the company and jobs, when the slump ends the CEOs can hike their salaries again, and the chain reaction of positive effects continued throughout the organization.

All of these PACEsetter leaders, even those who did not hold official positions of authority, but whom others admired, put themselves at risk for the sake of their organization. And this imbues within those they affect a sense of trust and cooperation, and a willingness to follow their leader's example of self-sacrifice. These PACEsetter leaders foster a feeling of belonging, where contributors felt safe and protected, and were therefore free of the constraints to protect their jobs so that they could express more creativity and promote others' success without the fear of reprisal. Those who serve with or at the effect of PACEsetter leaders feel like family, with similar protections as those afforded to children of benevolent parents, who would never consider divorcing their children, or laying off a family member but instead remain steadfastly committed to training, disciplining, coaching and encouraging their loved ones.

Perhaps no better examples of PACEsetter leadership exist than those of our heroic contributors who sacrifice themselves for the betterment of others—inner city teachers, relief workers in impoverished parts of the world, and embattled soldiers. People like Sergeant Dakota Meyer, who received the United States Medal of Honor for rescuing 36 soldiers under heavy attack in Afghanistan.

United States Medal of Honor recipient and PACEsetter leader Dakota Meyer (left) shakes hands aboard the assault ship USS Boxer while noting, "I was part of something bigger" (than survival).

Surrounded by ferocious enemy fire, Dakota jumped into a Humvee and drove straight into the killing zone, his head and body exposed to a thunderstorm of fire from AK-47s, machine guns, mortars and rocket-propelled grenades. He wedged the Humvee in the line of fire, jumped out with all of the enemy guns aimed on him, was wounded in the arm, and yet despite believing he would die, Dakota one-by-one delivered all the wounded to safety by going back several times, all because, said the brave soldier, "That's what you do for a brother…I was part of something bigger," part of a team "that worked together, lifting each other up and working toward a common goal. Every member of our team was as important as the other." Spoken like a true PACEsetter leader.

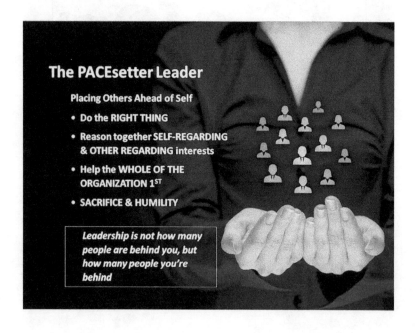

The PACEsetter Leader

Placing Others Ahead of Self

- Do the RIGHT THING
- Reason together SELF-REGARDING & OTHER REGARDING interests
- Help the WHOLE OF THE ORGANIZATION 1ST
- SACRIFICE & HUMILITY

Leadership is not how many people are behind you, but how many people you're behind

DISCOVERING THE PACE FORMULA FOR THRIVING

Over the years, my colleagues and I researched numerous sources while sharing models for behavior that can make anyone who adopts them a PACEsetter. As the CEO overseeing biotech and biomed companies, an advisor to many charities, an executive with companies like Johnson & Johnson, and a trainer of several thousands, I've gleaned countless pearls of wisdom from accomplished PACEsetters.

As a research team at the strategic development firm TenorCorp, we analyzed thousands of cases spanning the lives of high-profile achievers, like Joni, and private contributors, such as notable volunteers, leaders in companies, education, politics and non-profits, and countless people who command genuine admiration. We asked people who they admired, and why.

We researched several other studies to uncover the traits of high achievers whom people admire, some of which confirmed the growing recognition of "non-cognitive" skills like self-control, sensitivity and grit. We looked at famous world changers, like Thomas Edison, who said that "genius is mostly just perspiration." We reviewed volumes of works, such as those conducted by researcher, K. Anders Ericsson, who argues that high achievement mainly results from deliberate practice, about putting in those 10,000 hours or so of intense training or so.

Our reviews included quotes from high achievers such as Michelangelo who said, "If people knew how hard I worked to get my mastery, it wouldn't seem so wonderful at all," as well as contemporary PACEsetters like Bill Gates, whose success has been linked to extraordinary execution. As the most "admired person in the world," according to a survey of 14,000 people by the *Times of London*, what qualified Gates as a PACEsetter, in addition to developing *Microsoft* that had long held the record for the most valuable public company in the world, is that he is one of the most generous philanthropists in the world.

As we studied volumes of works about admired achievers, some researchers such as Yale Law Professors, Amy Chua and Jed Rubenfeld, suggested common traits amongst achievers with some PACEsetter qualities. They published an article in the New York Times claiming a striking similarity amongst successful groups in America who share three traits: a superiority complex (a deep-seated belief in their exceptionality), a feeling that you or what you've done is not good enough, and impulse control. In PACEsetters we studied, a "superiority complex" was more accurately translated as a resolute confidence in one's abilities, minus the arrogance that often defines self-seeking (non-PACEsetter) aspirants. As to the second trait described by Chua and Rubenfield, "a feeling that you or what you've done is not good enough," translates into a healthy mindset of continuous improvement for the PACEsetter.

These achievement factors mostly deal with behaviors, rather than skills, though. So we dug deeper as to what common skills could be developed to create PACEsetter qualities. We discovered that most people understood the *behaviors* required for them to achieve their highest goals, but not nearly as many possessed the skills or knowledge to get there. Quite honestly, many integrity-based people who aspired to display commensurate qualities with those they admired struggled with the skills necessary to get there.

Finally, there was the question of integrity—how does one develop integrity? We discovered that a healthy attitude combined with the ability to live out one's purpose contributed immensely toward personal integrity, as well as, interestingly, maintaining a high energy level. It turns out that when people feel drained, they find it challenging to function with integrity, and may even give up entirely. People with integrity also feel the need to improve their planning or communication skills, or to adjust their attitude, in order to function at their best potential for the benefit of all concerned.

Of the hundreds of high achievers we analyzed, less than half met the criteria for a PACEsetter. Again, integrity and a healthy attitude served as equal components to achievement for the PACEsetter in our study, which translated differently from many achievers who practiced a more self-focused perspective. Some achievers in the non-PACEsetter category lived with deep dissatisfaction, and some became so self-centered that they almost forgot others shared their world.

True PACEsetters time and again excelled in four basic areas, with an ongoing commitment to plan, grow, learn, and free themselves to stay motivated. About 40% of the high achievers we studied lacked a high measure of satisfaction in life. Those who valued money or status as their primary goal expressed the least satisfaction. Even more telling was the fact that those who were not actively involved in some form of charity or loving-kindness (e.g., helping the disadvantaged or caring for a loved one) applied negative terms to describe their state of satisfaction, using phrases like: "I just can't get enough done," "Nothing I do seems to last," "I'm not really sure if I'm making a difference," "The people I care about really don't appreciate me," and "I'm never content." Satisfaction proved to be the most elusive quality for most high achievers, including even those who attained high levels of status and wealth. So why is satisfaction in life so elusive or complex?

Finding Satisfaction

Researchers like Sonja Lyubomisrski at the University of California and others determined that satisfaction with life is comprised of part DNA, part "intentional attitude," and part life practices. Our genetic make-up has been thought to largely determine our level of happiness or satisfaction. A mere 10% of satisfaction with life resulted from circumstances, and attitude resulted in 40-50% of overall satisfaction. These studies concluded that each of us tends toward a "set point" of satisfaction based on how we're wired, determining much about how we react to life. The "disruptive force" that can move this set point in a positive direction would be the "intentional activities" we take to create a positive attitude, such as living purposely, helping others, communicating effectively, expressing gratitude, taking care of ourselves, and fostering resilience.

PACEsetters were able to advance their set point by leveraging these types of disruptive forces. What's interesting is that PACEsetters view their life as a series of steps rather than viewing the macrocosm of their world. In other words, they remain focused on their goals without getting lost in the constant demands of life. They live, as PACEsetter and mega-church pastor Rick Warren would say, "a purpose-driven life." This way they can measure their progress in achieving something worthwhile without trying to control factors outside of their ability to directly influence them.

PACEsetters also set goals mostly based on intrinsic factors such as personal development, social contributions, and connection with others—all within their sphere of control. Those who focused on extrinsic goals as wealth, status, or attractiveness over a long period of time found it difficult to stay motivated, and the majority of them eventually felt dissatisfied with their overall wellbeing. This happened in large part because many of these extrinsic goals were either fleeting, elusive, difficult to maintain, or outside of the control of the person striving to achieve them.

Through our research we discovered that the most significant advance in the PACEsetter's set point toward greater satisfaction in life resulted from faith. Those who overcame extreme obstacles, like Joni Eareckson Tada, stated that their faith allowed them to claim promises beyond their own comprehension. They laid claim to absolutes like those found in John 14:27: "I am leaving you with a gift—peace of mind and heart. And the peace I give is a gift the world cannot give. So don't be troubled or afraid." These kinds of assurances supplant reason with trust. Demanding less from situations and people, and expecting more from these statements of faith served as a positive lifestyle choice for the faith-based PACEsetter (See Figure 1.1a to view a summary of a 30-year study to determine the PACEsetter—a high achiever who thrives with integrity, and someone we tend to admire).

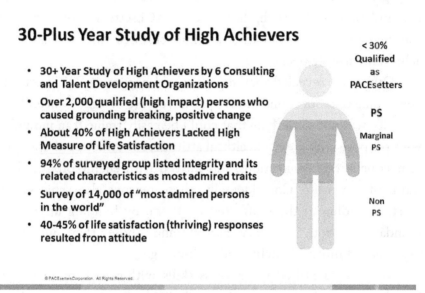

30-Plus Year Study of High Achievers

- 30+ Year Study of High Achievers by 6 Consulting and Talent Development Organizations
- Over 2,000 qualified (high impact) persons who caused grounding breaking, positive change
- About 40% of High Achievers Lacked High Measure of Life Satisfaction
- 94% of surveyed group listed integrity and its related characteristics as most admired traits
- Survey of 14,000 of "most admired persons in the world"
- 40-45% of life satisfaction (thriving) responses resulted from attitude

< 30% Qualified as PACEsetters

PS

Marginal PS

Non PS

© PACEsettersCorporation. All Rights Reserved.

(Figure 1.1a - 30-Plus Year Study of High Achievers)

The Four Foundations of a PACEsetter

Not all of these PACEsetters were in traditional leadership positions, with followers. Some performed as individual contributors, and others gleaned their influence informally through others who became impressed by their works. These latter types include people such as students who volunteer their time and efforts, stay-at-home parents who raise exemplary children, and retired people who counsel others with their experience and wisdom.

These PACEsetters chose to make a big impact on others without needing the position power to do so. Their PACEsetter skills also spilled over to help countless others with their struggles and aspirations. Those PACEsetters that held official positions of leadership only served in their role primarily because of the respect they gained through others—not because of some form of political manipulation. And as such, these leader-PACEsetters fostered healthy, learning organizations with thriving cultures more than their achievement-only peers.

Our study revealed that anyone could become a PACEsetter by developing the four foundations to achieve a life of significance. While integrity was not something that could be easily trained, an individual with purpose who grew a healthful attitude, communicated optimally in making strong connections, and thrived with energy produced the most integrous life. Coincidentally, these persons also achieved the most, according to those affected by them. By building upon these foundations, both the PACEsetter and those they influenced experienced mutual benefits and well-being.

We also identified the success skills within each of these four foundations required to potentiate an individual's effectiveness. When fully activated using proven practices, these four foundations invariably lead to the highest level of positive achievement (coupled with integrity) and satisfaction:

> 1. **Purpose** produces passion, and passion motivates people to excel. For lack of purpose, people slowly drift into a confusing milieu of competing demands that steal away their joy and can lead to defeatism. The key is finding purpose in everything we do. We must begin by living intentionally, producing a life of abundance, and then

analyzing our situation in order to make the big impact. People who not only define their purpose—but also follow a well-defined pathway toward its optimal outcome— thrive. This takes a series of disciplines for making our dreams reality.

2. **Attitude** plays an essential role toward gaining optimal achievement. A healthy attitude sees the possibilities in life. However, being a possibility thinker doesn't naturally happen. An undeviating attitude of optimism and gratitude requires a reframing of our thoughts that triggers a positive momentum for overcoming trials, resulting in the wisdom to succeed forward. A positive attitude may be the single most important foundation for healthy living, but it is also one of the most difficult ones to maintain in an increasingly demanding world.

3. **Connection** reflects the way in which we relate, and there are five essential skills for effectively connecting with others: Unselfish listening, empathy, adapting, relating and ("harmonic") negotiation. These represent the most important bridges to connecting us with others, so that we can enjoy mutually beneficial relationships. All effective communication hinges on our ability to L.E.A.R.N.— Listen, Empathize, Adapt, Relate and Negotiate—using subtle techniques that can turn anyone into a phenomenal communicator with strong relationships. Creating a harmonious relationship that resonates with synergy happens when the pinnacle of connection is reached, and this leads to joy.

4. **Energy** ultimately dictates whether we can sustain the momentum for achieving lasting results. Extrinsic habits of

eating and exercising efficiently provide us with the energy to perform at our maximum capacity. Then there are the lesser-known intrinsic factors that, according to research, create sustaining energy. Like faith, which is an expression of hope for a better future. The other intrinsic energy producer is "prioritized" rest, which revitalizes and restores. But, it's not just rest that is needed, rather it's a paradigm change that will produce more with less. In other words, we can stop striving and start thriving!

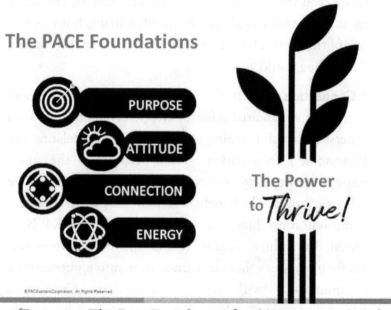

The PACE Foundations

PURPOSE

ATTITUDE

CONNECTION

ENERGY

The Power to *Thrive!*

© PACEsetters Corporation. All Rights Reserved.

(Figure 1.2 -The Four Foundations for the Power to Thrive)

WHEN YOU WERE MADE, THE "MOLD" WAS BROKEN

While these four foundations must be fully developed for anyone to thrive in life, no PACEsetter can ever achieve someone else's finish. After each of us was made, the "mold" was broken—no one else can assume our exact make-up. Joni's example of someone who overcame horrible tragedies to live a life of tremendous meaning can never be exactly replicated, because of course, there is only one Joni Eareckson Tada…just as there is only one *you*, and there is only one journey specific to you. If we try to be like someone else, we miss the purpose of our own journey and may end up living an unfulfilled life.

Take for example my friend, Michael, who spent most of his life trying to live out his father's dream. He developed an anxiety disorder associated with cardiovascular disease. Only after he practiced the Mapping In Reverse (MIR) method, which I will explain a little later, did he start living out *his* dream. Now, at the age of close to 80, he can run circles, even figure eights, around people half his age. If we replicate the formula for achievement that assuredly will lead us on a unique path while remaining true to our singular personhood, limitless possibilities await us.

The Same but Different

Who we are is reflected in our physical, psychological and spiritual DNA. Most understand the basic principles of the body. The psyche (or mind) is less commonly understood but contains most of the drivers that can or should determine our mission in life, such as our passions, talents and values. Even fewer understand their spirituality. The spiritual self was thought to be too ethereal or incomprehensible by the majority of people we surveyed, and yet spirituality was rated as "important" by almost all of those people. Later we will dig deeper into all of the DNA imprints of our singularity as we build a roadmap to your one-of-a-kind destination, because who better to understand than yourself?

Whereas our design is unique, the pathway to being a PACEsetter ("someone we admire") is fairly universal. Think if you will, of the PACE set of foundations as "nutrients" for your body, mind/psyche, and spirit. Just as there are four basic food groups (fruits & vegetables, grains, dairy and protein) required to supply your bodily functions, there are four basic achievement groups that feed your ability to achieve like a PACEsetter (purpose, attitude, connection and energy) as shown in Figure 1.3. In life, purpose fuels meaning, attitude fuels satisfaction, connection fuels joy, and energy fuels vitality.

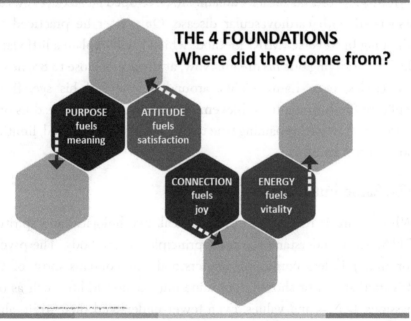

(Figure 1.3 - The PACE foundations fuel the power to thrive with meaning, satisfaction, joy, and vitality.)

The four food groups nourish the body, and the four "PACEsetter" groups nourish your ability to thrive in life. The basic food groups are needed for each person to live a healthy life, however, what kind of life each person chooses to live varies. No one lives the same life, or travels the same journey. Similarly, the basic PACEsetter groups are needed for each person to live a life of significance, however, their talents, abilities, values, passions, opportunities and purpose largely determine what kind of achievements each person produces.

To achieve a life of significance, we all need to apply the same basic principles, however, the unique journey and destination that define our success will be different. For example, what defines success for a minister may be very different than that for an agnostic. A young student may consider success differently than a senior retiree, as both will have different aspirations. The charity worker, Mother Teresa, considered her purpose differently than the wealthy industrialist, J. Paul Getty. To begin our process of discovering the success principles for everyone, let's go back to the PACE formula, and finally we'll attempt to apply this formula for your unique design.

BEGINNING STEPS TO SET THE PACE

At TenorCorp, we uncovered the core characteristics of PACEsetters and then developed the foundations upon which these exceptional achievers standout. The chief commonality amongst all PACEsetters is that their purpose, attitude, connection and energy foundations are exceptional in comparison to those who struggle. We discovered that PACEsetters thrive primarily because of their strength in these areas

For each of the PACE essentials, there exists a clear roadmap for maximizing potential, and we've established acronyms for each one to help you remember the skills required to build your foundation as a PACEsetter. During the course of this book, we'll first explain the P.L.A.N. formula for "planning with purpose" through a fresh analytical approach that challenges existing paradigms. At the beginning stages of planning our purpose, the "arbiter" of any activity must be identified, followed by a sequence of identifiers for answering the what, why, how, and when of making a *big impact.*

To develop a consistently positive attitude, we'll describe how to G.R.O.W. your perspective to create a cycle of renewal that not only overcomes obstacles but welcomes them as the most important pathways toward a healthy mindset. High achievers continually seek out their own personal development, often as autodidacts (self-learners). Self-directed personal growth manifests itself through a productive attitude that attracts and motivates others as well as ourselves. The signifier of a healthy attitude is then reflected in wisdom—the most important aspect of success, because wisdom assimilates knowledge with the truth for making good decisions.

At the heart of effective connection we'll explain how to L.E.A.R.N. and unlearn habits in order to engage people through an "ego-peripheral" vantage point. Deferring our agenda in order to genuinely listen to someone calls for a transformation of our perception from a separatist viewpoint of "them and me" to a collective viewpoint of "us" (*We're in this together.*). There are five basic skills that must be fully developed in order to achieve a level of harmonious connection. We'll take a look at the "pyramid of connection" to show the various levels of connection, targeting the highest level of connectedness and how to get there.

Finally, we'll give you the means to F.R.E.E. yourself from those energy suckers that have drained your ability to stay in the "zone," that place where we experience peak performance, sometimes exceeding our natural abilities. Athletes typically get in the zone during game time, with their emotions peaked and their focus unyielding. Individual contributors can free themselves to achieve this same peak state through the substantiated benefits of healthful exercising and eating, with suggestions that don't take a lot of time and won't require you to eat cardboard tasting foods. Then we'll look at what we call the intrinsic energy producers of rest and faith through a fresh perspective. We'll also look at distinct ways to create a passionate form of energy that keeps you motivated toward higher levels of achievement that may change your way of thinking.

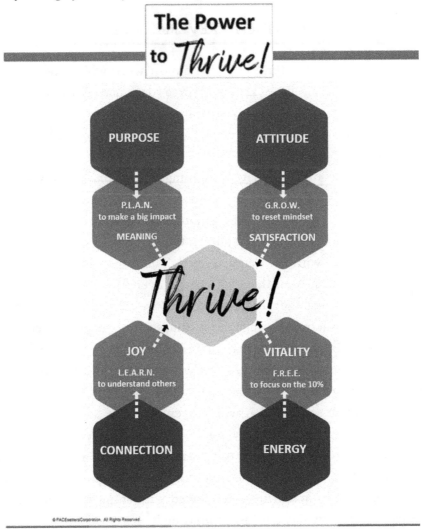

(Figure 1.4 -The Power to Thrive Diagram)

What I've just explained represents the PACE formula for breakthrough achievement (Figure 1.4). By looking at the achievement factors and skills that cause PACEsetters we admire to do the things that merit our admiration, we can now pinpoint the universal characteristics of these PACEsetters, and how to achieve your own unique definition of success using proven principles.

MAPPING IN REVERSE (MIR)

Growing as a PACEsetter is one of the most worthwhile exercises of your time. We all have 24 hours in a day, and what separates PACEsetters from dawdlers is *how* they use it. We also have this one life to live on earth, and it's never too late to make it the fulfillment of our dreams.

When our dream—that consuming aspiration, gives way to encroaching responsibilities, we tend to give up on our dream to achieve something more practical. Dreams need not include some grandiose plan to become someone on the world's stage. They simply evoke a passion within when imagined. The desire for it may even draw you to tears. And, they can change over a lifetime, just as my dream of becoming a journalist at an early age evolved into dream of helping others succeed through my writings and seminars. Experience is a great modifier of our dreams as long as it doesn't dampen the calling that tugs at your heartstring. Our dreams must be nurtured the same way we nurture our bodies, with not just the hope, but with the expectation that someday…it will happen.

That someday can be today, now. We enter our dream as we take the first step from imagination to action. It starts with an action plan. Dreams that turn into reality have a purpose—a destination—a goal. After all, we as human beings are created with an innate desire to do something worthwhile, not just to imagine it.

PACEsetters typically start with a goal and reverse engineer it. While achievements present some level of satisfaction, they pale if not congruent with our dreams. Envision the best that you wish to be and do—therein resides your dream. Once discovered, work backwards from there. This concept is called Mapping in Reverse (MIR). After you first create the endpoint in your imagination, you draw up a blueprint for getting there.

The key is to flip that blueprint in reverse so that you are starting immediately with the endpoint. In other words, you are doing what you dream about first, and then finding a way to support your continuance and development of the endpoint/dream. In this way you won't become frustrated through the twists and turns of getting there, which causes many people to just give-up on their dream.

MIR is about immediately connecting with your dream. For example, Erin dreamt of writing a book to leave a legacy for her family—so she started writing, without delay. Realizing your dreams does not always necessitate uprooting yourself from job or home. Many choose volunteering as a way in which to immerse themselves in their dream. Sometimes our dream is not a position but rather a change in attitude. PACEsetter Naomi wished to be more patient, so she carved out a sabbatical to relieve her stress and worked weekends at a soup kitchen as a means for stabilizing her emotions.

By jumping immediately into the dream we connect the sequence of our steps in reverse beginning with the desired endpoint as our reality. PACEsetter Steve Wozniak, co-founder of Apple, used MIR after dreaming that he would have a computer someday—so he made one. MIR allows a person who dreams of being a master chef to start cooking classes, or a banker who dreams of being a police officer can start as a police volunteer or by filling out an application for becoming a police officer.

MIR allows people to get real with themselves. Author Po Bronson writes about defining the "New Era," wherein those who thrive focus on the question of who they really are, and instantly connecting that to work that they truly love. In his article *Choosing What to Do with Your Life*, Bronson recounts the story of a catfish farmer who used to be an investment broker, an academic turned chef, and a Harvard MBA who found his calling as a police officer. These examples of people who stopped waiting and started living out what they truly love give testimony to the fact that all of us can do the same.

The average person spends 40-60 minutes a day waiting, usually for fairly unimportant things such as another person to show-up, or for an event to happen. Waiting too long can lead to a lifetime of regret. Over time, those who endlessly wait for tomorrows waste their todays until they casually accept their situation as inevitable. They become resigned to what seems normal or inevitable. And then instead of living out their dream, someone else hires them to live out theirs.

Have you ever been left wondering, "If I could do it over again, what would I do differently?" Once you've got the answer, the response must be to do it. As Lao Tzu said, "The journey of a thousand miles begins with a single step."

We know this as children, but somehow false rationalization convolutes the concept of just stepping into our purpose or dream. As children we learned to dream big and as adults we learn to accept reality, except, reality need not be in exception to our dreams. In truth, we can enter into our dream without delay by working backwards from its endpoint in order to justify our reality. PACEsetters plan their dreams, not just their tasks. That's because PACEsetters qualify all of their plans by defining their purpose first.

If your heart still beats with your dream, even though nothing seems to be happening, keep at it and don't let it go. Other times, you may feel it best to step away for a while and come back when it calls you again or circumstances change. Don't become overly concerned about this or put too much pressure on yourself about clarifying your purpose or dream. Your purpose might indeed be something spectacular, or it may be as simple as treating others with encouragement and caring.

Leaving a Lasting Legacy

If you quit on your dream, how will you ever know if you could have achieved it? Of course, you can never know if just a little more time or effort would have seen the dream come true. The fruits of living your dream could bear out today, or ten years from now. No one really knows. What separates PACEsetters from others is the fact that they never quit. Quitting was removed from their list of options, even if it meant that their dreams would only benefit the next generation—or those thereafter.

Even when they reached their dream, they created a new one, a new reason for going forward—people like Galileo who invented the telescope, allowing him and generations thereafter to discover the galaxies. He was largely criticized and even accused of heresy by Pope Urban VIII, who placed him on house arrest until his death.

The famous painter Vincent Van Gogh's 2,000 pieces of art were never discovered until his death—and today they are worth millions (his Portrait of Dr. Gachet was valued recently for $134 million). Many of these unheralded achievers followed their dreams knowing full well that their dedication might never be recognized, but they never quit—they were willing to leave a legacy for others.

PACEsetter Florence Nightingale helped revolutionize the service of nursing and the treatment of patients as she volunteered to nurse soldiers during the Crimean War. Martin Luther King Jr. inspired millions of people black and white to aspire for a more equal and just society. Dietrich Bonhoeffer, a Lutheran pastor, was executed in 1945 after being an influential critic of Hitler and Nazism. Emile Zatopek (1922-2000), won three gold medals at the 1954 Olympics for long distance running and served as a principled supporter of Czech democracy, being sent to work in mines for his opposition to the Communist government. Susan B. Anthony (1820-1924) was an active member of the American Anti-Slavery Society, and despite facing hostility, pressed for an amendment to the U.S. Constitution to outlaw slavery while pushing forward the women's suffrage campaign.

For these PACEsetters, their breakthroughs came *after* they left this world. You don't know when your breakthrough will happen. So don't guarantee your failure by quitting now. You can develop, adapt and change, but never stop. Be content with leaving a lasting legacy for others who may follow after you. Create an inheritance built upon the foundation of your efforts.

Just like a farmer who plants a crop knowing he won't taste its fruits, a legacy is a gift you leave behind for others without any expectation of a return. The values and life lessons that you can impart to those around you can benefit countless others. Just make sure that your legacy is a labor of love, not a chore. Pass on your talents, the benefits of your work, your inspiration to illuminate the lives of those who come after you.

It's all about giving back, as psychologist Erik Erikson stated poignantly when he said, "I am what survives of me." Doing whatever matters to you should not only be motivated by the desire to accomplish something through a "never-quit attitude" but also by the desire to share it with others. As American philosopher and psychologist William James said, "The greatest use of life is to spend it for something that will outlast it." That achievement may require a change in direction. Maybe your life is not what you wish it to be. Perhaps you need to start making *your* difference now.

Writing Your Signature Purpose

The story of someone who turned around his life illustrates how anyone can start afresh. One crisp morning, a man of great wealth opened his newspaper. As was his daily curiosity, the man reviewed the obituary column to read about the poor souls who had recently departed. One obituary immediately struck him with blood curdling horror—his own. After nearly fainting, the man called the editor to ask why the paper had reported him as dead. "We are so sorry, sir, we reported the death of the wrong person by mistake…" and on and on the editor profusely apologized for upsetting the accomplished gentleman from fashionable society.

After calming his nerves, the man sat down and began contemplating his life. He again picked up the newspaper and decided to fully read the article. The obituary read, "Dynamite King Dies." Another startling commentary read: "He was the merchant of death." The man threw the newspaper down and gasped, wondering to himself—"Is this how I will be remembered?" The question circled in his head until a resounding "No" blurted from his mouth.

Thoughts of what he had done in his career exploded out of him with mournful lamentations for those who would be affected by his research and discovery. "I will not accept what I have done as my final legacy," he said. From that moment forward, the man dedicated his life's work toward peace. The man's name was Alfred Nobel, the inventor of dynamite, and his legacy is known as the Nobel Peace Prize—the award he funded.

What would you like your legacy to be? Do you need to redefine your values as did Alfred Nobel, or will you be remembered for your generosity and loving-kindness based on your contributions today? The legacy you leave is the based on your final chapter—how your story ends, as well as how you got there. And it often requires that you think higher than the environment in which you currently find yourself.

Your legacy comes from the storyline that expresses how you've made a difference.

Thinking about it forces us to consider where we've been, where we are in the present, and where we are going in the future. A positive legacy explains our journey from success to significance. By living our lives with intention, we determine our desired legacy. We make our own world a better place than before we influenced it. We can choose a life of lasting significance over temporary success. It takes determination and purposefulness. Try writing your signature purpose today, *before* the future becomes the past.

Just please understand that nobody's past can dictate his or her future. Don't let the past dictate your future, or who you are as a PACEsetter. The point is to live according to the wise advice from an old Native American saying: "When you were born, you cried and the world rejoiced. Live your life in such a manner that when you die the world cries and you rejoice."

purpose

 You can be anything you want
to be, do anything you set out
to accomplish if you hold to
that desire with singleness of
purpose. "

—Abraham Lincoln

CHAPTER 2: PURPOSE—TO FIND MEANING

Thrive Drive is to...
P.L.A.N.
PLAN YOUR FUTURE AND FRAME YOUR LIFE WITH PURPOSE

SHERI BRIGGS GREW UP IN an alcoholic home located within a pernicious cult. At 19 she left the cult to marry a man who eventually abused her during drug and alcohol induced rages. Two years later she divorced him, and then two years after that became pregnant. After the birth of her son, Sheri found herself without much money and in need of help. But, while people from her church kept giving her advice, no one provided the practical help she needed. "Christians were telling me this and that about my choices and that they would pray for me to have the things, finances, and support I needed," said Briggs. "But, no one really came along side of me and offered this help practically or spiritually. I saw it was easy for them to look at my situation and tell me what to do, but not participate in it."

Sheri found no tangible help because of the common human phenomenon known as deferred responsibility—people typically do not want to become involved in another's hardship. PACEsetters overcome this tendency by seeing another human's suffering as an opportunity, not a burden. As did some individuals at a new church Sheri attended after moving with her 18-month old son to San Diego. These opportunity-inclined PACE setters finally gave Sheri what she needed: beds, a kitchen table, and one thousand dollars. "This tangible giving, coming to my house, delivering these things to us, was a huge revelation to me," said Briggs. "These acts were saying to me, from our heavenly Father, 'I see you. I know you. I love you. I am with you. I will provide for you.' I took note of this in a big way, as God was planting seeds in my heart for a journey I could never imagine."

Sheri's journey included meeting a surfer in San Diego, Brewster Briggs. They grew to love each other and married. The newlyweds managed a women's shelter for a couple of years until feeling called to move out of the shelter while remaining involved with its residents. Sheri remembers this experience as another turning point. "I began to understand the challenges of women leaving recovery, or prison, to start their own life over with nothing. They needed a bridge of some sort to help them up and over to the other side to live successfully on their own, and in turn encourage others."

Through zealous prayer Sheri explains that God began giving her visions about a safe place for women, and a storehouse filled with all kinds of essentials. Another vision that remains clearly visible in her mind to this day was that of a cross. "He (God) showed me the vertical piece is the plumb line of his word - the truth. The other horizontal piece is the practical. The needs that are met." She explains it from the perspective of Jesus feeding the poor, as well as teaching them. "It was the complete deal," Sheri said. "He showed me the cross, the two intersect. They work together. When I was a single mom, the practical provisions coming to me were what I needed to feel, taste - to see the Lord is good."

Sheri joined a women's prayer group, and received confirmation for fulfilling the vision of a storehouse for those in need. She founded *Bridge of Hope* by renting a 400 square foot space near her home with only one month's rent in her savings. Her faith that God would provide the clothing and other necessities, as well as each month's rent, proved enough. Then a larger vision happened after almost a year. An article about an African refugee boy who had lost his limbs in a rebel war and was relocated to San Diego, tugged at Sheri's heart. "I kept hearing in my heart, 'go to the city.'" So Sheri moved *Bridge of Hope* to the City Heights area of San Diego, home for many immigrant families, refugees, gangs, drug addicts, and the poor. She found a 900 square foot shop that cost $675 a month. Thanks to donations the *Bridge of Hope* account could pay for most of the six-month lease, except for $100. A volunteer found a piece of copper in the building left behind by the prior tenant. Sheri recycled it to cover the remaining $100 owed.

Soon after relocating, *Bridge of Hope* began supplying donated clothes, furniture, cookware, food, and other items to hundreds within its community. Those who came included refugees from Uganda, Iraq, Nepal, Burma, Vietnam, and other African countries. People from all faiths and backgrounds frequented the storehouse, including Hindus, Muslims, Buddhists, Christians, local gang members, drug addicts, and prostitutes—all were enthusiastically welcomed. Sheri and Brew offered games and crafts to children on the property. Word spread, and soon volunteers from all over the country contributed supplies, and planned community events. They delivered furniture to refugees freshly arrived from war torn countries, and fed thousands unable to pay for groceries.

Today, *Bridge of Hope* operates both a large warehouse and a community center. Families of those victimized in the crime ridden area all-too-often hold their funeral services there. Volunteers at *Bridge of Hope* conduct classes such as teaching English to foreign speaking children and adults, music classes for those used to hearing only emergency sirens in "the hood," and dance or art classes for those who seek to escape their desolation. Private tutoring, after school programs, sports camps, *Alcoholics Anonymous* meetings, and vocational training also happen at the community center. College and university students from across the nation serve internships at *Bridge of Hope* while gleaning a practical understanding of why this charity has become so successful. Sheri's plan is to someday purchase an apartment building to house families in transition.

Founder and CEO Sheri Briggs supplies thousands of desperate families and refugees with food and other critical necessities through her organization, Bridge of Hope, which also provides inner city housing and career training.

Bridge of Hope distributes about 6,000 pounds of food each month—and that number is growing exponentially. This organization serves about 1,500 families a month with essentials. Countless people as desperate as Sheri was as a single mother have benefited from her solution for the needs she once struggled to meet.

Instead of succumbing to her severe circumstances, PACEsetter Sheri turned her trials around to find a solution that could benefit others. She chose "betterness" over bitterness. Faith superseded doubt as Sheri learned complete dependency on God. She now plans intentionally, not missing the opportunities for miracles to show-up, but also planning with purpose. Her confidence is greater than the sum of her understanding, so she never loses hope. She has learned the art of giving-*up* means not abandoning the "dream," rather it means lifting it up to God and other PACEsetters so that the unseen can become reality.

Discovering an unmet need and meeting it is the mark of a PACEsetter. Sometimes the need we cannot meet through others serves as the impetus for meeting that need through ourselves. Sheri used her deep empathy for the needs of the poor to create purpose through pain. Brew and Sheri Briggs are PACEsetters, because they live with intentional purpose.

A THRIVING PURPOSE STARTS WITH AN *INTENTIONAL* PLAN

Mark Twain said, "The two most important days in your life are the day you are born and the day you find out why." PACEsetters have discovered why they were born. They also know the reason for which they should wake up in the morning. The answer to knowing oneself can be found in a corner of the world in which some of the most satisfied people live—Okinawa Island.

In the Okinawan language, spoken by natives on the island of Okinawa in Japan, there is not a word for retirement. They use one word that encompasses everything, the word Ikigai (eek-y-guy). Roughly translated, ikigai means "the reason for which you wake up in the morning." Ikigai, or, your "sense of purpose," is a very personal experience—and it manifests itself uniquely to each individual.

One of hundreds of Okinawan centurions (which can boast the highest percentage of centurions in the world), this woman practices Ikigai, a "sense of purpose," which helps explain why Okinawans happen to be the oldest, happiest, and healthiest people in the world.

These purpose-driven Okinawans happen to be the oldest, happiest and healthiest people in the world. Their average life expectancy of 83 years old is the highest in the world, they have more people over 100 years old by population than anywhere else in the world, and they have exceptionally high energy levels and a low rate of chronic illnesses. Retirement is rare in Okinawa, not because others cannot do their work, but because these people genuinely enjoy their jobs. This enjoyment stems from a culture that values each person's contribution to the whole of society and an individual commitment to planning even the smallest activities in life with gusto.

Okinawans have a strong sense of purpose. They are known for maintaining a positive outlook on life and for pursuing their ikigai, or "reason for being." Whether it be working in their community, taking care of their families, tending to their households, or anything in their daily activities, each Okinawan cultivates an ikigai—a sense of purpose in everything.

Purpose, the kind that drives high achievers who overflow with satisfaction, is the starting point for the PACE Formula. It's the fuel for achieving *meaning*. Whether it is on a large scale such as embarking on a career or helping people survive the rigors of desperation. Everything done with intention has purpose.

Only one of two things can happen in life—either outcomes happen to us through someone or something else, or we cause outcomes to happen. If we do not live with intention, life happens to us. If we are intentional with a purpose for everything we do, we make life happen. How far we get depends on the type of goals we set and how we meet them.

Intrinsic Versus Extrinsic Motivation

What is it that keeps PACEsetters, like many in Okinawa, intentional and motivated over the long term? How are they able to achieve their goals, whether big or small, and keep that passion alive? And how do they thrive in *both* their personal and career lives? What makes the difference between PACEsetters…and followers?

The answer to all of these questions, according to the PACEsetters we reviewed, resides with the values these PACEsetters believe in as they determine their goals and go after them. Their perspective focuses on the end of their plans rather than the beginning. Whether they are dealing with the minutia of life or pursuing aggressive goals, or trying to achieve their dreams, at the close of their purpose, it is *not* the recognition and rewards that will be most highly valued, but what they have achieved on the inside.

The meaning behind the goals they seek cause the PACEsetter to feel genuinely satisfied. In other words, the *real* value lies in how their efforts and labor will benefit the ones for whom they do it, not necessarily in the award itself. This is what most PACEsetters hold in highest regard, for it is the reason in putting forth these efforts that will motivate them to persevere in even the most trying times.

So the question then becomes, where should you as the PACEsetter place the most emphasis in order to reap the *most* benefits from your efforts? It is through prioritizing intrinsic "rewards" (motivators) as a means toward self-satisfaction rather than the extrinsic rewards that cause others to applaud your works. Some examples of intrinsic "rewards" (motivators) include:

- The prospect of improving someone else's life or aspiration

- The enjoyment of getter better along the way and testing one's limits

- Mentoring someone

- The fun in just doing something worthwhile

- The competition, primarily against oneself to do better (Because when we compete against someone else, our standard becomes that person. When we compete against our self, there is no standard. The sky's the limit.)

- The opportunity to make a positive difference in the community

- Pride in a job well done

- Just enjoying doing what is pleasing

- The prospect of reaching one's potential

- Mastering one's skill set and developing new skills

Not only are these self-satisfying and long-lasting, but they help to perpetuate an *internalized* form of motivation as the PACEsetter seeks to maintain these feelings through processes within their control. This is far different than the *external* types of motivation that are so common in the workplace and in many personal lives. These external factors that tend to decrease in value over time are:

- Seeking the approval of others

- Gaining wealth at the expense of important relationships

- Reaching for higher level positions ill-fitted to one's abilities and passions

- Overemphasis on "winning at all costs"

- Pursuing fame and fortune foremost in the absence of priorities in life

These goals tend to be less fulfilling in the long-term. Contemplate Sam Walton, for example, founder of Walmart, who uttered, "I blew it" as his last words, despite an estimated wealth at his death of $65 billion, supposedly because he had neglected some of his important relationships, such as "being there" as a father. Imagine that! Extrinsic motivations, like pursuing fame, and to a lesser extent wealth, are outside of one's direct control, which makes them highly variable and therefore often outside of a person's innermost longings.

Some extrinsic goals may indeed satisfy, like seeking approval from respected individuals who can help build esteem, and achieving rewards that bolster confidence. Still, PACEsetters are motivated primarily by intrinsic goals, even if their extrinsic goals are used to instill something of significance. An example would be an individual whose healthy esteem is bolstered by achieving an award or position of influence but whose ultimate intrinsic desire is to help others achieve their own success through the individual's more influential position as a result of his increased status. In this case, the motivation is "outside-in," such that the extrinsic goal serves an intrinsic goal to pay the reward forward.

The difference might be subtle. However, it could be the difference between gaining significant value from one's experiences or receiving only superficial value from those same experiences. Investing in goals that can perpetuate the good that results from them can lead to a more positive frame of mind.

In his book, *Why We Do What We Do*, Edward L. Deci cited that researchers have found that the extrinsic aspirations for fame, wealth and appearance made the individuals who sought them more likely to experience poor mental health. In contrast, he states, "Strong aspirations for any of the intrinsic goals—meaningful relationships, personal growth, and community contributions—were positively associated with well-being. People who strongly desired to contribute to their community, for example, had more vitality and higher self-esteem (like the Okinawans). When people organize their behavior in terms of intrinsic strivings (relative to extrinsic strivings) they seem more content—they feel better about who they are and display more evidence of psychological health."

So achieving intrinsic goals like personal growth, health and meaningful relationships can give the PACEsetter a greater sense of well-being. Having the right kinds of goals, along with a purpose that finds meaning in the small as well as the large parts of life, fosters significance.

Finding Purpose in Everything

Some of the most hidden opportunities toward being a PACEsetter are found in the minutia of life. Purpose need not be some grandiose culmination. Each day represents an opportunity to find purpose. Wasting any moments by discounting vast sums of our daily activities misses the nuances of life. Time is a fleeting resource that can't afford to be wasted. If we do not choose to spend it intentionally, the circumstances around us will choose to spend it for us. To live intentionally means that we pay attention to the opportunities, the environment, the people, and the needs around us. And we try to remain alert to the right choices, as well as "secondary opportunities."

Primary opportunities are expected outcomes, such going to a meeting with a planned course of action. Secondary opportunities include the unexpected that happen along the way. One psychologist shared with me a good illustration. He went to his hair salon on a Thursday but was informed by his stylist that his appointment was actually the next day, Friday. The doctor looked over to the stylist's chair, noticing a fifty-something woman with her hair wrapped in a towel. Admitting his error, the psychologist began walking out the door. "Wait," yelled his hair stylist, as she came running up to the psychologist. "That woman, my client, lost her husband yesterday. She's been crying the entire time and is beside herself. Can you help her?" Being a PACEsetter, the psychologist said "absolutely," but also asked the stylist why the grieving wife was, of all things, getting her hair done. The stylist answered, "She's lost, and just decided to keep her appointment as some sort of coping mechanism, I guess."

In that situation, the psychologist realized his second and more impactful opportunity was to counsel and console the grieving wife, despite not being able to satisfy his far less important first opportunity—to get a haircut. These kinds of *second opportunities* happen frequently, such as traveling someplace only to intervene in an emergency, or helping a desperate person, like Sheri Briggs, on a day intended for something else, or just brightening someone's day with a compliment. The key is to be ready for them. Don't allow second opportunities to pass unnoticed. In reality, there are more second opportunities than first ones, so the intentional life looks for them. Even in times of rest and relaxation, those opportunities to help someone, or even oneself, are all around us.

The intentional life of a PACEsetter doesn't just hang out. It breathes quality of purpose based on the resources we either create or find in our midst. Free time is never really free—it's borrowed at a cost that must be repaid with either satisfaction or regret—and satisfaction comes with earning it—regret from simply letting time pass with no investment whatsoever. If you decide to listen to the wind rustling through the trees, then make sure it's done with intention—that it renews your strength and inspires you rather than being a moment spent just "killing time." The key to being a PACEsetter begins with staying on purpose as to how you can apply what resonates with you into your daily life, while taking advantage of the opportunities in our midst.

An intentional life responds versus just reacting. Pick the right foods that will make you healthy and not just satisfy your sweet tooth or appetite—decide when you will sleep, and exercise, and devote time to your most essential needs. Choose the work that fits with your vision and dreams instead of just getting by, because we are by nature purposeful people in need of more than a paycheck. And if the job is not what you love to do, then give it your all as a means to your end by loving what your job gives you.

Invest your resources—your time, your money, your energy—into what's most important to you by consciously asking yourself, "Has my first priority been paid?" Then ask, "Am I helping others' primary needs" or "Who else can I help?" After that's been taken care of, you can go onto the next and so forth. Seek people in need of your help. Don't wait for someone to fall over in front of you crying "help me"— look out for the frowning face and turn it up with your smile. Offer to help someone. Choose the memories you wish to create and make them happen. You make life intentional by giving it meaning—don't hand the keys over to someone else by not driving it yourself.

Brew and Sheri began with a purpose to help people who needed food, clothing and shelter. Their intention was to help people escape a life of desperation, and to show the love of God in real terms. A purpose must not only accomplish something, it must have meaning. Satisfaction will come when we test our ability towards some meaningful purpose.

P.L.A.N.—Plan with Purpose

The P of P.L.A.N. starts with a Plan –*intentional* planning (see Figure 2.1). Every intentional purpose starts with a plan to do something. A person who decides his plan is to lose weight may establish that as a purpose, setting a goal to lose two pounds a week. That's a well-conceived plan if the intention is to get healthier, but it is not a purposeful plan until that person executes a regular exercise schedule and a fixed diet of acceptable foods, and then measures their success. An example would be a person spending 20 minutes of aerobic exercising at the gym each day coupled with 20 minutes of a weight-lifting regimen every other day, and a healthful diet plan for each day of the week. The more specific the plan, the more intentional it becomes.

P.L.A.N. - The PACEsetter in everything—even the minutia of life, must intentionally define **PURPOSE**.

In the exercise example, the *big impact*, which should be defined for each plan, is to run a half marathon, let's say, after six months. It's that motivating force for pressing on—that galvanizing, blood-pumping goal that signifies an outstanding achievement at the end. Everyone needs some key driver to keep going. The *big impact* tells us we have arrived! It's the proverbial "carrot," or the "pot of gold" at the end of our efforts. For Sheri, the big impact was giving the underprivileged what they need so that they could lead a life of significance—one person at a time. Her and Brew's joy fed off of the joy of helping others succeed, and serving God. Each plan should begin with a purpose and concluded with a big impact that declares, "I've made a positive difference!"

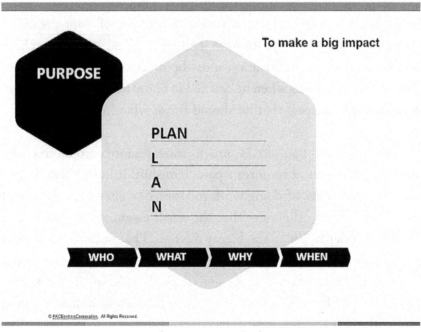

(Figure 2.1 - Plan)

Love What You Do

Sheri's dream didn't start with a large organization. It started with the steps needed to feed, clothe and house herself and her son. She just needed to survive. Dreams don't usually start with the love of your life. They're often small endeavors born out of necessities that lead to some grander purpose to expand one's personal success. Big impact plans usually start as personal needs, and grow to satisfy others' needs. The difference between a PACEsetter's plan and a non-PACEsetter's plan, is that they can apply "the oxygen mask" to themselves before handing it over to "their child" to benefit *all* concerned. They take care of the minutia, or their basic needs, before attending to the macro— making a big impact. In fact, those who skip over the laborious tasks in order to shoot for their dreams usually do not succeed.

Doing what you love to do, as a fulfillment of your dreams, is complicated. Not all passionate endeavors lead to a paycheck. Sometimes delayed gratification must be practiced first. Even Albert Einstein had moments when he wanted to enjoy his love of sailing right away, but told himself that he should finish what he was working on first.

Loving what you do is much easier, more productive, and healthier. However, it requires a paradigm shift. It begins with halting your common view of doing work for someone else or a company. It also means altering the view that the small essentials are tasks to be hurried in order to get to the bigger mission. That outlook of working for "the boss" feeds into a fatalist perspective that fails when others disappoint. And, when dreams get delayed because of the tactical requirements, the dream tends to slowly fade away unless we think differently.

"PACEsetter thinking" considers work as a journey for developing one's skills and relationships. So the journey is not thinking about your next job, or that big expectation, it's about realizing how all of your efforts comprise a mosaic of experiences that make you a richer human being. This way your title or occupation or even achieving your dream (or not) does not define you. Consider instead how you want to spend your time—What skill do you want to develop? What kinds of people will teach you something? What work instills within you the desire to do more? PACEsetters are all about personal growth, because they know that growing themselves will fashion their purpose as a result, often with the realization of their dream as a byproduct.

Sometimes as a PACEsetter, you can grow opportunities in your current position. Sometimes you need to make a change. Steve Jobs of Apple said he looked in the mirror each day and asked himself: "If today were the last day of my life, would I want to do what I am about to do today? And whenever the answer has been 'No' for too many days in a row, I know I need to change something."

Most of the time the change starts from within. There's a quote from the movie, *The Peaceful Warrior,* that speaks to loving what you do: "A warrior does not give up what he loves. He finds the love in what he does." We may compromise our passion for a while, but only to rekindle a new experience that can enliven our dream with deeper understandings. Discover the love of what you do in all aspects of your life while keeping in mind opportunities for the next adventure. Self-experiment with new ideas and insights, and push your physical and mental limits. Keep learning until your brain hurts. Surround yourself with people who've accomplished what you admire. This way your journey can evolve into something truly inspiring.

Getting and Staying in the Zone—Doing the Right Thing

Staying on purpose requires consistently focused performance. We've all heard about sports players "getting in the zone," that place where their mental and physical abilities are at peak performance. That sense of exhilaration comes from the thrill of competition, which stretches the athlete's trained abilities to reach their maximum output. We can also attain that same level of positive energy in our activities.

That same focused energy can be achieved with any goal. Instead of being distracted by the activities around us, we can gain control of our actions through a mental discipline of driving our personal limits toward a challenging and meaningful outcome. That adrenaline rush that athletes experience during game time releases endorphins that create an invigorating sense of sharpened purpose within them. Those who stretch themselves toward increasingly more challenging and definitive goals instill a consuming sense of meaningfulness that has the same effect.

Doing something with meaning triggers a subconscious effect that overrides the conscious mind's tendency to overthink or to think via "circular reasoning"—referring to the error of basing one's conclusion on an assumption, often a form of the conclusion that may be incorrect. PACEsetters are great at challenging existing paradigms to avoid these distractive thought tendencies. There's the well-known example of Steve Jobs, disappointed with the boot time of the Macintosh. So he walked into the cubicle of Larry Kenyon, who explained why it took as long as it did—but Jobs cut him off. "If it could save a person's life, would you find a way to shave ten seconds off the boot time?" Kenyon ended up finding the time—he shaved not ten but 28 seconds off the boot time. Imagine how reframing Kenyon's approach to something that would make a vital impact switched him from circular reasoning to a zoned process of getting it done.

Getting in the zone is both intrinsic, relating to what you view as important, and extrinsic, relating to the effect of how what you do will be perceived by others. An intrinsic value would be like the "saving lives" scenario Jobs used, while an example of an extrinsic value is "having prestige"; in the case of Kenyon, he impressed Steve Jobs and many others at Apple. Finding purpose often requires framing the goal as something noble and worthwhile for others. The more vitally important a goal becomes, the stronger the forcefulness of its purpose. One famous case study illustrates how rating an intrinsic value "of doing the right thing," ahead of an extrinsic value of "making lots of money" can cause a "zoned decision" that does both.

In 1982, someone laced Tylenol capsules with cyanide resulting in several deaths. At that point, Tylenol represented Johnson & Johnson's (J&J's) greatest profit maker. Losing it would potentially ruin the company. Within weeks, its market share dropped from 37% to 7%, and the company's stock plummeted. Governed by J&J's Credo (value statement) without regard to the consequences, then Chairman James Burke ordered a halt to production and pulled all 22 million Tylenol capsules from retailer shelves.

By 1985, Tylenol's market share was fully restored with J&J's new tamper-resistant product. Burke stated, "Later we realized that no meeting had been called to make the first critical decision. Every one of us knew what we had to do. There was no need to meet. We had the Credo to guide us." The Credo statement expressed values about doing what's best for the customer, the public, and the employees. As one of the greatest market recoveries in history, this story represents a "zoned approach" of doing something vitally important.

By overriding the extrinsic need to maintain its market share with Tylenol with the intrinsic need to do the right thing, employees' resolve at Johnson & Johnson increased exponentially. I know, because I was an employee working near Chicago during that time, and I discussed the plans to recall Tylenol with the McNeil (the division that made Tylenol) executives during a dinner meeting. My employee counterparts and I had never been so zoned into the mission of making J&J successful again. This purposeful zeal was company-wide. We were proud that our company acted honorably, and our customers responded in kind. This profound experience taught me a lesson that has been reinforced over the years: getting in the zone requires a meaningful purpose, by doing the right thing, and a goal with *big impact.*

This truth applies to individual PACEsetters the same as it applies to companies. Getting and staying in the zone requires a passion, an almost-religious conviction in what you are doing, believing wholeheartedly in the importance of it. It seems that for PACEsetters, their time spent in preparation (e.g., planning and training) for a crisis, or a game, or a project makes them able to almost intuitively focus on the sheer importance of what they are doing during the moments of action. A keen sense of purpose happens when they can relax and let the knowledge of what they're doing just burst out of them. That's when they slip into the zone and just do it.

Zoning—"Know the Score"

The intrinsic value of making a big impact, or doing the right thing, serves as the most powerful fuel for peak performance. Of course, other elements enter into that formula for "zoning in," like our biological clock—understanding our peak work times. I work best in mid-afternoon; some find their peak time to be early in the morning.

Discovering your peak time allows you to schedule your performance during that period of optimal rhythm. But no time is a productive time unless the goal, and its big impact, is inculcated into our very fabric. When the end goal is clearly understood, demanding, and within reach, and we can see the "score" (how we are performing against some measurement)—we can enter the zone. For a sports player, he or she can see the scoreboard. All contributors in life can track their progress against their goals. It's important to know the goal, and then to stretch it a little—just enough so that it's within reach. And it's also important to know the score (the results versus the goal) to sustain the drive for winning the goal or final reward.

Dopamine "zoning" is triggered when you can see the end result or reward. When you see a finish line, your brain releases dopamine. It's our body's reserve tank of energy. Dopamine keeps you going until you catch the prize you've been thirsting after, even when the "game" is long and frustrating. Studies in rats have shown that dopamine is crucial for reward motivation. If we were surged with dopamine all the time, our energy would be depleted when we really needed it. We can pump that dopamine at the right time for those moments when an important goal is within reach.

So how do you increase your dopamine levels? One way is to exercise. Another is to create a meaningful purpose. Another is through eating. Increase your intake of antioxidants such as fruits and vegetables rich in beta-carotene and carotenoids (e.g., greens, orange vegetables and fruits, broccoli), and eat foods or supplements with vitamins C and E. Eat foods rich in tyrosine such as almonds, avocados, bananas, fish, meat and poultry, dairy, lima beans, sesame and pumpkin seeds. And avoid foods that inhibit the brain's function, such as those that contain refined white flour, caffeine, saturated fats, and cholesterol.

A team of Vanderbilt scientists recently mapped the brains of "go-getters" and "slackers" and found that those willing to work hard for rewards had higher dopamine levels in the striatum and prefrontal cortex—two areas known to impact motivation and reward. Among slackers, dopamine was present in the anterior insula, an area of the brain that is involved in emotion and risk perception. The brain can be trained to feed off of bursts of dopamine sparked by rewarding experiences. You create the dopamine environment by zoning in on the desired outcome, and the brain does the rest.

One way to achieve this is by setting incremental goals, according to neurologist Judy Willis. In essence, what you are doing is rewiring the brain to attach a dopamine response to the task you want as a reward. Allow yourself to experience frequent positive feedback as you progress through a series of goals. Dopamine will flow as a result of your brain's positive reinforcement every time you complete a step and meet a challenge.

Be the Answer

Staying motivated isn't easy. We sometimes get restless. Things aren't going according to plan, or our interests change. New technology is being developed every day, and life is moving at a faster pace than ever before. The frenzy of life makes some fatigued, others anxious, and a many symptoms like dopamine depression, insomnia, and scattered thinking. George Miller Beard was the first to diagnose the symptoms of restlessness due to overstimulation as "neurasthenia," an ailment he believed to be caused by modern civilization's taxing effect on the nervous system.

Even those who didn't feel they were suffering from neurasthenia's physical symptoms can feel plagued by a sense of shiftlessness and restlessness. Society has changed dramatically from the pioneer days when most lived off the farm, guided by the predictability of changing seasons and growing crops. Now we live in temperature-varied environments using the modern resources of high technology that are ever changing. It's hard to satisfy our expectations in the midst of so much instability. Or, as one person said, "As soon as I learned all the answers, they changed all the questions."

If our modern feelings of restlessness are caused by the disconnect between our wants and expectations, then the cure must be to bridge the two. Instead of being overwhelmed by the seemingly endless demands in life, simply hone in on those things you truly *want* to do and *can* do.

Once you understand what you *can* do and what you *want* to do, you can start taking steps toward those things. Sometimes the purpose for what you do will be revealed later. You just have to choose one thing at a time to accomplish. Making small, steady victories will cure your restlessness. Your mind always wants to feel as if you are moving forward. So make that first step. Staying on purpose requires the daily discipline of doing our best with the situation in which we find ourselves. Instead of continually seeking after the answer for something better, why not focus on "What I can *do* better?" This calls for *being the answer.*

I learned how to "be the answer" from a man who interacted with heads of state from countries all over the world. United States Marine Corps Lieutenant General Martin Steele served on several special intelligence projects that merited his stellar reputation as a leader in both the military and as a corporate leadership trainer. He has served presidents, and has functioned as a dignitary who communicated sensitive messages between countries like China and the United States. One day while speaking to a group, General Steele articulated an enlightening message prefaced with this often spoken statement: "Grow where you're planted."

He explained that many find themselves feeling restricted by the confines of their work environment, or other limitations in their life, so people find themselves looking for another opportunity, or some other place where the grass appears greener. The principle of making the best with what you have doesn't preclude anyone from making a change, it just means that today, now, each of us must make the best of our present opportunities. General Steele recounted his experiences in warfare, stuck in battle with nowhere else to go, and he and his soldiers having to fight their way out of a trap. In other words, instead of waiting for answers, they needed to be the answer to their situation. If each person didn't execute his or her survival plan, nobody would do it for him or her.

Then he related a somewhat similar dynamic in the workplace, where people feel trapped, and the only alternative is to do what you can to succeed with where and what you're given. No matter where you are, with whom you share your life, what you do or what age you're at, we all need to make the best of our situation by growing and pushing forward. By not expecting answers from others, we force ourselves to be our own answer. That concept is tremendously freeing, and it is indicative of how PACEsetters live. Growing where you're planted means giving your best in the here and now, with what you can do. Stay focused. Look to make a difference. Grow your abilities to do more and be more and to reach new heights of success. There will be a better place for you in the future. It starts with what happens inside of you now.

Finding Significance

Once you find satisfaction in the present, the future appears less daunting. Intrinsic value is not measured by your status or wealth, rather it's measured by making a difference, being purposeful, responsible, and helping others. Is that your definition of success? Or are you motivated by something else?

In the context of living a life worth imitating, success isn't so much about doing something monumental beyond what you can do now. In fact, success relative to our prosperity ends on the day we die, when all of our possessions and contributions go to someone else or someplace elsewhere. A wise person once told me that the mark of a significant life is the accumulation of many significant moments.

This perspective caused me to realize that significance is not tied to some great achievement. Instead, we can live a life of significance by seeking significance in everything we do. Significance is a moment-by-moment opportunity to enrich the lives of someone else as well as ourselves. We can choose to make each moment significant or not. It is up to us to find meaning and value in our daily life.

Most think of significance as a position or major achievement. That kind of perspective robs us of the chances to make each moment significant. Significance starts with a moment, and then by making each moment count, the accumulative effect leads to a life of significance. Staying focused on each moment with an ever-present attitude increases our focus, allowing us to get things done one opportunity at a time.

Keep life simple by focusing your thoughts and actions only on what's significant. Consider something fresh within your familiar surrounding with what some call a "beginner's mind"—a different perspective with no need to judge it.

Significance finds itself in taking advantage of the present circumstances, over and over again. Its signifier is not just the sense of doing something great, but of how we have grown, and what we have gained through learning. Finding meaning and purpose leads to significance through living life to the fullest as we see it, not as others expect it. Positive first experiences, whether a specific occasion, or a career, or in relationship, create lasting impressions; however, too often we forget what made those things special.

The thrill of the "first time" gives way to a life of monotony. Reignite those passions by remembering what made them special in the first place, and then infuse those qualities back into your life. Perhaps it was the first time you met someone, the thrill of a new opportunity, or the first time you did something together with the people you met in your career or in your personal time.

The moments we dedicate to building relationships form the building blocks toward significance. Living life afresh makes everything a new beginning. See things as newborn discoveries and opportunities. View people as opportunities to contribute to their joy, their needs, and their growth.

You are significant not because of what you have, but because of what you did with and for others in the moments that defined your life. Create a vision for the future that appreciates the process of making it happen along the way. Attempt to refresh life through the lenses of your first-time experiences.

Your life centers all on this moment, and each moment represents a significant part of your life. If you're not living in the present you're relinquishing your life. Now is your most precious possession; don't waste it on anything else. Make a difference in someone's life—maybe even your own.

PLANNING WITH PURPOSE

Significance and purpose go hand-in-hand. Living out one's purpose moment-by-moment maintains a life of significance. There is the art of living with purpose by living "the dream," and there are the "nuts and bolts" of building something significant—by doing something worthwhile in the moment because of who we are, and what we can and want to do. PACEsetters do both. They are both dreamers and doers—both curious and practical. They begin with being curious, and they conclude their curiosity with doing something meaningful—one footprint at a time.

Curiosity

We tend to dismiss curiosity as a youthful, naïve trait, but it can actually help us experience life in a refreshing way that gives new meaning to our purpose. Curiosity focuses us on possibilities, even when facing the old, by turning the tried-and-tested into the "untested-and-try (it)," through a fresh perspective of discovery. Seeking the unknown in what is new or previously understood as "known" opens us to new possibilities—maybe even a revitalized purpose.

Children are natural curiosity seekers, however, as we mature, we tend to lose our questioning ability through a growing need to conform. Society dictates an adherence to rules, which tends to stifle inquisitiveness over time. Those who are the most risk-adverse tend to be the least open-minded persons, which in turn makes them less curious about life as they seek greater security, even if that security is false. An example would be a person trying to hang onto his/her job by adhering strictly to the job description, instead of thinking of creative ways to improve the job. Sometimes, that narrow-minded approach can actually cost that person his/her job, as more curiosity minded persons discover new and better ways of doing things.

Harvard psychologist Ellen Langer conducted a study that demonstrates how being curious can transform risk-aversion. She asked a group of volunteers to give unprepared speeches to an audience, and at the same time randomly assigned them to one of three groups. The first group was told not to make mistakes because "mistakes are bad." The second group was told that any mistakes they made would be forgiven. And the third group (in the so-called "openness to novelty" condition) was told they should deliberately make mistakes, then include those mistakes into the speech itself.

The speakers in the last group not only declared themselves more comfortable, but their audience also rated them the most composed, effective and intelligent of the three. Langer's experiment confirmed that if we can shift our focus from what frightens us to what sparks curiosity in us, our inhibitions fall away.

We noticed a similar dynamic in PACEsetters versus non-PACEsetters. PACEsetters almost invariably seek the "newness" in situations versus the tried-and-true inclination of the non-PACEsetters. Their success is largely determined by their ability to see the unseen possibilities through curious lenses. They question more, and they welcome new ideas more than their non-PACEsetter counterparts. To cultivate this type of "PACEsetter curiosity," we found that a series of questions must be answered. And how do you develop a more curious attitude based on your specific interests? Why, beginning with a question, of course.

What makes you curious? Do you find outer space fascinating? Perhaps you stay awake at night wondering about relationships and what makes them tick. Those things that spark our curiosity tend to serve as our primary drivers and motivations. They are not observations; rather, curiosity compels us to delve into the research for finding answers, and this compulsion impacts both our personal and our career lives.

There are simple curiosities that serve more as fleeting desires to know more, like wanting to know more about the American Civil

War; and, then there are complex curiosities that can drive a lifetime of discovery, such as a career scientist wishing to discover a treatment for multiple sclerosis. And then there are life-transforming curiosities like wanting to know the meaning of life, or how to discover God.

Curiosity within us sparks discovery, it feeds meaning, it helps direct our paths, and it may even define our careers and our approach to life in general. The antithesis is being bored and stagnant, and because curiosity leads us to learn more and do more—the lack of it can result in an unfulfilled life.

To develop our curiosity, we must tap into that inner child that always wants to know the hows and the whys. That type of thinking triggers a chain of causation: what causes that, and what's the meaning behind that, and how can that make my life and others' lives better? Said another way, just be like a kid discovering something new. Getting to the root cause of a curiosity, like what causes obesity, or what causes people to fail, can lead to the solution.

Author, speaker and PACEsetter Bruce Wilkerson went through this exercise of curiosity to uncover the reasons why people in Africa were unable to feed themselves. He determined that a permanent solution would never be in place until these people could irrigate their crops, so he started a movement to engage others in an irrigation project throughout Africa. This is the type of positive outcome that can arise from a robust curiosity about things. It begins with a nagging question that won't go away, and it ends with an answer that can't be dismissed without doing it.

The Nuts & Bolts of Making a Big Impact

Just like Bruce Wilkerson, each PACEsetter must establish his or her own purpose with a plan. That's not perhaps as alluring as dreaming, but as Winston Churchill said during World War II, "If you fail to plan, you plan to fail." We can dream about flying through the air, but it's only after the training and planning to parachute out of a flying plane that the dream can be realized and satisfying (e.g.—we live).

After identifying their intentional purpose, PACEsetters follow a definitive pathway for making the *big impact*—that something which says, "I've arrived." PACEsetters identify the who/what/why/when/and how of executing their plan—in that order.

THE *WHO* OF A PLAN IS THE ARBITER

Managing the Arbiter

Many plans fail because the planner fails to identify the arbiter—the person who will assess whether the outcome of a plan is successful or not. The arbiter may be the boss, or the customer—or in the case of an entrepreneur—an investor. The point is everyone is influenced by an arbiter, whether he or she knows it or not. Even chiefs of large organizations must be accountable to one or more arbiters, people or groups with the final say as to their success.

WHO: The Arbiter

The ARBITER will ultimately determine whether your big impact is a success or a failure, and gaining buy-in from this ARBITER is essential to success.

Arbiters tell us whether we've been successful or not. The "primary" arbiter is typically the individual(s) who gives a responsibility or inspiration to you. Identifying this person to whom you are responsible is critical to success.

Say, for example, you plan to write a book intended for fiction readers. A publisher may be your final evaluator (arbiter)—that person who will ultimately judge the book's merit, before readers or critics do. Asking the arbiter to *exactly* define the key measurement(s) that will be used to measure success, as well as consistently checking in with the arbiter as to whether the objectives/measurements of success have changed, will prevent any surprises on evaluation day. Making sure to keep the arbiter consistently informed of your progress helps gauge your progress.

I remember a young man (I will call him Jimmy) who graduated from the prestigious Wharton School of Business and came to work full of great ideas. My immediate assessment of Jimmy caused me to think, "This guy's an intelligent go-getter who can make things happen!" He wanted to re-engineer our computer system to link all of the departments together. He enthusiastically entered his bosses' office to tell the boss about his idea, and received only a tacit acknowledgement with a nod of the boss' head.

So Jimmy preceded to invest hours of his time, and the time of others, to integrate the computer systems—without gaining an explicit buy-in from his boss. Jimmy could have done so by asking his boss where this project fit into his (the boss') priorities, and if the boss would fully support Jimmy's idea. Jimmy just assumed that if he did a good job, everyone would applaud his efforts.

After rushing into his bosses' office to explain his "success" in one of the pilot operations, Jimmy's boss began to criticize him for not addressing the most important issue in the department—an overrun on the expense budget. Jimmy's hard work went for naught. Jimmy did not base his plan on the arbiter—the ultimate decision maker—

but rather on an unverified assumption. And eventually, this expensive error cost Jimmy his job.

Jimmy did not effectively *manage* his arbiter. First mistake, Jimmy did not discuss his manager's priorities irrespective of Jimmy's own personal agenda. Neither did he try to convince his arbiter of the consequence of not satisfying the need he had identified. Finally, he did not keep his arbiter well informed. To manage the arbiter requires knowledge of whether the arbiter is detail-oriented or outcome-oriented to fit his or her style, and knowing when and how often the arbiter would like to be approached.

Another mistake Jimmy made was not sending background information ahead of meetings. Most arbiters don't want a huge data dump; they want information that is properly analyzed and filtered. On a couple of occasions, Jimmy did not back up his resource requests with enough justifications, which made him appear less credible. After picking up on his boss's lack of enthusiasm, Jimmy became frustrated, causing him to complain about his arbiter/boss with others, which undermined any ability to manage up. This increasingly convinced the arbiter that Jimmy's project was more a detriment than a benefit.

Instead of supporting his boss by acknowledging the boss' strengths, Jimmy downplayed his boss' strengths and emphasized his weaknesses. Maintaining positive communications is key to managing the arbiter. Keeping them updated on what what's being done is important and making sure not to complain during meetings is even more important. Occasionally expressing some sincere appreciation to the arbiter and asking him/her/them if there's anything that can be done to improve your performance builds support and confidence.

If you want to impress the arbiter, show that you are on top of things by taking responsibility, and coming up with options so that both of you can make informed decisions. Let the arbiter know exactly what is needed from their side. If problems occur, prepare a sound plan to correct the root cause and to prevent future such problems.

Make sure that the arbiter is never blindsided with information, especially when he or she meets with key stakeholders.

Also, make sure that information about your area comes mainly from you, not others, and make an effort to bring good news to your arbiter so that he or she can associate you with a positive mental image. Managing your arbiter is an important skill that will benefit your career and performance.

Achievement only can happen when clear and measurable requirements are identified with the arbiter and then aligned with your personal goals so that the end result is meeting or exceeding each aligned requirement. Again, these are just cold and hard facts, but if the arbiter is not happy, chances are you won't be happy either.

STEP ONE OF A PLAN: Identify who will ultimately determine whether the plan is a success or failure, and gain buy-in from this arbiter.

THE *WHAT* OF A PLAN DEFINES OUTCOMES AND MEASURABLES

Create the Picture—Create the Passion

Wilting intentions can happen to anyone. Those plans that once inspired enthusiasm become monotonous, and you can't find the energy or focus to keep going. You feel defeated and burned out. All of those visions of making a difference—like an important project, an amazing relationship, turning that job into a mission, attaining financial freedom, or turning your dream into a thriving reality—start to fade. You don't know what to do.

Many times I've heard from people who say things like, "I start with good intentions, but I can't seem to maintain my motivation for a long period of time." Or, they will say, "I struggle with keeping focused." I get started, but I can't seem to follow through." I usually tell these people not to worry—this only shows that you are human. I've felt the same. My standard response is to ask these types of questions: "Do you have a clear picture of your vision?"; "Does your dream make a big enough impact—a big difference—one you can get behind with all of your passion?"; "If you could design your relationship, or your career, or your goal any way you wanted it, what would it look like?"

WHAT: The *Desired* Outcome

Feeling the big impact draws us to a more intentional outcome, and motivates others to join us in making it happen

Defining:
- **What is your vision?**
- **Is your vision inspiring?**
- **If you could design your outcome any way you wanted, what would it look like?**

PACEsetters can answer these questions with crystal clarity, because they've gone through the exercise of creating a picture of what success looks like—and it's big—*really* big—to them and those they can influence. By envisioning something important that evokes passion, the 'chances of staying motivated increases exponentially. That's because by creating a powerful vision, we create a physiological response in our mind and body as well. Now as a demonstration of this phenomena, allow me to create a situation that will engage within you so much passion that you will cry.

Imagine this visual: Envision yourself sitting at the kitchen table, peeling a large onion with a carving knife. You peel the first layer, then the next, and finally you hit the core of the onion. Hold the onion core, that most pungent part of it, up to your nose. Tear the core in half and take a deep breath of it into your nose, sensing the smell deep into your nostrils. Keep the onion pressed to your nose. Inhale the sulfur compounds responsible for that "biting" odor and taste. Plop the onion into your mouth and start chewing on the crunchy white chunks. If you were like most people after thinking through this scenario in detail, assuming you really did the exercise, your eyes or mouth would be watering at this time. You would actually sense the effect of the onion even though it really never existed. Did I make you cry?

The upshot is that the clearer the vision, the more impact it will make both to our psyche as well as our senses. When we immerse ourselves in the vision, meditate on it, make it as stimulating as that imagined pealing of an onion, our brain brings us to a state of peak preparation. As a confirmation of this phenomenon, a large number of studies of the impact of meditation upon the brain and behavior show that centeredness, focusing and mindful attention enhances both our cognitive powers and the strategic actions we need to undertake to bring our dream or vision into reality. When our senses come alive, our brain starts accepting our concept as a reality. And that serves to motivate us forward.

There's a lot going on in your mind, so you need to focus by envisioning something that evokes a deep response. The clearer your vision, the quicker your brain will respond. We generally do this when watching a truly great movie as we become completely absorbed in it. While watching the movie our anxieties about life start to vanish. Depending on the type of movie, we find ourselves emotional, laughing, thrilled, inspired—even motivated. What we focus on influences our passions. Our circumstances haven't changed, but our changed focus while watching the movie determines our feelings. When we readjust our focus, we can find our motivation for any given plan.

Inspiring Visions and Outcomes

MICROSOFT: A computer on every desktop and in every home.

INSTAGRAM: Capture and share the world's moments.

AMAZON: To be the world's most customer-centric company

CHARLES SCHWAB: Helping investors help themselves.

JOHN F. KENNEDY (for the United States): Landing a man on the Moon and returning him safely to Earth (before the decade is out).

WIKIPEDIA: Imagine a world in which every single person is given free access to the sum of all human knowledge.

Justified Motivation

A caveat is that we need to make sure that the focus itself is cause for motivation. Make it worthwhile by answering the question: "What is the desired outcome—the big impact?" The most innovative and impactful achievements result from learning to "forget yourself," in the sense of putting your energies into something larger than just your own ego-gratification. PACEsetters thrive because they believe that what they're doing is making a difference, a positive impact for not just them, but for *everyone.*

Inspiration arrives when we see ourselves as a giving individual. A study published in *Psychological Science*, a journal of the *Association for Psychological Science*, suggests that thinking about what we've given, rather than what we've received, may lead us to be more helpful and motivated toward others. Researchers Adam Grant of The Wharton School of the University of Pennsylvania and Jane Dutton of The Ross School of Business at the University of Michigan hypothesized that reflecting on giving could lead a person to see herself as a benefactor, strengthening her identity as a caring, helpful individual and motivating her to take action to benefit others. These and other studies show that a giving attitude, seeing the goodness in a goal, is one of the most powerful motivators toward achievement.

The second most powerful motivator is related to the onion peeling exercise—making a vision or dream come alive. Vividly imagining the end result keeps us moving forward. PACEsetters often write a script detailing what the big impact will look like to create passion. It's called a *dream statement.* A dream statement is different from a vision statement, in that a vision is a more specific and developed description. A dream statement inspires a chain reaction of thought that can tip over and multiply for the benefit of countless others.

Martin Luther King Jr.'s "I Have a Dream" speech inspired a national transformation, through the power of making a "dream statement."

It's more of a picture of something that you can envision tugging at you, like from a magnet or rubber band pulling at the "heartstrings." Martin Luther King Junior's 'I Have a Dream' speech on August 28, 1963, inspired a movement for generations as one of the most compelling dream statements of all time—because it came with a big impact that stretched the possibilities at the time, and inspired people of all colors. Dream statements envision the ultimate effect of a movement or plan through a stirring vantage.

Movie scriptwriters turn dreams to dream statements for each setting, often to produce emotions or passion for a scene. In the 1997 Academy Winner for Best Picture, *Titanic*, Best Director and scriptwriter James Cameron wrote the following description of the "Blackness" scene:

> Then two faint lights appear, close together... growing brighter. They resolve into two DEEP SUBMERSIBLES, free-falling toward us like express elevators.
>
> One is ahead of the other, and passes close enough to FILL FRAME, looking like a spacecraft blazing with lights, bristling with insectile manipulators.
>
> TILTING DOWN to follow it as it descends away into the limitless blackness below. Soon they are fireflies, then stars. Then gone.

Notice the attention to detail that allows the movie crew to precisely replicate the scene. There's no doubt as to the finished product. Even the emotion of the scene comes through its description. We can see the blazing lights of the submersibles fading into the darkness. We can almost feel their free falling at the speed of express elevators. The description doesn't *tell* the crew what to do—it *shows* them—that's the key to inspiring emotion. Showing, as in describing each intention and its effect, allows others to engage their emotions with their abilities. Showing, as MLK did in his "I Have a Dream" speech, which showed people what the end result will look like, is much more powerful than telling, as in, "This is what we're going to do." A dream statement says something like, "This is how it's going to look!"

It's not enough today to just take on responsibility. To do it spectacularly the goal must be imbued with passion and emotion through focused aim. When passion meets ability, big impact happens. To make a big impact, we need to envision the goal as vividly as if watching a movie, or reading a script, or tasting an onion. When the goal or impact becomes real, and consuming, so does our intention. That's why dream statements that focus on helping *everyone* should always precede important plans. A plan without a dream statement can turn into a long, tedious grind. A dream without a plan never becomes reality. However, a big impact dream accompanied with a well-executed plan makes an inspiring difference. All PACEsetters are dreamers. They start there and find a way to make their dream a reality.

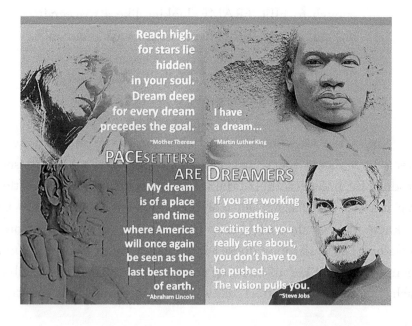

Growing Passion or Money?

I've been asked numerous times to define the single most important factor for success. Believe me, I've researched and lived out that question for thirty plus years. My answer? Passion! If someone chooses money over passion, chances are they will always strive for more. When you are passionate doing what you do, you are in the moment. That's why PACEsetters achieve personal, business and career goals by pursuing them in the moment; by deliberately *not* getting ahead of themselves through the pursuit of wealth. In relationships, those whose goals are not so much to "find" a new partner but who want to experience the pleasure and enjoyment in relationships and then find that one that may grow and develop, over time, demonstrate the same proven principle.

Passion centers us in the present with an abundant attitude toward work and life, which tends to attract more abundance in life, including oftentimes, money. So in essence, money can't buy passion, but passion can lead toward money. It's been observed in the business world that people who are passionate about what they do tend to work harder, and produce more. When we are tied to money, or to some other egocentric goal, we lose some of our freedom. Sometimes we stay at a job we hate so that we can earn enough money to make us happy. It's a vicious cycle—we buy more things to cheer us up and have to work at less than ideal paying jobs to pay for it, and feeling oppressed we need to buy more.

Contrary to conventional wisdom, money doesn't drive performance. Individuals striving for material success can easily become too focused on prestige and money, too concerned with external measures of their own worth. PACEsetters focus instead on the positive impact their service or product has on others, whether the customer or someone else. Consider marketing or sales people in the pharmaceutical industry who are best motivated by a desire to help heal cancer patients or the customer service agent who is driven by making life easier for people. In my 30+ year experience I found that these kinds of passionate, big-hearted contributors perform best.

Whether it's through higher quality, making a positive difference, or quicker delivery time, the new paradigm calls for anyone trying to make a difference to speak or write about the impact they can make. Providing context and challenging others with a noble purpose makes work meaningful.

When the PACEsetter talks to the customer or the worker, she can ask them, "How will that person you're trying to affect be different by what you are doing?" If every conversation includes that question, that by itself will make a big impact on what is accomplished.

The Titanic scene mentioned earlier evokes the kind of dramatic effect that should drive every goal, each step along the way. Make the goal come alive in the mind of everyone working on the plan, so that anyone with the talent to work on the plan knows it and feels it— including you. A plan comes alive only after the big impact feels like it will make a positive difference. Martin Luther King's famous *I Have a Dream* speech created a vivid picture of the big impact that motivated people of all colors to "look to a day when people will not be judged by the color of their skin, but by the content of their character." Wow! That was an inspiring dream statement each of us could get behind!

Feeling a *big* impact always draws us to a more intentional outcome, and it motivates others to join us in making it happen. However, we have to *feel* it first. Big impacts are often bigger than ourselves, which grows us, and makes them more inspiring, as long as we get specific as to how to achieve them.

Specificity with Big Passion

Once passion enters into a plan, the rest is detailing the process for completing it—the "nuts and bolts." For any plan, measuring the desired outcome will let you know when your success has arrived. It's a little like planning a vacation by noting your stops, the attractions you will go to, and your meals. Knowing where you want to go sets in place the means for getting there.

Each dream should start with a mission, a destination. Walt Disney started his with a fantastic mission statement—"To make people happy." Great mission statements are pithy, short and to the point, so they're always on the forefront of everyone's thinking. I love catchy mission statements—and hate those lengthy (more than two sentence) statements that most forget. Everything Disney did after his company's inception, each plan, had to remain faithful to the mission. If it didn't *make people happy*, it didn't qualify as a plan.

After qualifying the plan with a mission statement, typically, success for the mission is measured by some quantity like time or an amount, such as a person's goal to lose two pounds a week, or a salesperson's quota to exceed her revenue base by 10% at the end of the month. Measurements also can be accomplished through satisfaction surveys—achieving a 95% or higher approval rating based on a survey of customers. PACEsetters are masters of specificity without getting too mired in the details.

Regardless of how or when success is measured, it must be as specific as possible. Goals like "enjoy life more" or "get healthy" are too vague. A goal of reading "one book a month" is good. Saying "I will lose 40 pounds by mid-year" just OK, but stating "I will lose an average of three pounds each week" is even better. These goals are *measurable* with a quantity and a deadline. The smaller the detail, the bigger the impact it will make on our ability to achieve it.

Through being specific and detailed you can routinely track your progress by planning regular updates to gauge your progress. If a plan cannot be measured by its effect on you or others it is not a plan, it's a hope. In some cases, you may want to keep a log in order to track progress against the goal. Your goal should inspire you to change by offering enough motivation to do so. Having an accountability partner or being a part of a group may help maintain your mojo during lower peak times. Don't establish goals that are not under you control, such as a goal for your "boss to be nicer"—goals for other persons typically are not readily *attainable*.

The goals of a plan should require you to stretch your capacity without being impossible. *Realistic* goals may need to be broken down into smaller goals, with a corresponding plan to graduate their degree of difficulty based on time and quantity. Once you've done all this, revisit and revise you goals consistently to incorporate any changes that may have occurred along the way.

STEP TWO OF A PLAN: Show the desired outcome of a plan using descriptive details that express the big impact to everyone involved.

THE *WHY* OF A PLAN BEGINS WITH A QUESTION

Questions are the best way to develop richer understandings and create more breakthrough solutions. Questions prevent false assumptions and help to clarify intentions as well as solutions. When we ask good questions we can expect good outcomes.

Think like a Child

Children are great at asking questions. "Children are designed by evolution to be extremely good learners—to be able to think about anything that's interesting and important in the world around them," says Alison Gopnik, a professor of psychology and an affiliate professor at Berkley's University of California. "When you look at their brains, they're extremely flexible, so they can change what they think based on new evidence very quickly and easily."

She further explains that as adults we tend to focus only on the things that are most relevant to us, making us more close-minded and unable or unwilling to consider the broadest possible range of opportunities. We stop asking questions, causing us to stop learning new ways of thinking. Gopnik suggests adopting more of the inquisitive approach to things that adults tend to lack by becoming more hesitant to ask questions. Keeping an open mind and releasing preconceptions is key to not overthinking a problem with prejudiced answers. Kids are always asking "Why?" Or more importantly, "Why Not..?"

WHY: ASK QUESTIONS TO GAIN INSIGHT/DEVELOP UNDERSTANDING

Ask these questions:

- **Will my plan add value?**
- **Will my mission be served through this plan?**
- **Will others grow as a result of what I do?**
- **How will this decision affect how I want to be viewed?**

Consider the true story of a seven-year-old boy who was caught in a traffic jam with his mother on the freeway. As the two approached an overpass, the reason for the congestion became apparent—a semi-truck was stuck underneath the overpass, and the emergency crew could not get the truck unstuck, regardless of how hard they tried. This quandary triggered a host of questions in the boy's mind: "Could they make the truck smaller?"; "How flat can you make a truck?" Then a possibility ignited within the boy, and he insisted that his mother pull over so that he could offer the solution. His idea? To let the air out of the truck's tires so that it could be driven beyond the overpass. Sound simple? Perhaps, but several adult minds could not come-up with it. The boy's unfettered questioning devised the answer no one else could imagine.

Most of my personal success has resulted from asking, not telling. When I became responsible for the corporate operations of the fastest growing pharmaceutical company at that time, I simply sat down with my staff and asked one question, "What can we do to make things better?" I then followed with another question, "What is the one thing we could do today to make our customers delighted?" I knew that at an early stage that I could learn more from my team than they could learn from me. These questions resulted in some great ideas that helped us to bring four separately operating companies into a single well-functioning organization.

Albert Einstein revolutionized common scientific practices by asking many questions. All the great inventors and scientists asked questions. Einstein asked, "What would the universe look like if I rode through it on a beam of light?" Isaac Newton asked, "Why does an apple fall from a tree?" Steve Jobs asked, "What if we could give everyone a computer?" By asking these kinds of provocative questions they were able to trigger thinking that lead to transformational inventions.

PACEsetters spend their entire lives asking questions about the meaning of what they do. They ask the deep questions about the situations they face: "Will the plan add value?"; "Will my mission in life be served through this activity?"; "Will others grow as a result of what I do?"; "How will this decision affect how I want to be viewed?" These types of questions serve as the best way to get the information and insight we need to make informed decisions, and for people trying to gain buy-in from others (e.g., sales people) it is the single most important skill they need to succeed.

So Why Don't We Ask Questions?

If it is obvious that asking questions is such a powerful way of learning, why do we stop asking questions? For some people the reason is that they just assume they know all they need to know, so they do not bother to ask more. They cling to their beliefs or prejudices and steadfastly adhere to their assumptions—yet they often end up looking foolish.

Other people are afraid that by asking questions they will look weak, ignorant or unsure. They like to give the impression that they are decisive and in command of the relevant issues. They fear that asking questions might introduce uncertainty or show them in a poor light. In fact, asking questions is a sign of strength and intelligence—not a sign of weakness or uncertainty. PACEsetters constantly ask questions and are well aware that they do not have all the answers. Others are in such a hurry to get things done that they do not stop to ask questions because it might slow them down. They risk bullheadedly rush into the wrong direction.

One of the most effective ways to plan with purpose is to check assumptions and gain a better appreciation of the issues by first asking questions. Start with broad and open-ended questions ("Tell me what's going on?") and then move to more specific clarifying questions ("What is broken?"). Open questions are the best way that we learn—they give the other person the chance to open up about matters. Examples of open questions are:

- How would you explain the current situation?

- Why do you think this has happened?

- What are all the things that might have caused this problem?

- Why do you feel this way?

- What possibilities have you considered?

Additional questions may arise as we listen carefully. We can further clarify an understanding or deduce the root cause of a problem by asking, "Why?" Our tendency is to plunge in with our proposals, opinions or conclusions. The better approach is continuing asking questions to deepen our comprehension of the issues before drawing a conclusion. Once we have uncovered the key points, we can use closed questions to get specific information. Closed questions give the respondent a limited choice of responses—often just yes or no. Examples of closed questions are:

- When did the problem happen?

- Was the customer satisfied?

- Who is the person responsible for this area?

- Did you give permission for this action?

By narrowing the choices that the respondent must give, we get specific information and deliberately move the conversation forward according to our agenda and desired conclusion.

Asking several questions can be very effective, but it can also make you appear overly intrusive. So it is important to ask questions in a friendly and unthreatening way. Do not ask accusing questions. "Please give me your take on what happened?" will most likely elicit greater cooperation than, "Why weren't you more responsible?" Try to frame each question with the intent of moving forward with a solution and ensure that your body language is relaxed, facing the other person, and open (e.g., arms to the side). Do not point at the other person or shake your head from side to side as you ask the questions.

There exists four basic types of solution based questions, and framing questions in this order will help lead to a positive outcome.

TYPES OF QUESTIONS

**POSSIBILTY—Thinks outside the box
as to possibilities**

**UNDERSTANDING—Checks assumptions
to gain a better appreciation**

**CLARIFYING—Investigates the root cause
of a problem or challenge**

**PROBLEM SOLVING—Offers a solution
framed as a forward focus**

© PACEsettersCorporation. All Rights Reserved.

STEP THREE OF A PLAN: Be curious about a situation by asking questions in order to uncover information and develop relevant insights.

THE WHEN OF A PLAN CONVEYS URGENCY

Developing a mindset of urgency requires a transformation from what non-PACEsetters just **say** to what PACEsetters actually **do**. Notice in the next diagram what people *say* on the left side that can delay or paralyze a plan, and what PACEsetters *do* on the right side to expedite or empower action. For example, non-PACEsetters think they need to be on the winning side which can lead to a sense of complacency when 'winning' causes political stagnation; whereas, PACEsetters make things happen sooner and better by thinking they are on the losing side, which instills an 'underdog' perspective and makes everyone 'try harder' by creating breakthroughs.

At the base of this diagram note the measurables on the left that can cause delays, and the contrasting measurables on the right side that can make big-impacts happen quickly. "Sayers" focus on hindsight while "doers" focus on foresight. For example, revenues are measured in hindsight of what has been accomplished (a 'rear-view' mirror focus), whereas learning and growth measurements determine future success (e.g., tracking the outcomes of training to determine if learners are increasing their competencies so they can perform better - and that is looking through the 'windshield.')

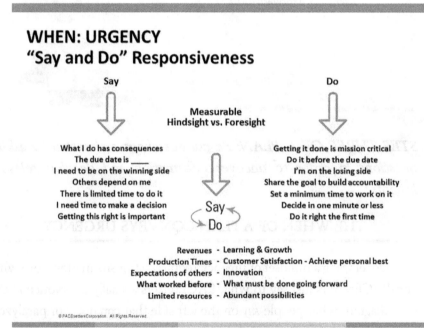

W. Clement Stone, founder of an insurance empire that grew to one of the largest in the world, made all of his employees recite at the start of each workday the same phrase over and over, "Do it now!" Make that your mantra each day. Here's a method for getting it done: Once you've thoroughly completed all of your agreed upon requirements for a task, including assembling the necessary information, click on an imaginary two-minute timer to make a confirmed decision.

The same goes for multiple priorities—once you've made an informed decision, do it. PACEsetters have a high tolerance for ambiguity, because they are able to act boldly without overanalyzing. They can cut through the red tape and make it happen. Decisions tend to vacillate until the status quo takes over—that is, until you as the PACEsetter impart a sense of urgency to drive the process forward to completion. Use the vast majority of your time for taking action, not for decision making. In the professional world, experience and thoroughness take a back seat to accomplishment. Delivering or exceeding the expected results means everything.

If you want to make things happen, your skill in adapting others to your objective is key. Begin by evaluating what decisions have been simmering on your mental stove for a while, and make a 60-second decision to implement your decision now. When others see you as being decisive, it engages them to act as well. This includes getting tasks or reports done for others that have been sitting for too long. Likewise, ask yourself what responsibilities from others are due to you.

Try moving up the due date or quickening the process by making what's owed you move to the top of the other person's to-do list—without sounding too pushy. It can be tricky, but try it by saying something like: "I fully trust in your ability to make it happen because I believe in your skills and abilities!" Establish a deadline and challenge others to beat that deadline if at all possible by offering a reward for doing so.

Deadlines establish a parameter, but the deadline usually means the least acceptable timeline. PACEsetters will generally complete tasks well before the deadline and have enough time to spare to volunteer for other responsibilities that will further elevate their value in the organization. Postponing a task should only be done if another more important and more urgently needed task takes its place. Procrastination is a lethal temptress.

If you are a constant procrastinator, ask yourself the tough questions—are you afraid to fail, are you avoiding something? The common perception says that procrastination is a problem of time management. It is not. Procrastinators *actively look* for distractions, like getting sidetracked with the Internet. These diversions serve as a way of regulating their emotions, such as the fear of failure. By saying "I work better under pressure," they lie to themselves.

Consider the consequences of postponement as way to keep on track. If interruptions consistently interfere with your ability to complete things, determine which urgent ones actually require your attention, and decide if they can be scheduled (such as setting up a meeting), delegated or managed in some other way (i.e., "send me an email"). If an interruption exceeds the level of importance of your top priorities, then deal with it then. Developing and keeping a schedule factors not only planned activities but also inevitable interruptions.

With only 24 hours in a day, do your activities in order:

1. Do goals and commitments first.
2. Do the things you want to do, but don't *have* to do, second.
3. Do your small busy (more irrelevant) work third.
4. Do your chit-chat or idle entertaining things last.

Don't go onto the next set of tasks until you've completed the first. This way you'll master your time. Urgency is a state of mind. Instead of accepting the status quo, we can ask others and ourselves why something can't be done better, and sooner. We tend to accomplish what we expect. An ever-present attitude of getting it done urgently inspires the will to accomplish something vigorously and expeditiously.

STEP FOUR OF A PLAN: Creating a sense of urgency is the most important driver toward success, so stretch the target to make it sooner and better.

HOW EFFECTIVELY WE PLAN DEPENDS ON EXECUTION

Execution is the discipline of getting things done. Since execution is even more important than strategy, the PACEsetter focuses on execution by creating the team motivation *and* connecting people's actions to the organizational goals so that each person understands how their role fits within the whole. This creates a healthy learning organization that is both people and results oriented.

However despite many knowing the importance of "doing it" instead of just "thinking about doing it," effective execution continues to be one of the biggest problems facing people who need to get things done. The July-August 2010 edition of the Harvard Business Review survey of 1,075 readers found that the most significant execution obstacles facing organizations were those associated with making strategy meaningful to those responsible for getting things done. Once the strategic plans have been developed, executing them through aligning jobs to the strategy was among the biggest obstacles to fulfillment.

Management apparently is not clear enough when relaying the strategy to employees. People in organizations don't have the foggiest idea as to what the strategy is or how they fit into the overall scheme. Simply communicating the strategy through a systematic approach is the key to more effective execution.

Getting Rid of Futile Initiatives

PACEsetters excel at execution because they get rid of futile initiatives or programs that either unnecessarily drain resources or have never met expectations. Letting go of these drains is key to making progress. PACEsetters only solve problems *once* using widely applicable solutions that can be easily understood and used for a wide variety of problems. They realize that doing nothing is actually an acceptable option because busyness without a big impact leads to futility. Most ventures fail from being too bloated with busyness rather than from a starvation of ideas. Organizations and individuals suffer from doing too many things at the same time and for lack of doing a few things very well.

Only widespread problems merit a top priority for action. Once these general problems are surfaced, the final part of an effective execution plan is taking action, which means making it a part of someone's responsibility.

Effective execution follows five rules:

1. Spend time and resources based on the importance of returns—those activities that are "mission critical" (don't major in the minors).

2. Tap into peoples' strengths as well as your own strengths by fitting yourself and others in roles ideally suited to your or the person's talents, experiences and passions.

3. Identify the gaps in a job or project and fill them.

4. Concentrate on the highest priorities one at a time and complete each one before moving onto the next (multi-tasking is actually *not* a productive means to get things done).

5. Make goals that are simple enough to apply across a broad range of areas, and that are executed by assigning responsibilities.

In the mid-1990s, I had the pleasure of being a department leader at one of the fastest growing companies within Johnson & Johnson. This diabetes company trained all of its employees in a quality improvement process, and I was one of the quality trainers. Part of the indoctrination was that everyone had to complete training on the company's value statement, and each person's commitment was tested as to whether they had established the "rules of quality" and the organization's values to memory. This way everyone was speaking the same language of quality and values.

Upper management met mid-year to establish the company's 5-7 strategic plans that were communicated to employees at a winter meeting. These plans were the basis for determining a company-wide bonus program that paid on the number of goals met. As a department leader, I met with my teams to develop objectives and action plans directly related to the 5-7 strategic plans, and each individual was required to align his or her goals with the department's strategic plan. The results were up-reported to senior management.

Each person's merit pay was linked to the achievement of these objectives, as measured by well-defined criteria for productivity. The execution strategy always remained linked to the top 5-7 strategic plans which were funneled down to each individual's own personal set of objectives so that everyone was operating from the same general benchmark. This company rose from obscurity to the number one position in its market.

Great execution follows four basic rules:

1. Clear goals for everyone in the organization.

2. Buy-in to the overall strategy.

3. A means for measuring progress toward goals on a regular basis.

4. Clear accountability for all teams and individuals

STEP FIVE OF A PLAN: Execution is more important than strategy because strategy only maps out the intention—whereas execution gets you there.

MAKING THE BIG IMPACT

Dr. Phil Johnson works to find a cure for mitochondrial disease, a group of disorders that is caused by dysfunctional mitochondria, that part of the cell that generates its energy. His young son Kyle eventually died, most likely because of this disease (at the time little was known about the human genome). Recalls Dr. Johnson about his son, "I will never forget his beautiful blue eyes, his blond hair, him not wanting the oxygen tube on and holding his gentle hand. He would look at me with assurance because his dad was with him as he always had been. It wasn't long before Kyle passed away. Despite the fact that he was on a ventilator, in my mind's eye I remember hearing him say bye bye while waving his hand to me. He was then gone." During those moments of deep suffering, Dr. Johnson found the problem he was created to solve. One might even say he was destined to solve the problem that caused his son's death. As of this writing, Dr. Johnson is working to cure mitochondrial disease.

You also must all discover the problem(s) that you are tailored to solve. There exists something that really bothers you. Not a mere annoyance, but a grating, gnawing problem that eats away at your ability to enjoy life. Perhaps it's some terrible injustice, like world hunger, or disease, or the lack of good education in high schools. PACEsetters work to undo what bothers them the most. A truly inspired physician must eradicate the problem of mitochondrial disease. A dedicated teacher must ensure that the problem of illiteracy is eliminated. An inspired children's caseworker must prevent the problem of abuse. The problem may be something in the neighborhood or at work that causes others to suffer or fail; or, it may be a disease, a shortcoming, or an injustice that has plagued your own life.

That intolerable problem will lead you to find your Big Impact. You need not dedicate your career toward solving that problem—you can simply do something positive or you may instead serve as a volunteer or do something else without receiving an income, but you must do it. It may be some irritating problem at work or in the neighborhood. You were created to solve a problem, and your satisfaction in life depends on your success in finding that significant problem and making a Big Impact to solve it.

PACEsetters look outside of themselves and find a problem, and the solution can define their life. Most PACEsetters don't develop themselves first and then lead a life. They are called by a problem, and their calling forms their development gradually, just as Sheri Briggs started *Bridge of Hope* through the hardship of homelessness. Sometimes a tragedy defines your intolerable problem. A loved one may have become the victim of a violent crime, which compels a family member to become a police officer. Or some problem that prevented a person from attaining a goal may serve as their driving force for correcting that problem.

When a problem becomes a blood-fueled living force that boils over into consistent anger or frustration, not solving it would be tantamount to being disloyal to you. So finding your intolerable problem and making your life's work to solve that problem is the best way toward satisfying the purpose for which you were created.

Then once you've discovered that one problem you are meant to solve, focus on making that one Big Impact. So how do you find your one big impact? Look for the intersection of three factors:

A   The problem you are passionate about solving

B   What you can solve based on your abilities

C   An opportunity that will either make you money or will enhance your position

D   At the intersection of these three things lies your Big Impact (Figure 2.3)

PURPOSE—The BIG IMPACT

**PACEsetters are led by a purpose:
to make an impact that matters**

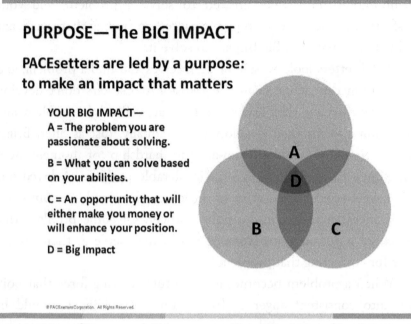

YOUR BIG IMPACT—
A = The problem you are
passionate about solving.

B = What you can solve based
on your abilities.

C = An opportunity that will
either make you money or
will enhance your position.

D = Big Impact

(Figure 2.3 - Discovering Your Big Impact)

Clarifying Your Big Impact

Ask yourself this question: "What separates me from 90% of others?" Is there something that others consistently ask you to do? What would you do for free just because of the fun or satisfaction of it? What is your driving instinct—that compelling force to do something? The steady attention to making that one big impact based on a compelling inner voice is the sure mark of a PACEsetter.

The courage to think BIG breeds power, opportunities and amazing adventure. If you have a product or service that others have validated through their encouragement or praises, and you feel passionate about doing it, then you owe it to yourself and the world to bring it to as many people and places as possible. Most people do not reach their potential because they don't listen to their inner driver and they think too small. If you *reach for the stars*, the worst that can happen is you end up with some elevated understanding of the possibilities under those stars, higher than you were before stretching yourself.

THE P.L.A.N. ONLY SUCCEEDS THROUGH LEARNING

LEARN

Expanding Our Vision

We all live within our isolated worlds, however PACEsetters understand that expanding one's outlook to different people and communities will help create a larger view of the possibilities available to them. The more people, places and experiences we can include into our envisioning the better. Broadening our horizon doesn't have to be as complicated as planning a trip to some distant land. It can be as simple as networking with others or retreating to a relaxing environment.

Just by expanding our visual horizon, we can extend our range of thinking beyond the parameters of our normal thought processes. When we get stuck in a rut, the creative juices tend to dry up. That's because left to our limited environment, we fail to see the possibilities.

We can't expand our vision without first expanding our view beyond just ourselves. Our vision needs to include the larger context of the world around us. Just by expanding our current skills and abilities, we can make a broader impact by learning new and better ways, so that the habits of old do not consume our way of living.

Habits

So what happens if that person with a plan to lose weight and run a half marathon gives up? That sometimes happens. Or what about the one bad decision that ruins all of that hard work? We can have the best intentions but life begins to happen to us, and we lose control. It happens mostly due to making bad choices and bad habits. This is where the L of P.L.A.N.

becomes so important. L stands for Learning, or relearning as the case may be. During our unique journey, we've accumulated an abundance of habits and lessons learned. PACEsetters practice healthful habits and are byproducts of a full life with experiences. No one can make a big impact if his or her tank is empty, or if the habits formed are counterproductive.

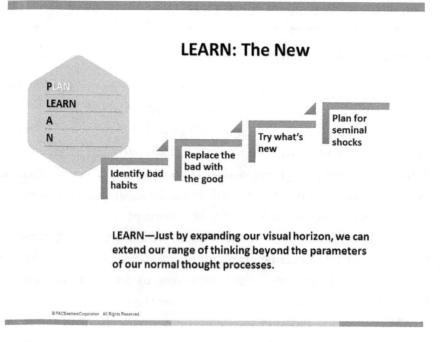

LEARN: The New

PLAN
LEARN
A
N

Identify bad habits

Replace the bad with the good

Try what's new

Plan for seminal shocks

LEARN—Just by expanding our visual horizon, we can extend our range of thinking beyond the parameters of our normal thought processes.

Bad habits often result from anxiety caused by fears that typically begin from an inability to resolve hurt or insecure feelings. Look for habits of thought, repetitive stories or words that feed into a negative narrative. Replace those bad habits with good ones, like a healthy change in your daily regimen (e.g., exercise) that can stimulate your brain and cause increased focus. When damaging habits keep looping within the brain, a new routine must be established to essentially short-circuit the existing signal/temptation. It takes about twenty to forty days of repetitive practice to cause a change in behavior to become a new habit.

Dieters wishing to lose weight can adopt new routines of eating and exercising that can pre-empt old eating habits. Trainers use the technique of masking bad habits by overlapping old responses with new stimuli, like rewarding runners each time they increase their distance or finish time. The key is to create incremental wins that gradually rewire the brain, by starting small and working bigger. Smokers can be trained to cut down on their nicotine use before cutting it out all together by using this incremental method.

Changing bad to good involves discovering the root cause of the habit in the first place. Someone who cracks their knuckles, for example, may discover that he/she does it whenever he/she receives bad news. Janet L. Wolfe, Ph.D., a clinical psychologist in New York City and author of several books including *What to Do When He Has a Headache*, suggests keeping a log to help establish a baseline. "Put down the antecedents, the emotions surrounding the knuckle cracking and what goes through your head when you crack your knuckles," she says. "This will make your bad habit more conscious."

Replacing Bad Habits

The next phase of retraining the brain is to replace the bad habit with the new one. Wolfe says about knuckle cracking, "Try getting your hands in a position where you won't be able to crack your knuckles." Maybe doodle or stroke your sleeve. Start with small wins, and work your way to a new routine. But don't just try to suppress those bad habits. Attempting to push a negative thought or a bad habit out of your consciousness can actually bring it back even more powerfully. Our mind seems at times to work against us—we want to get a good night's sleep, but thoughts keep racing through our head—we want to stop that craving for sweets but pictures of chocolate fudge sundaes go dancing in our head.

Psychological research has found that trying to forget about a bad habit can actually make the condition worse. Professor Daniel Wegner and his colleagues initially researched the effects of thought suppression in 1987. Participants were asked to try not to think about a white bear for five minutes, then for the following five minutes were asked to think about a white bear. Participants were asked to articulate their thoughts throughout the process, and to ring a bell each time they thought of a white bear. Those who tried to suppress their thoughts rang the bell almost twice as often as participants in a control group.

Other researchers have confirmed Wegner's findings, such that this phenomena is now called the "post-suppression rebound effect." This principle is particularly pronounced when people attempt to suppress their emotions. Trying to suppress depressing thoughts or bad memories can double psychological distress. Apparently our mind initiates an unconscious monitoring process to check if we are continuing to think about what we are trying not to think about—a sad twist of irony. Anything that remotely seems like the suppressed idea triggers the mind's looping response.

So the key is to give-up trying to repress negative thoughts. If you want to change your ways, ask yourself, "What can I do instead?" For example, if you're trying to lose weight, devise a plan that when you have that craving, go for a walk or do something active as a form of replacement therapy to stave off a reoccurrence of the habit. Eventually if you remain committed, your bad habit will start declining until is vanishes completely.

Planning for Seminal Shocks—"Disruptive Proactivity"

Allow me to tell you about a person who was forced to change his way of looking at his life. Skip's life changed dramatically six years ago when he was fired from his job. Now he looks back on his former life, slightly depressed and a little overweight, feeling sorry for the old Skip. Seminal events by their very definition influence later developments, like getting fired, turning a certain age, the diagnosis of a serious illness, a lost relationship—events that cause us to pause and reflect: "What am I going to do now?"

After Skip got fired, his contemplations led to branching out on his own as a small business owner after fifteen years in a totally new industry. He now owns a bakery and coffee shop and loves it. When Skip turned 40, he faced another seminal event. He started examining what the heck he was doing in life, which lead to an exciting new life.

What about you? What seminal events helped shape your life? Any regrets? Any turning points that made things better? After all, it's your life and only you can live it. Those seminal events force us to reflect, to reconsider the path we're on, and though sometimes beyond our control they're to be welcomed—not dreaded. They make us more capable of any change that comes our way. PACEsetters in particular don't wait for crises to happen, they plan for them. They also frequently engage in what-if scenarios in order to be more proactive. What person doesn't wish to be more?

And yet, when the occasion to do it arrives via a shock, or a dramatic turn of events, our human tendency is to go back to what's most comfortable. Yesterday's habits tend to win-out in our desire for a better future. The key to fulfilling the desires you construct in your mind is to alter your response to seminal events, since they invariably happen in life. These events can turn the impossible (opportunities) into the inevitable decision points that force us to think, "Why not?"

It's called being "disruptively proactive." Consider planning these events in advance—that's right—what would you do if you were diagnosed with a terminal illness today? What about if you were fired—then what? If you lost your closest loved one today, how would you reroute your life? What would you do in a crisis? The truth is, these events can quickly turn wishes or shoulda-coulda's into reality, if we don't just look for another replacement. Don't try to go back. Sameness truthfully is never really the same. We can never *fully* go back. Awaken yourself to a new perceptual reality of what you can do if the foundation underneath you suddenly evaporates. These seminal events are finite—don't waste them—they present the ways we grow and develop.

Seminal shocks, seemingly daunting adventures, changes, risks, and stretch goals are all challenges. There exists an inverse relationship between challenges and growth. One cannot happen without the other, just as strengthening our muscles cannot occur without bodily resistance.

As long as we learn from these lessons and apply our newfound understanding or perspective, we can create a more meaningful plan for anything we do. As challenges happen, we can grow. We can strengthen our ability to plan more effectively with purpose. Being purposeful allows us to be more intentional with our plans. It prevents us from simply surviving so that life doesn't just manifest to us by happenstance.

A P.L.A.N. REQUIRES THAT WE ANALYZE THE SITUATION

ANALYZE

Socrates, Isaac Newton, Abraham Lincoln, Orville Wright, Albert Einstein, Ralph Waldo Emerson, Winston Churchill, Thomas Edison, Mother Teresa, Frank Lloyd Wright, Marie Curie, Henry Ford, Steve Wozniak, and Bill Gates all are or were *critical thinkers*. They demonstrated an individual's ability to reasonably reflect on an issue and subsequently decide what to do or believe.

The ability to analyze an activity or process is a key skill for the PACEsetter. It means assessing what you are doing using your critical faculties to weight the evidence and considering the implications and conclusions of what you and others are doing so that you can make a good decision.

How to Practice Critical/Analytical Thinking—to Avoid Being Reactive

Imagine two situations. On the first, you plan a vacation to Yosemite National Park. While hiking you come across a sign that warns you not to attempt go down a trail because of some erosion from a waterfall. Would you consider whether to heed the warning? As to the second situation, suppose you were to receive a call from a friend that he would like you to join his wife and him on a trip to Hawaii. In this situation, would you not be more likely to think about the reasons for saying yes or no, considering the implications for you and your family? In the first situation, you were thinking reactively and in the second, you were thinking analytically. PACEsetters think primarily from an analytical vantage point, because analytical thinking forces them to consider higher possibilities than does simply reacting to what life throws at them. New and innovative paths are forged through analytical thinking.

ANALYZE: to Synthesize

PLAN	MANAGE	SYNTHESIZE
LEARN	MAINTAIN	CREATE
ANALYZE	☐ Evaluate	☐ Integrate
N	☐ Inspect	☐ Orchestrate
	☐ Short-term Impact	☐ Long-term Impact
	☐ Execution	☐ Breakthrough
	☐ Problem Elimination	☐ "Go on Offense"

Analytical thinking processes the following possibilities:

- How strong is the evidence for moving forward?

- Can you spot any flaws in the plan?

- Is the desired outcome based on clear rational thinking or emotion?

- How does the plan compare to others in the field who have done similar things?

The key to analytical thinking is to develop an objective approach that evaluates facts and sets aside personal bias and rash emotions. A fair analysis of anything considers these factors:

- Different opinions and viewpoints

- What other successful people have done in similar situations

- A logical order of justifications for what must be done to reach the desired outcome

- Evaluating the strengths and weaknesses of decisions

- Playing "devil's advocate" in considering why not to do something

- Making sure well-substantiated evidence supports your conclusions

- Removing any emotions or prejudices as much as possible

- Eliminating anything that does not support the desired outcome (the Big Impact)

Analytical thinking skills will distinguish you from the average person any day. Analytical thinking means not accepting something at face value but using your diagnostic skills to assess the evidence and consider the implications of information based on its value and affect. To think analytically, you can engage in what-if thinking—"If we do this, how will it affect my desired outcome?" Choose a problem and systematically think through how your decision will make an impact: How relevant is it to solving the problem? How a problem or situation is defined determines not only how we feel about it, but also what information is crucial, how we should act upon it, and the implications it will have on us.

Each situation can be defined in more than one way, so analytical thinking is about finding the best approach. In order to find that answer we must be able to spot false assumptions (e.g., All the people I see have two legs, so all humans must have two legs), and it must be challenging (e.g. "How can I be wrong? Is there a better solution?"). Make it a habit to require evidence for your decision. Consider your sources as well—how reliable are they? Ask yourself what bias may have factored into others trying to influence your decision, such as whether the sales manager may have underforecasted in order to exceed quota.

Effective analytical thinking factors in the myriad of possibilities based on an objective or a problem to be solved, which can lead to a do's and don't list of what you should do. If you can prioritize your objectives and problems, you can then assess what information will best help to achieve the big impact.

PACEsetters Synthesize Information, They Don't Just Manage It

In an article by Dr. Howard Gardner, *The Synthesizing Leader*, which appeared in *The HBR List: Breakthrough Ideas for 2006*, it was explained that the single most important trait of future leaders in the development of the world is the ability to synthesize information. Synthesizing which information to utilize includes, in addition to other things, developing standards for selection, such as discerning credibility and relevance. It also includes the ability to answer the question: "Does this information form a coherent story?" and "Do these trends make sense?" With a plethora of data coming from multiple and global sources, selecting which chunks of information are worthy of one's limited attention is a key competency for success, and ultimately, for being a PACEsetter.

A leader synthesizes information, while a manager evaluates. A leader requests that his or her managers provide status reports and other critical statistics, and then the leader considers all of the data and tries to synthesize it into a basic statement followed by a direction for the entire set of problems. Essentially, synthesis entails dealing with abstract concepts to create a vision or broad strategic plan, whereas evaluation deals with details to provide a tactical response.

Leadership assesses the long-term impact of the information and circumstances, whereas management considers short-term goals. Leadership defines the next big impact to bring the organization to the next level of success, whereas management is concerned with effectively executing the plan by controlling processes and tracking progress.

PACEsetter leaders use information to see the broader view. They take various facts and observations and connect the dots to create a clear picture of what is likely to occur in advance of it happening. In other words, they put their organization on the offense. PACEsetters understand how to clear through data by looking for the 10-20% of information that will return 80-90% of the value. They think in terms of a sequence of importance and consequence, laser focus on goals, factor in constraints, formulate alternative courses, and develop back-up plans should a decision go wrong. Being a PACEsetter in the 21st century and beyond will require a new paradigm that can form information into breakthroughs.

Being a Strategic-Thinker-PACEsetter

The concept of problem solving versus strategizing is comparable to fixing potholes versus building a new road. Strategic thinking is a critical skill for achieving success in both your personal and professional life, and it's a hallmark of the PACEsetter. It includes setting short-term as well as long-term goals, establishing effective plans, anticipating unexpected situations, analyzing all facets of your surroundings, and tapping resources that will help to meet goals.

Most focus on what's ahead, but strategic thinkers (i.e., PACEsetters) look in all directions to look for blockbuster solutions. They question the status quo by challenging accepted beliefs, uncovering unproductive habits within organizations, and rethinking problems to identify hidden root causes. They are great at connecting the dots by engaging thought leaders and identifying key links between solution providers that should be interrelated.

Trusting their gut as well as their mind, strategic thinkers, which defines all PACEsetters, can assimilate information, cut through hidden agendas, and make decisions that factor in the divergent views of their wide network of sources without overanalyzing. They are constant learners, looking for cutting-edge information while challenging others to rethink approaches.

Are you a strategic thinker? If not, try overcoming the tendency to think tactically in favor of looking at things more critically from a higher level, so that you can view systems instead of parts. In other words, instead of looking for the defective part in a malfunctioning process, evaluate how the overall process can be improved by means of something different.

Strategic thinking focuses on relationships, the environment, possible outcomes, totality, the larger processes, and looping feedback. Start at a 10,000-foot view and drill down from there. Don't focus on the problem, focus on the larger system to identify why problems happen, and then don't jump to conclusions without a comprehensive solutions approach that insists on a new paradigm.

Pause, and Make Good Decisions

The information age that has birthed technologies at a faster rate than any time in history has overwhelmed our ability to think clearly. Thoughtful consideration has been replaced with this hurried human impulse that all of us have toward taking action, even at the risk of taking the wrong action. The classic way of thinking is that we have to just get things done. The myth is that we can multi-task effectively—the brain doesn't work maximally when rushed, as confirmed by recent studies. We need to pause.

Have you ever taken a time-out in the morning just to wonder? Consider the trends that are happening in the world, in your environment, or in your industry. Over time, that dedicated pondering allows your subconscious to bubble-up an idea that could lead to a breakthrough. Unplug yourself from the computer for a while, and you might be surprised at how refreshing it can be. Stop the outside interruptions that can cause you several minutes to recover from, and try not to interrupt others so much.

Getting to a breakthrough decision requires dedicated reflective time. All too often, companies reflect on situations only after a disaster happens. Say, a recall is forced on a business, and a post mortem meeting of the directors occurs to deliberate on what went wrong. Why can't we conduct those deliberations upfront? Think through the different possibilities, and the potential downsides and upsides before they happen. That requires dedicated time each day to either individually or collectively (as a self-directed team) create opportunity instead of deconstructing misfortune from making rash decisions.

Great leaders are oftentimes thought of as decisive. They get it done. But decisiveness is not always the mark of a great leader or even a great performer. Only *good* decisions merit a seal of approval. Quickly-made judgments can be wrong or right depending on the skill of the decider. PACEsetters understand how to balance emotion with reason in determining what will constructively and positively influence themselves, those affected by the decision, their stakeholders (customers), and the organization as a whole.

Leading Change—Tipping Point Decisions

Being able to accurately assess the tradeoffs between the positive influences of change, and the possible downside to others (like stress and uncertainty) will determine whether the impact is worth it or not. Knowing when to act, and when to wait for additional data gathering or for the condition to be ripe is critical to making good decisions. The tipping point for moving forward depends on managing the variables without becoming overwhelmed with the chaos of too much information and too many advisors.

Important to the process is making a list of the desired outcomes (priorities) and objectively assessing whether the consequence of a decision will produce those outcomes. Another checkpoint follows the Rotary Four-Way Test, which answers these questions: Is it the truth? Is it fair to all concerned? Will it build goodwill and better friendships? Will it be beneficial to all concerned? Another technique for making quick decisions is called *heuristics*, which means drawing up lists of "for" and "against," and going with the longer list.

Sometimes "and/or" decisions can be turned into "both" or "all of the above" decisions. At times, we limit our options based on preconceived expectations, when in fact, a limited decision may not be necessary. Instead, we can trial our options in order to determine what works and what doesn't work.

Increasing options can be beneficial, as in selecting the two top candidates when interviewing job candidates so that if one candidate removes herself from consideration, you will have a readily available option. Positioning a decision in a narrow frame is only effective when signs tell us that the options we are considering are really not viable options at all. For example, if we think we're picking the "least harmful option," we need to start sourcing new options. Good decision-making isn't about just making a decision—it has to be the right one for all concerned.

Trust Your Gut—It's the Sum of All You Know

Some of the best decision-makers rely on their gut thinking once they attain a peace that enough analysis has occurred. Several studies have shown that instinct as much as intellect leads to the right decision. Professor Marius Usher of Tel Aviv University's School of Psychological Sciences and his fellow researchers found that participants who were forced to choose between two options based on instinct alone made the right choice up to 90% of the time. Usher as well as others point to a person's ability to average value based on a repository of stored information in the brain.

As we accumulate knowledge, the brain begins to recognize patterns, and then it unconsciously organizes these patterns into groups of information—a mechanism the late social scientist Dr. Herbert Simon called chunking. Our long-term memory stores these clusters of patterns into a larger composition that can be recognized as an impulse of intuition. Of course, that commonly called "gut feeling" is not flawless, but it can be an important part of the decision-making process. It's actually a form of unconscious reasoning resulting from our brain's stored information.

Athletes in particular excel by trusting their instincts after extensive study and practice. During game time, overthinking can impede their ability to react quickly, so they allow intuition to direct their activities. In the professional environment when time is limited, "gut decisions" often can lead to greater progress, especially if corroborated with others and the facts. Steve Jobs said about trusting his gut, "It never let me down, and it has made all the difference in my life." That small voice that nudges you when you're conflicted between two choices can be real. Trusting your intuition factors in the due diligence process described earlier that leads to an inner peace. That's when you know that you've made a good decision.

Decide: 7 Tipping Point Questions

1. Is is truthful and ethical?
2. Is it fair to everyone concerned?
3. Will it benefit all concerned?
4. Will it build cooperative attitudes or feelings?
5. Instead of an and/or decision, is there an "all of the above" solution?
6. Instead of choosing the least harmful option, can a new and better option be sourced?
7. What does your gut say?

A P.L.A.N. IS CONCLUDED WITH A NEED-SATISFY

NEED-SATISFY

After taking an extended vacation with the family, I went to the post office to retrieve almost two weeks of undelivered mail. After plopping the pile of mostly junk mail onto the table, I laser focused on the mission—to determine which items to open and which to throw into the recycle bin. My plan—to sift through the mail and prioritize those pieces that really mattered. My qualifying factors? WIIFM— What's In It For Me? I also looked for mail that would benefit someone else in the family—the WIIFT (What's In It For Them?).

As the arbiter in charge of managing the mail stockpile, I would decide which mass marketers were successful. Those mailers that successfully translated what they offered into my language ended up in the open pile. Their marketing piece got to the point, or the hook, right up front. Their message started with a problem I wanted to fix, and then indicated how the product or service could fix it for me, or the family. This is the crux of satisfying a need.

NEED SATISFY:
Maintaining an 'Others' Focus

PLAN
LEARN
ANALYZE
NEED SATISFY

In a comprehensive study conducted by TenorCorp, the most successful sales persons were able to place their personal agenda (or needs) aside initially so they could focus on the underlying needs of the arbiter. Their intent was to understand, rather than to be understood. Numerous other examples lead to the conclusion that the arbiter intuitively knows the difference between someone who wants to help him/her, or someone who remains focused on their personal needs. In almost all relationships, the 'others-focused individuals' achieve greater success.

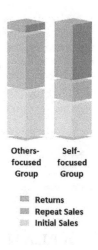

Others-focused Group   Self-focused Group

Returns
Repeat Sales
Initial Sales

I'm sure that each of the marketers who put together those mailers planned their ad campaigns by calculating how they could fix the target customer's problem. But, customers don't care about *how* someone or something can fix their problem; they simply want to know that the one they choose can deliver the results.

To the customer, whether internal (e.g., peers and supervisors) or external (e.g., buyers and consumers), *results* matter most importantly. So the first message to a customer or arbiter should always be about results that matter to them. For example, a project lead might say to the department manager/arbiter, "We reduced waste by 20% and increased production by 30%." That kind of transformational message almost always makes a big impact, and establishes a positive basis for continuing the conversation—because it focuses on what matters to the *customer*.

When I say "customer," I mean anyone for whom we're trying to do something. A customer could be a loved one who needs help. Anyone who could benefit from our services or what we produce is a customer. The problem in trying to satisfy another's needs usually starts from not properly identifying the customer's *real* needs. Most make their decisions on how they *perceive* other's needs, and the solution is determined based on anchoring a decision to a personal bias.

Avoid Anchoring

Anchoring or focalism is a common human tendency to rely too heavily, or "anchor," on one trait or piece of information when making decisions. Typically, individuals anchor, or overdepend, on specific information or personal bias and then adjust their decisions to align with their perception of what needs to be done. Usually once the anchor is set, there is a bias toward what appears right. Take, for example, a person looking to buy a new home—he may overly focus on the "curb appeal" of the house, and use that criteria as a basis for evaluating the value of the house, rather than considering the construction of the house or its value in comparison to other similar homes in the neighborhood.

That's one of the main reasons why people or companies miss the mark, as when the Coca-Cola Company started development on a new kind of Coke in early 1985. It was a variation of a product that reached back through American history, a response to the emerging challenge from an upstart called Pepsi. Coca-Cola, then two years into taste tests and research, was working with the secrecy of a military operation.

Then on April 23, New Coke was launched with millions in advertising, including prime-time TV ads. Company Chairman Roberto C. Goizueta proclaimed New Coke "smoother, rounder yet bolder," speaking of it more like a fine wine than as a carbonated treat.

But public reaction was overwhelmingly negative; some people likened the change in Coke to trampling the American flag.

Soon people were hoarding cases of the old Coke. In June 1985, Newsweek reported that savvy black marketers sold old Coke for $30 a case. A Hollywood producer, enamored with his comfortable beverage, reportedly rented a wine cellar to hold 100 cases of the old Coke.

On July 11, Coca-Cola pulled New Coke from store shelves. "We did not understand the deep emotions of so many of our customers for Coca-Cola," said company President Donald R. Keough. Indeed, despite hordes of market research sampling and numerous consumer experts working on the project, Coca-Cola had made one of the biggest corporate mistakes of all-time. Why the key decision-makers failed to identify the obvious can be debated, however, had they been able to step "outside of their minds" and "into the minds" of their consumers a far different decision may have resulted.

Maintain an "Others Focus"

In my experience, and based on studies done by my organization and others, most people succeed not because they have great minds or because of outstanding resources, but because they maintain an *others focus*. If the executives at Coca-Cola had not anchored their decision on their own personal wants or the wants of an internal few, and instead objectively focused on the customer, a far better decision would have been likely.

One of the purest forms of meeting customer wants, sales, supports this theory. At TenorCorp, we reviewed the success of more than 100 top sales performers, and about the same number of low (bottom 10%) sales performers, asking their customers, peers and supervisors about their key success factors.

The most frequently occurring comments about the top performers fit into an *others focus* phraseology, with words such as:

"attentive to my needs," "listens well," "doesn't push his agenda onto me," "goes the extra mile," "doesn't tell me, asks me," and "if I need something, my rep is reliable to give me what I need in a timely manner." When asked about who gives the most in their relationship (with the salesperson), the customer responded over 80% of the time that the (top producing) salesperson gave the most in their relationship.

Conversely, the customers of the low performers made comments such as he/she was: "pushing his product on me," "slick," "arrogant," "unreliable," "talked over me," and "not in touch with my needs." When asked the same question about who gave the most in their relationship, the customers responded overwhelmingly that the salesperson gave them very little, and in fact, many said that their time spent with the salesperson was wasted. These low performers were so hyper focused on their own agenda and needs that they mostly ignored the underlying needs of their customers.

When we looked at the two groups' actual sales performance, the others-focused group realized an initial close rate (reflected in first-time, initial sales) of almost double that of the self-focused group. More strikingly, repeat sales produced by the others-focused group were more than quadruple that of the self-focused group. An almost inverse relationship occurred with respect to product returns. The self-focused sales people experienced seven times the number of returns.

Successful people continuously look for opportunities to help someone else first, and themselves second, without sacrificing their own plans. As Zig Ziglar once said to a group of businesspeople—"Stop selling, start helping." PACEsetters maintain an emphasis on WIIFT (What's In It For Them) as a their modus operandi. By giving instead of expecting, the most successful people actually gain more in return as a result of their concern for others. This runs contrary to the commonly held belief that "me-first" people succeed over more altruistic people. To those with an others focus, the focus on the arbiter is always key to their own success.

Most people succeed because they maintain an *others focus*.

Overcoming Assumptions

I once thought a particular medical device would be a true breakthrough. It was safer than others in its category, and I was sure it would succeed in the marketplace. So I dove into manufacturing and promoting this device, fearing that if I did not, my team would perceive me as having just "given up." It failed miserably. Because of my personal bias and ego-based desire to be right, I pressed on without seeing the truth. I was afraid to be wrong, and in the end because of my bullheadedness, I *was* wrong. But, it took over a year of trying to make it work before I finally admitted it was a bad idea in the first place. Now (with perfect hindsight), I question how I could have been so self-deceived.

Instead of conducting the proper amount of due diligence, I took the easy way by applauding myself for my dedication. These kinds of assumption-based approaches can destroy effective planning, and sever once-healthy relationships. My device example was a hard but valuable lesson that later resulted in much better decisions. According to our research of PACEsetters, they are faithful in spending months, if not years of intentional research and practice necessary to master an effective plan or approach based solely on what works. It's really hard not to jump to conclusions, but those who persist with the facts end up making more of an impact.

To put it another way, if you're always busy, running from place to place, and giving in to distractive impulses and rapid assumptions that we're all subject to these days, you sacrifice awareness of the present and compromise your influence over the future. If you want to have control, first you have to relax and pay attention and face the reality of a situation. To put it more succinctly, if you're not aware of what's really going on around and inside you, your vision will be severely compromised.

In trying to discover what causes a thriving life, objective research confirms that egocentric decision-making is a common trap with disastrous consequences. It lulls us into a pattern of busyness that might have very little to do with real achievement. Egocentric thinking is when someone believes something and thinks everyone else should, too. For example, an extremely egocentric person would plan a vacation around his favorites, not taking into consideration the needs of his companions. Egocentricity blurs our objective ability. Reality-based planning always answers the question for the customer or team: *What's in it for them?* That's really all the customer or arbiter wants. Keeping that question top of mind focuses our efforts onto what matters.

So are all egocentric assumptions harmful? Not entirely. Most people make assumptions based on some level of egocentric reasoning. For example, if your friend tells you that she got four hours of sleep last night, the first assumption you would probably make is that your friend is tired. That's a fair deduction, but an egocentric one. Maybe your friend only *needs* four hours of sleep each night. Or perhaps four cups of coffee invigorated her. Egocentric assumptions can actually be offset by connecting the gap between the assumption and reality by asking questions, like, "Courtney, are you tired from getting only four hours of sleep?" It sounds simple, but the bottom line is that all assumptions must be challenged through objective reality-based assessments. Again, an others focus keeps us from focusing on our own assumptions.

Consider this story: Jerry's intentional plan is to get in shape. His purpose will be to live a healthier life, so he joins a gym. Jerry goes through the ritual of visiting the gym every other day after donning his pricey workout clothes, and does ten relatively easy repetitions on the same machines each time. Seeing no significant change in his body fat and muscle strength, Jerry has confused the discipline of going to the gym (his *perceived* goal) with his *real* goal to lower his body fat content by 20%. An honest assessment of his progress could be measured through a proven strength-training regimen as prescribed by experts. But, Jerry focused far too much on his schedule for training than on the outcome itself, and the prescribed regimen that would best achieve it. This example shows the faulty nature of egocentric productivity.

Some of us get so busy following a to-do list that we lose sight of the reality based planning required to get the job done. The perceived goal of working a lot can override the real goal of producing results. In the case of Jerry, an honest assessment of the W.I.I.F.M (What's In It For Me?) would have reminded him of the payoff that was motivating him. It wasn't just going to the gym.

Trying to plan from an egocentric point of view only distorts the reality of what must be accomplished. Being laser focused on the payoff (the WIIFM or WIIFT) coupled with a reality-based plan that is validated objectively tells us when we have arrived. Being right from an egocentric viewpoint doesn't always equate to doing the right thing. Instead, the assessment of a plan lies outside of our perception of what needs to be done and finds itself straight in the middle of what the arbiter sees as having been accomplished. This is true needs satisfaction that defines a successfully completed plan.

PURPOSE
(fuels meaning)
Reverse engineer dreams and intentionally define each purpose

The PACE Formula®

P.L.A.N.

PLAN—Who (Arbiter), What (the BIG IMPACT), Why (Question) When (Urgency)

LEARN—Expand Vision, Think the New, Be Prepared

ANALYZE—Synthesize, Strategize, Pause, Decide

NEED-SATISFY—Know WIIFT/WIIFM, Be Others-Focused, Check Reality

The Power
to Thrive!

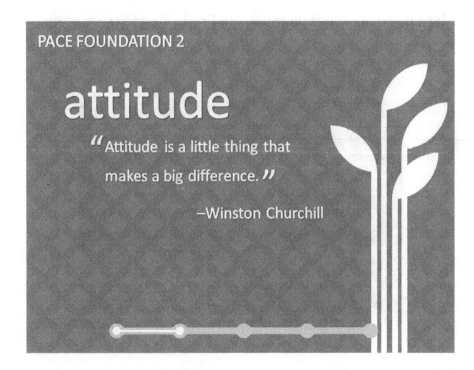

PACE FOUNDATION 2

attitude

"Attitude is a little thing that makes a big difference."

—Winston Churchill

CHAPTER 3: ATTITUDE—TO FIND SATISFACTION

Thrive Drive is to...
G.R.O.W.
A HEALTHY ATTITUDE BEGINS WITH THE ABLITY TO GROW

Self-Awareness

P.A.C.E.SETTER THOMAS JEFFERSON SAID, "Nothing can stop a person with the right mental attitude from achieving his goal; nothing on earth can help the person with the wrong mental attitude." One of the most critical steps toward achieving your dreams in life is to elevate your attitude and its impact on your performance and your ability to make a positive impact on others. Whenever I've faced a major project, one of the first questions I've asked the team is: "What is your attitude?"

Most people struggle with the answer because we tend not to be aware of our attitude until someone tells us. We understand our emotions, whether we are angry or happy, but as to our attitude—that's usually left for others to determine. Our effectiveness and ability to thrive could be greatly increased by recognizing our attitude, which will enable us to control our self-speak like self-motivation, self-pity, self-evaluation, and self-achievement. The key is to stop, be still, and know your state of mind. Self-awareness means understanding how our thoughts translate into our perception, and how others perceive our attitude.

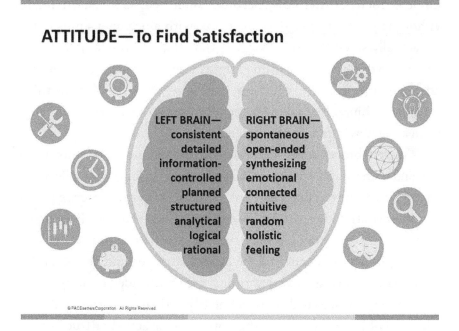

ATTITUDE—To Find Satisfaction

LEFT BRAIN—	RIGHT BRAIN—
consistent	spontaneous
detailed	open-ended
information-	synthesizing
controlled	emotional
planned	connected
structured	intuitive
analytical	random
logical	holistic
rational	feeling

Left and Right Hemisphere Thinking

Neuroscientists have long understood that the brain can rewire itself in response to experience, a phenomenon known as neuroplasticity. We can train our brain by virtue of how we interpret those experiences. Our right-brain hemisphere freely associates everything around us without any context of the past or future. Stroke victims whose left brain is disabled, leaving them with primarily right-brain functioning, explain their thinking as "free," "unencumbered," "unable to associate anything except their surroundings," "being one with everything," and "aware of the moment."

The left-brain hemisphere associates past memories in order to determine future performance. It tells us that because the phone rings, someone is calling, so we must answer. Or, it can tell us that because we failed at something, we must avoid doing it. Or, it can make a general conclusion that we are a failure, period—"so stop trying."

When patterns of negative attitudes arise, we need to train the brain to tap into the right-hemisphere way of thinking: stay in the moment, focus on the now, become connected to the surroundings without any need to judge them. Think with a beginner's mind. Stop and actually smell the roses. We can train our brain to stop, look and cross into a different programmed state of mind through re-routing the left-brain's propensity to think the same way. One way of doing this is to try new things, like taking an adventure to someplace different or inculcating newfound understandings.

The left-brain thinks methodically, by picking out events in the past and using them to predict the future. The longer we allow our experiences to be confined to what seems normal, the more we enable our left-brain thinking and disable our right-brain thinking. If the right-brain had its way, it would only consider the here and now, with no concept of the difference between people or places, and no perception of the past or future. Defining reality uses both sides by factoring in personal experience, reality as defined by others, and the dictionary definition of reality, which is "the state of being actual or true."

However, our reality is what we make it, by consciously choosing our beliefs. This takes the form of inner-speak—the reality of what we tell ourselves. Our inner-speak can also be used as the mechanism for re-wiring the left-brain to think more optimistically, which then comes across as a more optimistic attitude to the world around us.

Reflective thinking is the process of taking in one's surroundings without any thought as to what to do.

Sparking Creativity

Free association uses the technique of engaging the right-brain first, and then forcing a connection to the left-brain as a means for making an idea happen. This technique of rerouting the brain's synaptic pattern to create alternative perceptions uses disparate words or images to spontaneously suggest another way—say, by comparing apples to computers. Steve Jobs used this type of thinking to connect his left and right-brain thinking in creating the company, Apple. Apples have nothing to do with computers, but Jobs' right-brain was sparking creativity when he came up with the name. The company's later tag line, "Think Different," was a testimony of the free association that allowed Apple to revolutionize the computer industry through "out-of-the-right-brain" thinking.

At one advertising firm with which I worked, all of us at a roundtable session were challenged to tap into our right brain creativity, when an advertising instructor gave us the task of making a chemical company look "sexy." Sitting at a table strewn with little toys, putty and squeeze balls, we were asked: "Tell me an idea excited by the word chemicals," and then the moderator showed a picture of children playing in the field with a caption, "What chemicals should they be playing around with?"

We were given a few minutes to jot down concepts. That experience fostered greater out-of-the-box thinking—by providing a potential negative and turning it into a positive—which engaged right-brain stimulation with left brain associations. Providing prompts like those provocative questions provoke creative thinking by focusing concepts onto seemingly disparate words or phrases, while engaging some left-brain "formative" processing in order to prevent scattered thinking, by creating certain boundaries, like instructing the students that, "You can only create a concept that can actually be manufactured." Too much freedom can actually stifle practical creative thinking, so some framework is necessary without creating too rigid boundaries.

Try this exercise to "rewire" your brain's negative thinking by, for example, piecing together a story that positions your worst fear with your favorite place, and by creating a pleasant ending with these two diametrically opposed forces. Your brain may find an alternative way to reposition your fear in a positive light.

Spontaneous inspirations that challenge paradigms trigger the mind to go places seemingly unrelated to the challenge, and then force a way to funnel these ideas into a workable concept. Think of associations that seem totally unrelated, such as the words stars to vacuums, or oranges to cars. Most of the time when presented with outrageous links, you will become energized with a type of playful exuberance to place the randomness together. Try starting with a negative association, like toxic is to chemicals, and turn it into a positive, like life is to chemicals.

Consciously eliminate the filters of your thinking to begin considering the ridiculous or what may seem incorrect. Afterwards, you can mold it into something more practical. The key is to circumvent your programmed way of thinking in order to conceptualize something new and fresh. This is how we spark innovation. So why don't more people engage their right-brain thinking to solve problems with new solutions?

Changing Behavioral Patterns

Many of us are hard-wired with behavioral patterns that were established at an early age. Some of these can ground us, such as the feelings of security we gain in family. But, some patterns bind us to destructive beliefs. Being told we are dumb, or undisciplined, or any other such negatives are general indictments that can translate into painful and inaccurate self-perceptions. Left-brain dominance tells us that because we have been called "bad," then we must be bad in each circumstance of life. Habitual poor attitudes due to a controlling left-brain are usually the outcome of past experiences that can lead to fear, anger, stress, and poor self-esteem. It takes commitment to identify the root causes of our negative left-brain-speak.

Then after realizing the lies that we've been telling ourselves, we can begin to discipline our thoughts to enable right-brain thinking—being still, staying in the now, looking forward to the future with a fresh perspective—which disconnects those negative feedback loops and allows us to be free of those past negatives. So each time you become unfairly self-critical, consciously take control of your inner-speak in order to re-wire those left-brain loops. Engage your ability to think different by imagining new possibilities for your life as you become unchained to believe in here-to-fore unseen possibilities. This is the beginning of renewing our mind. As PACEsetters, we are fully aware of right-brain, left-brain thinking, and can integrate the two in order to grow our attitude.

TO IMPROVE OUR ATTITUDE WE MUST
G.R.O.W. WITH GRATITUDE

To reset mindset

ATTITUDE

GROW in Gratitude

GRATITUDE

R

O

W

An attitude of gratitude means routinely expressing thankfulness and appreciation in all parts of your life by concentrating on what you have. If you only concentrate on what you don't have, you'll always want more and will never be fully satisfied.

Attitude of Gratitude—Even in Times of Trouble

Have you ever been around a person with a great attitude? These persons don't live a trouble-free life. There are lots of people who suffer tremendous burdens, and they are joyful. It is not happiness that causes gratefulness. It is gratefulness that causes joyfulness. When something valuable is freely given, gratefulness happens. The good news is that this doesn't need to only happen once in a while. We can be people who live gratefully.

Each moment is a gift. There is no other assurance that there will be another moment. This moment with all of its opportunity is our only given moment. The gift within this gift is the opportunity. Opportunity knocks each moment as a new gift to be opened. Another piece of good news is that if you miss that opportunity, another moment with another opportunity awaits us. Of course we cannot be grateful for everything. We cannot be grateful for violence, war and exploitation. However, we can be grateful in each given moment. The key is how we can harness this moment by moment.

A dedication to—grow, improve, and move forward—instills a fresh way of thinking that reflects itself in a can-do attitude. The self-speak of gratitude says things like, "I can do this," "I am capable," "This is an opportunity for me to succeed," and "I have been successful before, and I can do it again." An attitude of gratitude reflects a positive outlook on what happens to us. The first ingredient required to **G.R.O.W.** is **G**ratitude.

Here are thirteen ways to develop Gratitude:

- Use positive self-affirmations many times a day (with powerful words of declaration and faith)

- Keep a journal

- Use visualization (think vividly of the day when you will achieve what you want)

- Reach out to thank others

- Be still and focus on pleasant surroundings

- Share good experiences with others (Studies show that people who share good news about a pleasant experience enjoy it even more.)

- Elevate your posture by smiling, sitting-up, puffing out your chest, and walking faster

- Use the W.O.W. (Watch Our Words) technique by noticing the words we speak to our self and others— and eliminate the negative ones as much as possible

- Meet others with a positive greeting (e.g., "I am so happy to see you!" or "This is a great moment")— studies show that others will be more encouraging of you if you are encouraging to them

- Practice being enthusiastic!

- For every negative, consider two positives

- Tap into your faith as a means toward being hopeful

- Use humor—there are actually health benefits to "lightening-up"

Sending Out "Positive Vibes" Through a Natural State of Thankfulness

The ability to align your thoughts and feelings with your actions allows you to send out what we commonly call "positive vibes." Feel gratitude for every act of giving by another person, and you'll attract others to you. If you feel entitled or dismissive, you will attract negative feelings like resentment, anger and regret. Once you've trained your thoughts and feelings, expressing gratitude becomes a natural process of being in a state of thankfulness.

When you retrain your brain to feel thankful with thoughts of gratitude, you are intentionally projecting those thoughts to people around you. This is what we commonly refer to as the *Law of Attraction*. The way in which we think and the thoughts that we hold most strongly in our minds have a profound effect on our lives in almost every way. What's called "thought energy" is sending the right vibe (vibrations) that will resonate to the other person in causing the same response. Positive feelings and thoughts will elicit a positive response, just as an attitude of gratitude will elicit positive feelings.

Gratitude extracts positive feelings such as joy, positivism, excitement and love. Not only will an attitude of gratitude create the positive responses you desire, but expressing gratitude also makes you feel satisfied. Anytime you find yourself in a negative situation you can quickly turn your feelings around by developing gratitude through coming to a STOP, getting STILL, and becoming SELF-AWARE. These approaches can transform our feelings. Feeling genuinely thankful is a failsafe way to achieve joy and realize your desire for success.

Choosing to be positive and having a grateful attitude will ultimately determine how you're going to live your life.

TO G.R.O.W. FORWARD REQUIRES A

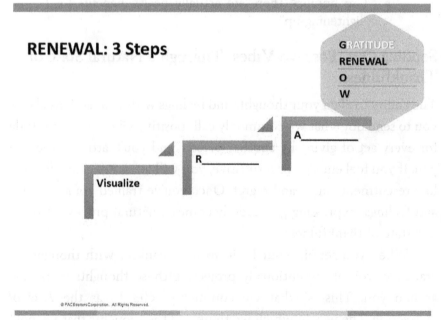

RENEWAL: 3 Steps

G RATITUDE
RENEWAL
O
W

A_____

R_____

Visualize

RENEWAL OF THE MIND

Three Steps to Renewing the Mind

Have you ever tried renewing your mind by declaring war on your thinking? Maybe or maybe not, but perhaps it's time to do so. It starts with remaining hopeful, which tends to attract resources for fulfilling your hope. Oftentimes increased hope signifies that the renewing of the mind is working. Making personal declarations, like "I'm an incredibly important person," or "I'm an influencer of many people," fuels it. One person indeed visualized himself as an important influencer of people, and succeeded as that for a nation, and world.

Nelson Mandela lived for 27 years in a narrow prison cell without any hope of ever getting out. He wrote extensively about how visualization helped him keep his sanity and health in place while being imprisoned. Each day spent in prison, Nelson Mandela thought about walking out of that cell and what he would do once free. That thought kept him alive and at some point became reality. Mandela wrote extensively how the power of visualization helped him maintain a positive attitude. "I thought continually of the day when I would walk free. I fantasized about what I would like to do," he wrote in his autobiography. Mandela visualized himself as a liberator of his nation from apartheid, which gave him confident hope.

Visualization is one of the three steps required to renew the mind in order to produce a healthy attitude.

VISUALIZE

How Does Visualization Work?

Many people use visualization to relax and renew. Visualizing positive images, like placing oneself in a dream position or a peaceful setting in nature lowers blood pressure as well as the bloodstream's level of stress hormones. Renewed, these visualizers are ready to face life's challenges.

Some use repeated visualizations to achieve personal or professional goals. By visualizing his release from prison, for example, Nelson Mandela could pave the way for his eventual position as a leader in becoming South Africa's first black chief executive.

I once coached an underperforming manager by asking her to visualize herself becoming more self-confident in a work situation that was uncomfortable for her, which resulted in her becoming more assertive. After 16 years holding low-level positions, Lynda overcame her self-perception that she didn't belong with the "high and mighty." Initially, whenever Lynda pictured herself in positions of greater challenge, fears of being in the spotlight highlighted her lack of self-confidence. Her thick New Jersey accent and use of slang words didn't quite fit the image of an executive, and she didn't want to embarrass herself. Staying unnoticed was safer, Lynda thought. Then she realized through visualizing herself as an executive that she had always demonstrated the leadership characteristics that people admired. People throughout the years saw her as the "go-to" person. So after Lynda bridged the fact that she had always been a leader even without the title, she decided to apply for a vice president position—and got it!

Leadership is a Mindset, Not a Position

Leadership is a mindset, not a position. Realizing this is not about being aware of one's *potential*, rather it happens when someone becomes aware of their current *ability* by visualizing both the past (successes) and future (possibilities), and connecting them to the present. That creates a healthier awareness of one's self. PACEsetters use visualization to search themselves in order to become more cognizant of their feelings, wants, and capacities. Through positive images, they can still themselves enough to connect with their emotions, thoughts, and intentions. They allow the visual to lead them onward.

Sometimes people need to resolve some conflict within themselves. A person who is feeling oppressed or depressed, for example, can use visualization as a means to find the answer. It starts by identifying the situation that has triggered the inner conflict.

Try this exercise: Close your eyes and visualize the situation or reason that triggered one of your problems. As you begin to ponder possible solutions to the problem, you see yourself in those possibilities, growing stronger like some superhero changing into his/her suit then flying over everything. The feeling of helplessness will begin to dissipate, replaced by the confidence that you are there, fully ready to assume the place in your visual. See your conflict from that 10,000-foot vantage point—as smaller...miniscule—and *you* as the conqueror of what caused the conflict. Think, "What are some new and better solutions I can use from this invincible position?"

Now open your eyes and consider what you can do based on your new empowering position of authority. Notice how much more powerful you feel. See how you've transformed that negative self-speak into a more confident narrative. Now, try doing this for those things that are inciting fear within you. Make those triggers of fear smaller and you bigger. View those intimidating relationships with people who ignite fear within you as insignificant in the overall scheme of things. Those perceived imbalances in relationship will need to be replaced with a sense of equal-power sharing, or even better, with you as the "superhero" on the "right side of justice." Believe it or not, this exercise has been shown to decrease the levels of serotonin in the body, the neurotransmitter that cause irritability, sleeping problems, depression and even migraines in some cases.

Other Visualization Techniques

Here are eight visualization techniques you can use:

- *Visualize the goal or result desired* (Imagine your environment and activities after you get that promotion and the processes you will go through for making your bigger decisions.)

- *Project your skill in a real-world setting* (Before making that sale, picture the customer and steps you will take, question by question, seeing the responses as they will happen.)

- *Be still* (Turn off the phone, get in a restful place, some serene location in your mind, feel the grass or sand between your toes, smell the crisp air, stretch and release your muscles.)

- *Visualize the type of person you wish to be* (If you want to be a sports player, see yourself on the field, focus on your motions, your practice, your opponent's style of play.)

- *Use affirmations* (If your goal is to lose weight, imagine your new body fitted in its new clothes, on the beach in a swimsuit, imagining how people will first respond to your more appealing body.)

- *Think baby steps to keep it real* (Instead of projecting yourself beyond what seems plausible, start with a goal closer to reality—before seeing yourself as president, see yourself as a manager first.)

- *Don't dwell on kicking a bad habit—dwell on its replacement* (If you're trying to quit smoking, don't remind yourself of the cigarette by picturing it; instead, dwell on what you will do instead, like going for a run.)

- Journal your visualization to keep it fresh and top of mind.

REFRAME

Turning Negatives into Positives

The second step for renewing the mind is reframing, and it is a step PACEsetters make frequently. It starts with a thought: Most of the disappointments we worry about are baseless, as amusingly expressed in a quote from Mark Twain, "My life has been filled with terrible misfortunes, most of which never happened." Our minds imagined them due to negative self-speak. Those trials that did actually occur made us stronger. Had we used a powerful renewal technique for those imagined or real disappointments, our attitude would have been transformed. That technique, *reframing*, involves identifying our destructive thoughts and replacing them with adaptive ones. Positive reframing means trying to reconsider things in a positive light, and it is a powerful way to transform our thinking.

2nd Step to Renewal—REFRAME

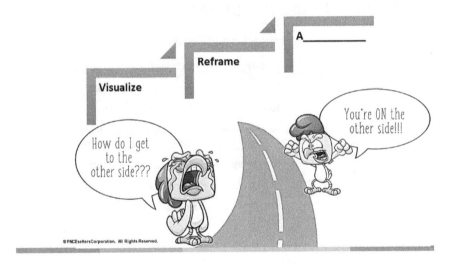

Can you reframe your obstacles as opportunities, even laugh at them as in, "Here goes another one—been there, done that!" It is not that easy, is it?—especially in the heat of the moment, but when we begin to trivialize problems, even laugh at them (even if we don't feel like joking about the problem), our brain accepts that dismissive attitude as acceptable. And the more we laugh at our problems, the more capable we become to perceive the solution. That's because our mind will start viewing challenges as insignificant in comparison to our ability to find a better way. When we get serious about determining a better approach, and trivialize the problem, only the answer seems relevant.

Seeing a problem as a place to shine requires that we place it in a different setting. Look at setbacks as times to learn and change direction. Out of the box thinking challenges assumptions, but it also reframes ideas to consider them in a new way, and it uses lateral thinking to look at problems from many angles instead of tackling them head-on.

COMMON FRAMING STYLES

	TENDENCY	REFRAME
Procrastinator	to delay	Do it earlier.
Over-Generalizer	to judge	Consider positive norms.
Over-Achiever	to fail	Accept imperfection.
Low Self-Esteemer	to withdraw	Focus on helping others and satisfying personal needs.
Self-Pitier	to give-up	Be vulnerable with others.
Clairvoyant	to regress	Learn and develop potential.
Risk-Avoider	to stress	Factor in past successes.

(Figure 3.1 - Common Framing Styles)

A situation might include someone saying, "I never have time to eat breakfast," and reframing it as, "I can wake-up a little earlier to eat something." Or an overgeneralizer might stub her toe and say, "I can never get a break," and then thoughtfully reframe the mishap as, "This is just a little fluke; usually I'm free of pain, and this is not the end of the world." Overachievers often need to reframe their high expectations that "I need to do more" with something like, "I'm not always perfect, but I accomplish a lot and I'm always trying." Those with poor self-esteem often misread situations as with, "My friend hasn't called me in forever—she must not like me anymore," and reframe those thoughts with a view such as, "Maybe she feels that I'm too busy with all of my work, so I'll just call her to check-in and see if she's OK."

Feeling sorry for oneself is a big one, with people often saying, "Nobody cares about me"; the reframing would be to think something like, "I need to be more vulnerable with others so that they can be more open with me." And then there are the "clairvoyants," who can predict the future by saying, "I know he's going to reject me"; they can respond with a positive future-focused statement as "I can't predict the outcome, but if he doesn't like me, he's obviously not the one for me, and I'll eventually find the right person." You can reference common framing styles people use in Figure 3.1, with the corresponding tendency elicited by each, and the reframe that can be used to overcome negative perceptions. Which tendency describes your pattern of behavior? Making a positive change begins by understanding that each reframe happens with a new mindset reset.

If you are afraid to do something new, try reframing your resistance to the situation by remembering how good you felt after getting something else accomplished that was once daunting. Think of the task as enjoyable, and you're more likely to do it. Also, try reframing the cause of your stress with a more positive perspective, such as looking at that traffic jam as a time to think through things and listen to some good music. Think long-term—is this really something that will be important in a month or year? If what causes you stress is something you need to live with, such as an illness or a job loss, just try to accept it and look for the silver lining, share your feelings with others, learn to move on, and find time for relaxation.

You can reframe literally any thought you ever experience into something more positive. Self-critical thoughts that limit our potential, such as "I'm not good enough for the job," can be reframed by first understanding that situations do not have any intrinsic meaning. They can only be internalized once we interpret a situation as having meaning. As humans we tend to second-guess ourselves, as in that meeting seemed to go well, but then we start remembering all the things we could have said or done to make it better. To reframe the event, we need to understand that our interpretation of a failure is only because of the way we look at it.

This is not to say that our emotions are not valid—they certainly are! However, we can interpret even a bad situation as having a good meaning. For example, it may be raining outside which can spoil an outdoor event, but reframing this as an opportunity to go to the gym in order to meet your weight loss goal gives the rainy outcome a positive meaning.

Each thought carries with it a frame of mind—our underlying beliefs and assumptions implied by that thought. For example, when you think, "I never do well taking tests because I get too nervous," the frame is that nervousness causes people to fail at tests. In reality, most people get nervous taking tests, so the opportunity may be to limit that nervousness through a more disciplined study process.

Behind each negative thought lies some positive purpose. That negative speak has deceived you into thinking that it will help. By finding the positive purposes behind this inner speak, you can retrain your mind to uncover a positive reframe. So don't ridicule yourself for those negative thoughts; rather, turn them around. Journaling can be an effective way for reframing thoughts by noting consistently negative thought patterns that you can turn around.

Words matter. So try to soften some negatives by using accurate descriptions of how they make you feel rather than making general indictments; like, instead of saying "I can't stand pushy people," you might say something like, "When people keep telling me to do something more than once, it makes me feel like they don't trust me to do whatever they're requesting." Maintain a forward focus toward some resolution, such as, "In the future, I'm going to confirm what others tell me so that they know that I am hearing them." By practicing a forward thinking solutions approach, people tend to feel that they are growing as in, "I can see if this new approach makes a positive difference."

As humans, we invariably make assumptions, but through reframing we can challenge these assumptions by changing our perspective about any situation to give it a more positive meaning. Turning assumptions into forward thinking solutions helps us provide meaning to situations that have no intrinsic meaning. Opportunity happens when we replace our negative thoughts with more positive ones by challenging them.

To help you counter each negative with a positive, think of the opposite of the negative; for example, a fear of drowning while swimming could be countered with being able to prevent drowning by taking lessons. Believing that a job loss will be financially devastating could be reframed as an opportunity to start a new business that will be more rewarding. Do this for each negative belief until you have reframed that negative with a positive purpose for each.

3rd Step to Renewal—ACT

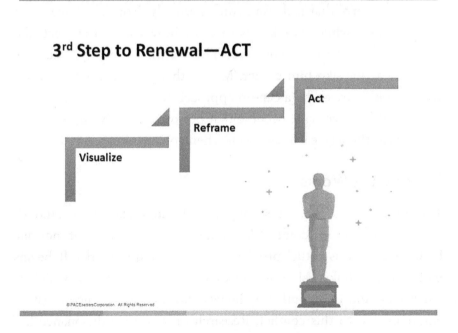

Act

Reframe

Visualize

ACT

Acting as Though It Is

Our attitude is really all about how we internalize what happens to us. At the heart of happiness is positive thinking—it's how we get our joy form our accomplishments by enjoying the present, looking forward to the future, and cherry picking the past with pleasant memories. Joyfulness is itself a type of positive thinking, because it comes from being content with what has, will, or is happening. By acting positive, even if we don't feel it, almost as though you were being hired as an actor to play the role of a positive person 24 hours a day, voila—we innately become that positive person. This is the process for changing the "want-to's" of life ("I want to be more positive") into the "have-to's" of life ("I have to be more positive—I am compelled to feel positive—because *that is who I am!*").

Don't worry that it doesn't come naturally. You may have to be an actor for a while. The key is to resist how you feel and act like someone that is positive would act. Think of that person you admire, and start acting like him or her. Maybe that person is adventurous, always polite, driven by a can-do approach to life. Pretend to be that person until you actually become that person. Don't give up—do this throughout the day, each day, even when you are alone.

Why Acting Works

The entire exercise may not seem practical, and it takes about a month to overcome the discomfort of doing it and to make it normal. However, there is actual proof that this technique works. It begins with the psychological principle of cognitive dissonance, which is when you hold two conflicting beliefs and then experience negative emotions due to this conflict. Research on cognitive dissonance has shown that our beliefs can change based on the way we act. If we act differently than we feel, our brain is shocked into re-evaluating its processing, subsequently altering the way we feel in order to match how we act. The Nike ad, "Just Do It," espouses this way of behavior. A right-brain action of just "doing it" tells the left-brain that this is a normative behavior.

Research Confirms That Acting Changes a Person's Mindset

Research on cognitive dissonance has shown that our beliefs can change based on the we act. If we act differently than we feel, our left-brain is shocked into re-evaluating its processing, subsequently altering the way we feel in order to match how we act. A right-brain action of just "doing it" tells the left-brain that this is a normative behavior.

*2012 study published in the Journal Psychological Science (smiling to reduce stress)
*Amy Cuddy, Harvard Business Business School social psychologist (TED Talk)
*2012 study published in The Quarterly Journal of Experimental Psychology
*Northwestern University's Kellogg School of Management (dress for success – lab coats)
*Journal of Positive Psychology, 2012 (The "happy music" effect)
*Harvard Business Review (mimic good leaders)
*University of Hertfordshire (UK 2012), pretending romance
*2013 Journal of Personality and Social Psychology ("faking confidence")

This is how acting positively can have such a dramatic effect on our overall mindset. When we act positive but feel negative, our brain is alarmed. Even though we know that we're just acting, our mind alerts itself to the way we feel and act, and realizes the difference. Over time, the brain accepts our positive acting as our actual mindset or state of mind.

As evidence that acting a certain way for a long period of time and really committing to it can work, Harvard social psychologist Amy Cuddy and Prof. Dana Carney at the University of California, Berkeley, completed a study. They found that participants who pretended to be more powerful actually felt more powerful over a period of practice. Cuddy says, "It is possible that our bodies change our minds." Those in the study who wanted to be more positive, say, smiled more often in order to evoke genuine positivity.

Cuddy used experimental methods to investigate how people judge and influence each other and themselves. Her research suggested that judgments along two critical trait dimensions—warmth/trustworthiness and competence/power—shape social interactions, determining such outcomes as who gets hired and who doesn't, when we are more or less likely to take risks, why we admire, envy, or disparage certain people, elect politicians, or even target minority groups. Cuddy's recent work focuses on how we embody and express these two traits, linking our body language to our hormone levels, our feelings, and our behavior.

Her latest research illuminates how "faking" body postures that convey competence and power ("power posing")—even for as little as two minutes -- changes our testosterone (the "dominance" hormone) and cortisol (the "confidence" hormone) levels, increases our appetite for risk, causes us to perform better in job interviews, and generally configures our brains to cope well in stressful situations. In short, as David Brooks once summarized in his findings, "If you act powerfully, you will begin to think powerfully."

In conclusion, renewing the mind involves a process of rewiring the brain to think constructively. Three powerful techniques for renewal include the ability to visualize events, reframe our thoughts, and act in accordance with our desired state of mind, or being. So in a sense, the French philosopher Rene Descartes was right when he said, "I think, therefore I am," with only one caveat: How we think defines our perspective. Doing what we want to become makes us the person we wish to be!

G.R.O.W. A HEALTHY ATTITUDE BY OVERCOMING

Overcoming Fear & Failure

Our fear of failure equates to the fear of being judged negatively, which causes anxiety, which can spoil our attitude. Unfortunately, expectations have been drilled into our heads by others—like parents, teachers, and even authors of success books. The truth is we are the authors of our own ambitions. But, if you are the type of person who feels uncomfortable when you can't be your best at something or when things don't go according to plan, you'll always be subject to feeling disappointed when situations fall out of your control.

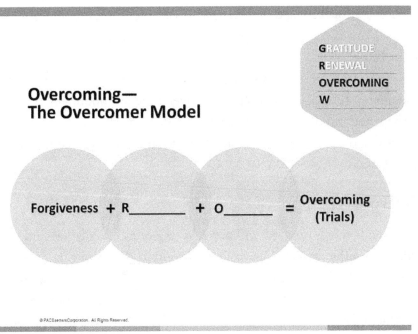

(Figure 3.2 - True forgiveness begins the process
for overcoming trials.)

Three responses can help us overcome our fears, anxieties, trials and those feelings of being judged. They are: Forgiveness, Resilience and Optimism. We know this from various studies, one of which looked at some of the most persecuted people in modern times, Holocaust survivors who had been interned in World War II concentration camps. The study was published as, *"Forgiveness, Resiliency, and Survivorship among* Holocaust Survivors" funded by the John Templeton Foundation (Greene, Armour, Hantman, Graham, & Sharabi, 2010).

About 65% of the survivors scored on the high side for resilience traits. Of the survivors, 78% engaged in processes considered resilient and felt they were transcendent or had engaged in behaviors that help them grow and change over the years since the Holocaust, including PACEsetters who left a legacy and contributed to the community. Those who became PACEsetters were able to forgive the Germans involved in their torture, not by excusing their actions, but by absolving these individuals of the debt they owed to the survivors. They also viewed their potentiality for turning their suffering toward the advantage of them and others. Many pledged to help prevent this kind of horrendous persecution in the future.

The study found that resilience, forgiveness and belief in the potential to turn "bad for good" could overcome just about any trial, any mishap, and any failure. Studies like this demonstrate that how far we progress in overcoming any obstacle depends on forgiving others' offenses against us.

Real Forgiveness

We cannot move forward without relieving ourselves of the burden of judging an offender. The Mayo Clinic reported that forgiving someone, even oneself, can lead to greater spiritual and psychological well-being, lower blood pressure, less anxiety, fewer symptoms of depression, and healthier relationships. Psychologists from Harvard as well as many other notable institutions say that holding onto the pain of a past event, such as an abuse or an unfair supervisor, is best overcome through the practice of acceptance. Accepting that what's done is settled means that we have accepted the past as the past and nothing more.

We cannot change the past and may not be able to control a situation, but we can make a conscious and deliberate decision to relegate negative effects to history by accepting them as simple fact and releasing our resentment. Bad habits often result from anxiety caused by fears that typically begin from an inability to resolve hurt or insecure feelings. Pledge today to release at least one excess baggage that holds you down. Your security lies in your inherent value irrespective of anyone or anything. Say something like: "That's just the way it is, I forgive _____, and I'm moving on."

Corrie Ten Boom did this in 1947 after being liberated from the Ravensbruck Nazi concentration camp almost three years earlier. She finished speaking to a group at a church in Munich with the message that God forgives. A man caught her attention. "One moment I saw the overcoat and the brown hat (he was wearing); the next, a blue uniform and a visored cap with its skull and crossbones," she said. "It came back with a rush: the huge room with its harsh overhead lights; the pathetic pile of dresses and shoes in the center of the floor; the shame of walking naked past this man. I could see my sister's frail form ahead of me, ribs sharp beneath the parchment skin..."

Corrie and her sister Betsie had been arrested during the war for concealing Jews in their home during the Nazi occupation of Holland; this man had been a guard at Ravensbruck where they were sent. "I was face-to-face with one of my captors, and my blood seemed to freeze. 'You mentioned Ravensbruck in your talk,' he said, 'I was a guard there.'" He did not remember her. "'But since that time,' he went on, 'I have become a Christian. I know that God has forgiven me for the cruel things I did there, but I would like to hear it from your lips as well, Fräulein.'" He stretched out his hand. "'Will you forgive me?'"

Corrie ten Boom, who helped many Jews escape the Nazi Holocaust during World War II and was imprisoned for it, practiced the power of forgiveness.

Betsie had died in that place, Corrie remembered—*could he erase her slow terrible death simply for the asking?* She thought about the home in Holland she began after the war for victims of Nazi brutality. "Those who were able to forgive their former enemies were able also to return to the outside world and rebuild their lives, no matter what the physical scars," she wrote. "Those who nursed their bitterness remained invalids. It was as simple and as horrible as that." Carrie stood there "with the coldness clutching my heart." But she realized that forgiveness is not an emotion, it is an act of the will.

As she mechanically stretched out her hand to the man, she explains an incredible thing that took place: "The current started in my shoulder, raced down my arm, sprang into our joined hands. And then this healing warmth seemed to flood my whole being, bringing tears to my eyes...I forgive you, brother, she cried, with all my heart." For a long moment the two grasped each other's hands, the former guard and the former prisoner. Corrie recalled about that moment, "I had never known God's love so intensely, as I did then."[1]

Just Turn the Other Cheek

The type of forgiveness that Corrie used runs completely contrary to human nature, and yet other PACEsetters like Martin Luther King Jr. and Abraham Lincoln practiced the concept of "turning the other cheek" as a means to accomplish hugely positive changes. The term "turning the other cheek" was popularized by Jesus from his famous Sermon on the Mount, in which he said not to resist evil, but "whoever smites you on your right cheek, turn to him the other also." Scholars say this teaching of returning "good for evil" represented the most revolutionary teaching during Jesus' life on earth. Prior to this transformational paradigm, the general population practiced an "eye for eye" way of responding to wrongdoing (as stated in the biblical book of Exodus 21:23), which King said "leaves everybody blind."

---

[1] Excerpted from "I'm Still Learning to Forgive" by Corrie ten Boom. Reprinted by permission from *Guideposts* Magazine. Copyright © 1972 by Guideposts Associates, Inc., Carmel, New York 10512).

Several studies now confirm that those who can turn the other cheek are more successful. Ask someone why he or she seeks revenge, and they're likely to tell you their goal is catharsis, says Kevin Carlsmith, PhD, a social psychologist at Colgate University in Hamilton, N.Y. But exactly the opposite happens, according to a study he published in the May 2008 Journal of *Personality and Social Psychology.*

In a series of experiments, he and his colleagues Daniel Gilbert, PhD, at Harvard, and Timothy Wilson, PhD, at the University of Virginia studied the reactions of students to an investment game during which they felt cheated by others. Those who *turned the other cheek* were able to trivialize the event, Carlsmith says, so it's easier to forget. But when we do get revenge, we think about it a lot. "Rather than providing closure, it does the opposite: It keeps the wound open and fresh," he says. And fresh wounds account for the greatest obstacle for people trying to overcome hardships. Unforgiveness mires us in the muck of cynicism.

PACEsetter and baseball great Jackie Robinson overcame hardships to become a legend. He broke the racial barrier by being the first African-American Major League Baseball player, faced vitriolic and harassing comments as well as death threats from angered fans. Feeling justifiably angered by these kinds of taunts and threats, Robinson asked Brooklyn Dodgers team executive Branch Rickey why he was chosen. "You want a player that doesn't have the guts to fight back?" he asked. Rickey replied, "No, I want a player who's got the guts not to fight back." Robinson accepted Rickey's challenge and demonstrated that he had the "guts" to not fight back. Instead of seeking revenge, Robinson went on to become Rookie of the Year, MVP, and World Series Champion.

Forgiveness has a reciprocal effect. It gives peace to the giver and conviction to the oppressor. Buddhaghosa, the 5th century commentator, said that "Holding on to anger is like grasping a hot coal with the intent of harming another; you end up getting burned." A similar yet different sentiment was expressed by the writer of Proverbs when explaining forgiveness: "In doing this, you will heap burning coals on his head…" The "coals of fire" are a metaphor for the penetrating effect of remorse and repentance upon the one forgiven. The last of what are termed the "Five Good Roman Emperors," Marcus Aurelius, said: "The best revenge is to be unlike him who performed the injury."

By forgiving an offender we can escape the consequences of anger and hidden hostilities that come with revenge, while often awakening the offender to his or her misdeed if he is not already repentant. Not forgiving someone maintains the burden of an offense upon ourselves. Confucius said, "Before you embark on a journey of revenge, dig two graves." Most people who harm us are acting out of insecurity, ignorance, abuse, or extreme unhappiness. These negative people then filter their thoughts and actions through their negative lenses and are either blind to the hurt they impose on others, or they choose to ignore their responsibility for committing something wrong. They become self-centered with a warped sense of judgment. Once you've realized that the person who offended you is damaged and will ultimately be the "loser" because of their toxic behavior (i.e., failed relationships, poor health, etc.), you can begin to forgive that person, and maybe even feel sorry for the offender.

This in turn releases you from the toxic burden of avenging yourself, and frees you to become stronger, more tolerant, compassionate and better. In Corrie's case, she forgave the prison guard for being such an insecure person that he needed to stoop so low as to participate in the brutalization of those imprisoned. The guard had already recognized his culpability for past grievances. In return, Corrie grew wiser and stronger. So did Jackie Robinson. Forgiveness is an attitude shifting approach for relieving the stress of pent-up hostility, and empowers you as a superior—and that builds confidence (see Figure 3.3).

Developing an Attitude of Forgiveness

- Relinquish the burden of judging an offender.
- Accept that's what is done is settled and in the past.
- Realize that the person who offended you is damaged and is on a course toward failure, or worse.
- Recognize that forgiveness is an attitude shifting approach that empowers you as a superior—thus building confidence.

Resilience

Forgiveness + Resilience + O_____ = Overcoming (Trials)

(Figure 3.3 - Resilience)

Resilience—Bouncing Forward (Not Back)

Have you seen the blockbuster movie, *Raiders of the Lost Ark*? The scriptwriter for this film, Larry Kasdan, was turned down dozens of times before his idea was picked up. Numerous times he heard, "No," but he kept going. If you keep persevering until you succeed, you're practicing resilience.

According to experts, one of the best ways to deal with life's disappointments and the anxiety they cause is to be resilient. Resilience is defined by the ability to adapt to challenging circumstances. Psychologists have identified some of the factors that make someone resilient, among them:

- Optimism
- Good problem-solving skills
- Positive attitude
- Loving support system
- Ability to plan effectively
- Ability to regulate emotions
- Ability to see failure as a form of helpful feedback.

Even after a life-altering trial, resilient PACEsetters are able to alter course and march forward because the mindset of resilience has been conditioned through the daily practice of seeing failures as opportunities. When you are resilient, your confidence is not dependent on your performance. You can play a lousy game of golf, shooting well over 100—someone's takeaway who is *not* resilient would be to regret that he/she is not a great player. But, if you're resilient, you can still get enthused with how much you learned from those mistakes and how you are building your abilities. You can also appreciate how much value the game brings to you regardless of your score. That's a very freeing attitude to adopt.

Unfortunately, we've been taught to strive for greatness while missing the benefits of just enjoying and learning the "game." The irony is that a resilient attitude actually leads to greatness—as a byproduct, not a motivation. The key is to acknowledge that one—or even two or a hundred—screw-ups do not define you. Resilient PACEsetters are consumed with the journey as much if not more than the destination, and that journey is about learning and growing.

They are curious about life and eager to embrace new challenges because their expectations are not self-limiting, not solely dependent on others, and they are not bound by the game's scorecard. When stuff happens not according to plan, allow yourself some flexibility to improvise. Reward yourself for just trying instead of criticizing yourself for not being the best, or even close. This attitude will allow you to try and try again—to face the next challenge with greater self-confidence and with a lot more fun in doing it.

Here are a few tips for strengthening your resilience to overcome trials:

- Remain objective from a 10,000-foot perspective by viewing trials as just a small part of a much bigger picture

- Set small achievable goals initially before moving onto bigger and more challenging ones

- Accept change as a normal part of life and avoid trying to change those things that are out of your control

- Foster positive strong relationships with family and friends through regular meetings, philanthropic organizations, and faith-based groups and try to be transparent with your own vulnerabilities while helping others

- Accept failure as an inevitable part of growing with the viewpoint that failure is a learning experience that allows you to move forward with better understanding

- Glean from others who have encountered similar problems to your own and seek out counsel from them

- Notice how you have overcome prior trials and use those victories as testimony that you can do it again this time (many persons report having more confidence in the themselves after a crisis as well as a deeper appreciation for life in general)

Resilience is not just about bouncing back from defeat. We need to learn from our mistakes. Good practitioners of resilience remain accountable while focusing on moving forward. Some problems occur outside of our control, such as those caused by natural disasters or large economic downturns. However, while we may not be able to overcome the cause of our problems, we can control our reactions to it, to find a new path. I have spoken before groups of people going through career transitions due to corporate downsizing. After our seminars many demonstrated resilience by expanding their abilities and skills to undertake new endeavors and discover new career possibilities through the MIR method discussed previously—Mapping in Reverse.

One client I advised, a pharmaceutical company, used the loss of its patent on a drug (which could have devastated the company because the drug accounted for 64% of sales) to initiate a consumer program to expand its presence in retail marketing, which more than compensated for its loss in patented drug sales, and also opened the door to an employee-motivating community drive to help people affected by the diseases treated by their products. These personal and corporate initiatives were driven by a strong sense of purpose that motivated all concerned, and in the case of the company, motivated the employees to help their organization survive and thrive—all because of a resilient attitude on the part of the company.

A purpose that can be altered in response to a challenge fuels resilience. Those willing to seek new opportunities may settle for less in the immediate in order to achieve better outcomes in the future. Consider PACEsetters Ben Carson, who escaped the gangs of Detroit to become a famed neurosurgeon, Abraham Lincoln who was primarily self-taught, or Daniel "Rudy" Ruettiger who despite his small size fulfilled his aspiration to play football at Notre Dame as depicted in the hugely popular 2005 film, *Rudy*. The story of Rudy also goes to show that despite our natural abilities in comparison to others, we still can initiate a pattern of success that can lead to alternate paths of success (e.g., Rudy's subsequent successful career as a motivational speaker). In other words, even though our primary objective may not fully succeed, the mere attempt of going after it will often result in building "bridges" to other opportunities.

Ways to Build Resiliency

- See the good through negative experiences—the 'silver lining'
- Learn and grow through trials—"what did I gain through enduring this trial?"
- Help others—give acts of kindness to others, and appreciate the kindness of others toward you
- Take care of your health—relax, take breaks, sleep well, ingest healthful foods and drinks
- Practice humor—even use 'dark humor' and uncover funny things

The key, as with Rudy, is to use failure as a motivator, not allowing it to derail us from our pathway to success. Resilience draws from strength of character, from a core set of values that motivate people to overcome their setbacks to move forward toward success. It involves self-confidence and the humility to acknowledge one's responsibilities for failure. Resilience also thrives in community—the desire to move forward because of a responsibility to others and because of those around us who want the same outcome. Resilience finds its voice in standing after falling—a new venture, a small goal that's been achieved, a ten-thousand-foot view of our world and the possibilities in it.

Trials happen to anyone who breathes, whether they stem from unexpected disasters outside of our control or individual mistakes. Whatever the cause, what matters is how we deal with them. The voice of resilience always says, "I am moving forward, getting stronger."

Optimism

Forgiveness + Resilience + Optimism = Overcoming (Trials)

(Figure 3.4 - Optimism)

How to Create an Optimistic Attitude by Overcoming Scarcity

Many societies operate from an attitude of scarcity. It's an attitude that says there is a deficit of possibilities in life and that the potential for more than what environment, abilities, and fortune can provide are close to nil. Our world economies are constructed mostly from a perspective based on the "Law of Scarcity," which states that there exists seemingly unlimited human wants in a world of limited resources. If everyone got what they wanted and needed, those resources required to fill these demands would eventually dry up. Advertisers play off of this belief in scarcity, implying through their ads that "We can only offer so much, so you had better buy our product before it runs out," which drives demand and cost.

From an early age, teachers and institutions, instead of encouraging the student to establish learning goals in relationship to life goals, teach us the law of scarcity as students vie for limited opportunities within an educational system where goals are established for them. However, new research now confirms that self-directed learners, or "autodidacts," will be the most successful persons in the 21st century and beyond. In an article published in *Perspectives on Psychological Science: A Journal of the Association for Psychological Science*, researchers Todd Gurecki and Douglas Markant discovered that self-directed learning exposes people to information they wouldn't normally learn through traditional means. Hence, autodidacts tend to assimilate information better than conventional students. In addition, they develop a more optimistic attitude because their primary interests and training fuel them in the direction of their genuine vocational choices, and that tends to make them more motivated and successful.

On the other hand, people who are "spoon-fed" information often view their possibilities from a narrowed perspective. They see their opportunities in comparison to others, versus through the lenses of their unique composition. Scarcity says that we all need to be made proficient through the same limited resources. Only advanced degrees, for example, qualify a person for a high-level position, when in fact, studies have shown that competency is better advanced out of an abundant perspective that qualifies candidates based on what they know, rather than what they are taught.

The attitude of scarcity teaches us that possibilities are always restricted by time, opportunity and potential. An attitude of optimism encourages the individual to search out their uniqueness, and then to tailor their opportunities based on unlimited resources available to them. That we must all drink from the same proverbial pool in order to succeed can be quite painful for the individual, and creates a lot of unnecessary fear, anxiety and desperation.

An attitude of optimism, on the other hand, tells you that there are always new chances and opportunities. This relieves much of the pressure someone may feel if they have a scarcity attitude that makes them think that they've only got one path toward success and one shot at success right now. Or an attitude of scarcity can make them feel like a complete failure just because they temporarily failed and something didn't work out. An attitude of optimism can help anyone improve their success since with it you're seeing the boundless possibilities that can be gained through learning to adjust one's approach.

Here are a few ideas to create and reinforce your own attitude of optimism:

1. **Identify an attitude of scarcity**. If you are continually stressed, controlled and pressured, chances are your attitude is one of scarcity. You may consider failure as the end, rather than seeing it as a stepping-stone to your goal. An attitude of scarcity may cause you to lose sleep over an important event, like a test, a presentation, an interview, or a meeting. Develop an attitude of optimism by reminding yourself that regardless of whether you succeed or fail, all that you've learned will inspire your

next journey, and the possibilities to continue your growth and contributions are endless.

2. **Focus on possibilities, not probabilities**. Possibilities evoke a future-focus within our mind that triggers unencumbered thoughts of what can be that here-to-fore seemed unattainable. Probabilities, on the flip side, factor in past experiences that create a cause-and-effect mentality that discounts previously untapped realities. What we focus on will determine how we view our options, and if our options are innumerable, we often stop limiting our prejudiced responses from a perspective of simply "what worked and didn't work," to "what might work that we've never tried before."

3. **Be thankful**. An attitude of scarcity sees what we do not have, while an optimistic attitude looks at what we have as being a treasure to invest into something even greater. Being thankful frees us from a sense of feeling that enough is never enough, to a feeling that what exists, in terms of our relationships, possessions and our overall being is quite enough—for now. Being content wherein we stand creates a springboard toward possibilities that will benefit us through our sure footing. If we cannot be thankful in even the small things, then how can we expect to be happy when bigger opportunities arise? Being thankful in all things frees us to expect a deeper appreciation for the next big thing.

4. **Greet everyone you meet with optimism**. There's a common thread of behavior that when people respond to us with an optimistic attitude, in saying something like, "I am confident that you'll succeed," or "I know in the end that we'll prevail," we feel empowered. The same happens when we express optimism about a situation to

others. In fact, others will perceive us in a more positive light as well. It's a well-known fact that people like hanging around optimistic people, because that attitude is contagious. Even if you don't feel optimistic, try faking it. That's right, even if you fake optimism, as we've learned through some aforementioned studies, we will begin developing a stronger attitude of optimism. And if your present circle of friends is typically comprised of naysayers, consider hanging around some more optimistic people to help offset those other negative influences.

5. **Give.** An optimist cannot be out-given, because the optimist's source of abundance never can be exhausted. Even with limited resources, there's a principle of giving that has been proven to increase one's wealth. At a Family Philanthropy Conference in San Diego, Arthur C. Brooks, president of the American Enterprise Institute and author of the book *Who Really Cares: The Surprising Truth about Compassionate Conservatism*, shared extensive research, which shows that giving leads to happiness and to more wealth, he said. He found that even a 1% increase in charitable giving leads to more than a 200% return. As to how giving feels, studies show that giving releases endorphins that makes us happier. What's more, those who give their resources and time to help others are generally perceived as leaders, and leaders attract success.

6. **Look for the win-win.** People with a scarcity attitude continually perceive choices as either a win or a loss, and relationships as either give or take. An optimistic attitude looks for the win-win, by creating a possibility well-beyond what the present situation affords—such as instead of allotting less money to growing teams in order to budget what's in the bank, investing that money into

growth funds so that everyone can be given more money. People with an optimistic attitude also are able to overcome their need to be right in relationships, such as winning an argument, by seeking a collaborative relationship that shares success, as well as failures.

7. **Overcome losses by releasing yourself to think anew.** After losing a loved one, or a job, or a relationship, instead of grieving over the loss for long periods of time, or worse yet, resenting what happened, look to fulfill those dreams that had been dormant. For example, a broken relationship may free you to find the person of your dreams. The loss of a job may free you to move to your ideal home—perhaps even to a resort location. A crisis that robs you of your wealth may open the door to a new entrepreneurial endeavor, or to get closer to supportive family and friends. Use the opportunity of a loss to find the time, space, and freedom to consider what might never have been possible before.

Optimism—Overcome an Attitude of Scarcity

People who adopt a negative attitude invariably operate from a position of scarcity. It's an attitude that says there is a deficit of possibilities in life and that the potential for more than what environment, abilities, and fortune can provide are close to nil. The attitude of scarcity teaches us that possibilities are always restricted by time, opportunity and potential.

An attitude of optimism, conversely, embraces each person's uniqueness, and then encourages each person to search out his/her uniqueness, and then to tailor his/her opportunities based on unlimited resources available to each person. An attitude of optimism tells you that there are always new chances and opportunities.

G.R.O.W. A HEALTHY ATTITUDE THROUGH WISDOM

Wisdom—Knowledge vs. Wisdom

GRATITUDE
RENEWAL
OVERCOMING
WISDOM

Wisdom at its core is about knowing the absolute truth in determining right from wrong, as opposed to knowledge, which is understanding information.

Consider hiring a highly educated, intelligent person who only sometimes does what's right for the organization, or hiring someone with moderate education and intelligence who always does what's right for everyone involved. Which one would you choose?

"Where is the wisdom we have lost in knowledge? Where is the knowledge we have lost in information?"

~T. S. Eliot

Vern left his lucrative job as a high-ranking executive at E.F. Hutton in pursuit of his dream to start *Hosanna Homes*.

There were some common characteristics reflected in these PACEsetters' wisdom. They were truth seekers with the capacity to process opposing ideas and reconcile them for the situation as appropriate. They could balance their self-interests and the needs of others, being neither extremely sacrificial nor extremely selfish, for example being able to "grab their oxygen masks before helping those around them in need of oxygen." They were able to find the proverbial win-win based on a hierarchy of needs. They challenged norms by taking calculated risks, instead of simply accepting the status quo. They also focused on purpose and outcomes over temporal pleasures, preferring the need to be true versus happiness, by following the principle reflected in Benjamin Franklin's words: "Who is wise? *He that learns from everyone.* Who is powerful? *He that governs his passions...*"

A Wise Attitude

As demonstrated by our PACEsetters, a wise attitude remains confident in who we are as a person and with the person we are becoming, *and* it also challenges our current understanding because— and this will seem obvious in concept but not in practice—regardless of our knowledge we know very little in comparison to all there is to know. Irrespective of our perspective, the truth is always the truth.

Many of us function with a bias, as we've reviewed in this book, and so we have established certain irrefutable beliefs regardless of whether we consider ourselves open minded or not. People tend to believe what they want to believe, even if the facts tend to refute their belief. This is how prejudice forms—through a bias that cannot be easily changed. For example, answer the question, "What is your favorite color?" Now, here's the follow-up to determine whether you have a confirmation bias: "Is there any way I can convince you to prefer another color as your favorite?" Most would say "no," because our prejudice favors a color even if we cannot explain why.

Wise PACEsetters that we interviewed could make valid observations from an objective viewpoint while remaining cognizant of their prejudices. For example, we asked some of them to evaluate a situation in which a youth was taking a hallucinogenic drug. On average, a young person taking a hallucinogen is not good. Those who exhibited a weak attitude of wisdom immediately judged it wrong for the youth to take this drug, some expressing indignation at the idea. Respondents with a strong attitude of wisdom asked more questions to clarify the situation, because there are situations when the average choice may not work. Perhaps, for example, the young man has a painful terminal illness. Or, the drug cured a movement disorder. Also, the young man may live in a culture with different values, or with foods that can elicit hallucinogenic effects. Those with a wise attitude were most willing to speak with the youth in order to determine his condition and state-of-mind before offering solutions. In other words, they didn't prejudge the situation without further investigation.

We found that those with the strongest attitude of wisdom could overcome their bias in favor of trying to understand the truth. They could risk challenging their own paradigm thinking to deduce something better. *Confirmation bias* is a cognitive bias whereby a person tends to believe and look for reasons to confirm his or her existing beliefs, at the same time ignoring anything that contradicts those beliefs. It is the type of selective thinking that caused so many to justify the injustices of slavery in the face of overwhelming reasons to think otherwise. Confirmation bias is what pits politicians against one another based on partisan bias, so much so that many politicians find it almost impossible to vote against their party even if when they are proven wrong. Couples that adamantly argue over firmly entrenched differences often choose their need to be right over their need for closeness based on their confirmation bias.

Overcoming "Hidden Confirmation Bias" or Prejudice

A very interesting test actually uncovers a person's hidden confirmation biases. The Implicit Association Test (IAT) developed by professors from Harvard, the University of Virginia, and the University of Washington measures the two levels that all people operate within—the conscious and unconscious. In Malcolm Gladwell's book, *Blink*, he describes the conscious level as "the decisions we make deliberately and things that we're aware of. I chose to wear these clothes. I choose the books I read."

The unconscious level, however, tells you more about an individual's true feelings. Gladwell describes this as "the kind of stuff that comes out, tumbles out before we have a chance to think about it. Our snap decisions. Our first impressions…how we think and how we feel (are) really important in things like prejudice and discrimination." The aforementioned study showed that our environment and the society in which we live cause these unconscious feelings. Societal influences like the news can bombard viewers with pictures of ethnic drug dealers and bias a person against that race even though consciously they do not think of themselves as prejudiced.

We are a product of our world more than we'd like to think. Dr. Tony Greenwald, one of the psychologists who developed the IAT, says we can change prejudice by showing positive images of the people against whom we have a confirmation bias, but the bad news is "that the change generally only lasts as long as the experiment (when the images are shown)." The key is to immerse yourself in an environment that reinforces these positive images in order to inculcate the goodness of those people into your unconscious mind. So we can change our prejudice (based on confirmation bias) by consistently exposing ourselves to positive representations of those for whom we hold a bias, so that we can understand the truth of who they are rather than the stereotype within our head.

The reverse effect also happens. Persons, for example, who felt prejudice from others could overcome their natural defensive response by immersing themselves in the culture of the prejudiced person(s). What's more, people tended to view others more positively when they did not "self-identify" as a "person defined by one specific quality or trait," or when they did *not* prioritize their identity by only one factor, but rather by other factors such as character, abilities and personality. Seeing oneself as multi-dimensional helped to overcome stereotypes.

How people view themselves either directly or subconsciously projects that image to those they encounter. So the most effective means for persons to overcome prejudice aimed against them would be to think of themselves in personal terms, rather than stereotypical ones. If one thinks of himself foremost as a "New Yorker" to a stranger, let's say, whatever stereotype that connotes to the stranger will be most pronounced in the stranger's mind. The key is to negate prejudice, or confirmation bias, by thinking of oneself in "real terms," defined by the inherent qualities most esteemed in one's personhood. Because by and large, others will see us as we see ourselves.

Changing our self-perception calls for an honest appraisal of our predisposed perspective. That usually means overriding our confirmation bias, and that requires an objective pursuit of the truth, even if it hurts in the short term. It also requires that we forego our need to always be right. Wisdom at its core is about knowing the *absolute* truth, and so an attitude of wisdom must challenge preconceptions or confirmation bias to better understand not just knowledge but also risking the application of this knowledge in accordance with the truth. An attitude of truth drove Abraham Lincoln to free the slaves despite overwhelming opposition at the time. It also gave some of the leaders of Europe and America the fortitude to fight Nazism in advance of any imminent threat. It inspired Einstein to create our current theory of gravity while disproving some of Isaac Newton's commonly accepted theories.

Wisdom also made King Solomon what many historians believe to be the wisest and richest man in history. People came from all parts of the world to see the wisest man in the world. The Queen of Sheba traveled with a train of attendants, carrying tremendous wealth from Arabia, about 1,500 miles, to test the wisdom of Israel's ruler—and she found him to be wiser than anyone. The Bible story tells us that God offered Solomon one wish, similar to the genie-in-the-bottle situation we all know. Solomon defied the norm by *not* asking for wealth, status or prestige. Instead he asked for wisdom. Asking for wisdom instead of these other commonly expected wishes pleased God, as the story goes, and ran contrary to every natural impulse—but the contrary decision to ask for wisdom produced the after-effect of all of these other things. Solomon was thus a contrarian—and being a contrarian defines most PACEsetters.

Risk-Taking: The Contrarian PACEsetter

PACEsetters not only understand the truth, they are often contrarians to the status quo in pursuit of it. Perhaps that's because they can best debunk destructive myths by overriding the herd mentality so often seen in societies. They're not apt to accept "good enough," like Bill Gates who when interviewed on *CBS This Morning* at the peak of his success, was asked whether he was happy with Microsoft's innovations, a company that had long held the record for the most valuable company in the world. "No, he (the current CEO) and I are not satisfied that in terms of, you know, breakthrough things, that we're doing everything possible," Gates answered. Gates wanted to push the boundaries of what at the time was considered "best" because he was a contrarian. His peer and competitor at the time, Steve Jobs, felt the same way—"great was never great enough."

Bill Gates observes plans to assist an impoverished area, part of his philanthropic work that includes asking billionaires to give away at least half of their fortunes, including his, which now funds the Bill & Melinda Foundation and totals over $40 billion.

All too often these leading-edge people are viewed as troublemakers instead of constructive forces. According to psychologist Sandi Mann, contrarians are not intentionally trying to be obstinate or gratuitously provocative. We may see contrarians as devil's advocates, she says, but their contrary opinions are often given in earnest, not just for the sake of putting across another point of view. "They have great talent for seeing things from another angle, are good problem-solvers and creative thinkers, unafraid to trust their judgment," said Mann. PACEsetters who are contrarians are also fiercely dedicated to the truth.

I once coached an executive who was let go by his previous manager, despite his stellar performance record and uncompromising integrity. "My manager championed my ideas," he said, "but in private he warned me I should be less vocal and focus on teamwork, or I'd create too many enemies." After using some reverse role plays, he learned to make himself more useful as a problem solver rather than as a naysayer. In becoming a PACEsetter, this executive grew to adjust his hardcore pursuit of the truth with the need to offer solutions. During one of our coaching meetings, I encouraged him to be a "solution-maker," not just a "solution-taker" or "problem-identifier." I asked him to provide at least one solution for each problem he surfaced. Now this PACEsetter is an exemplary performer while remaining true to his contrarian propensity.

There is a skill to being a contrarian in a conventional-thinking world. Counterintuitive thinkers often fumble with interpersonal relationships, says Karl Albrecht, author of *Social Intelligence: The New Science of Success.* "Often they haven't [acquired] the tactical skills of developing their ideas. They tend to blurt them out, making them hard to accept, or else they disagree with others in a clumsy way. Transformational people like Abraham Lincoln, Henry Ford, Martin Luther King Jr., and Bill Gates found a way to channel their contrary ways into being productive leaders who could discern an overall pattern for opportunity from a mass of detail or public opinion, to see the broader situation.

Some of the most influential change-makers have learned to adapt their contrarian tendency to a more socially acceptable way of making a positive difference. Education pioneer Sarah Winnemucca Hopkins, who with the financial wealth of Elizabeth Peabody, opened the once thriving Peabody Institute. As a Native American, she endured countless trials in pursuit of greater educational opportunities, eventually dying at the age of 47, to further education for her people. She said, "Much money and many precious lives would have been saved if the American people had fought my people with books instead of power and lead." Though a contrarian, she channeled her alternative view productively.

Instead of just protesting what she viewed as an injustice, as a PACEsetter she pursued the truth that an educated mind can bring, and then created the solution. She fought through the challenges of prejudice that invariably precede wisdom. Like all wisdom pursuers, she took a risk to defy destructive norms through a truthful understanding of what could achieve the desired result.

Being contrarily wise can apply to every area of life, even sports. Baseball relief pitcher Trevor Hoffman was the major leagues' first player to reach the 500- and 600-save milestones, and was the all-time saves leader from 2006 until 2011. He did this throwing a loopy looking change-up when just about every relief pitcher in baseball prior to him threw mostly fastballs. First up in relief, he threw a pitch around 12 mph less than his fastball, which was exceptional. The deception of the pitch was remarkable. While other fast baller relief pitchers were throwing the "heat," Trevor used his unique approach to set an all-time save record.

Another contrarian, PACEsetter George Van Vliet, is the most successful real estate investor I know. As a friend, I also know that he has helped countless people as both a mentor, a financial donor, and as a leader of various philanthropies. He came from a poor background as a neglected foster child working odd jobs as a young man until finding his career niche. George practices contrarian investing—a strategy that involves making investments based on factors other than market norms and current industry indicators. Essentially, George chooses to make an investment that would generally be considered to run counter to the usual procedures of investing. He enters this high-payoff mode of investing with the idea of getting in on a good deal before the rest of the investment world notices. He's succeeded in every investment made, which now totals thousands of properties.

While on the surface contrarians appear to base their actions more on instinct than factual information, this is rarely the case. Those who speculate in high-risk ventures and use abnormal approaches usually try to zero in on opportunities that are overlooked by others. For example, the contrarian investor may choose to focus on an industry that is not in favor right now, and make an investment in a company within that industry that is stable and doing very well. By choosing to invest in overlooked businesses that are part of an unpopular market sector, the investor stands a good chance of making a significant return on the investment while facing little to no competition.

Wisdom seekers, as I call them, look for new revelations through a contrarian perspective that challenges existing paradigms. They dare to seek the truth in exception to societal norms that govern the "herd mentality" of so many others. They are both truth seekers and risk-takers, because wisdom brings them to a place apart from social pressures in exception to counterfactual thinking. They display an *attitude of wisdom*. The attitude of wisdom is comprised of one part truth seeking and one part risk-taking (see Figure 3.5).

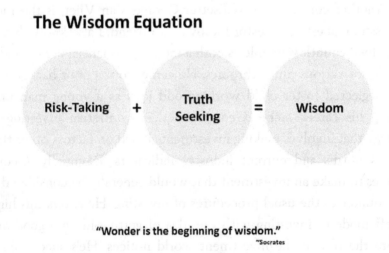

(Figure 3.5 - The Wisdom Equation)

So Now That We Understand Contrarian Risk-Taking, How Can We be Truthseekers?

We are all students in life, regardless of how much we know. Situations constantly unfold, and as soon as we find out the answers, someone has changed the questions. A truthseeker learns from experiences and from others but never simply accepts a majority rule or even social norms as the way it must be. The entire community around you may be wrong at certain points, and then as a truthseeker you may need to stand alone in determining the objective truth based on a compilation of sources filtered through your own finite understanding.

You will make decisions that may never be fully validated, yet the probability of your being right compels you to think that maybe you know the answer, and so you choose to act with all you know at the time. Realizing that you may be wrong is the voice of wisdom telling you that there's always more to know. As a truthseeker and PACEsetter, you deal with terms such as "probability," "likelihood" and "maybe's." That's not a bad thing—it just means you will never shut the door on new ideas or concepts that may enter into your world of reality.

A scientist seeking the truth arrives at a conclusion while recognizing the uncertainty in life, just as a professional must act based on the probabilities that he or she knows the answer. As long as we're aware that there may be more to know, we can be at peace simply knowing we did the best we could at the time. If we believe with absolute certainty, then our eyes may be closed to revelations that present themselves to us.

An open mind need not exist in unsettled state for perpetuity, it simply needs to revisit its ordered way of thinking should some disclosure arise, or should the truth surprisingly show-up from some unknown source. We can arrive at a conclusion without closing all questioning by critically analyzing our ideas based on new information. Creativity and innovation puts new ideas to the test, and when combined with critical thinking the truth may be revealed.

Take the time to reflect on whether your truth is based just on what you want to believe or some personal bias, or whether you've honestly appraised the value of your truth against a standard higher than yourself. Changing your mind is not always a bad thing. It means you are willing to factor new evidence into your way of thinking.

So Where is the Wisdom?

We live in an over-communicated world with so much information bombarding us and yet are we experiencing fewer problems? T.S. Eliot posed the question: "Where is the wisdom we have lost in knowledge? Where is the knowledge we have lost in information?" We've got knowledge—we need more wisdom. There's a difference between the two.

Knowledge is the accumulation of information and skills acquired through experience and education. Wisdom mediates that knowledge toward the achievement of a sound decision that results in the common good. In other words, wisdom makes you do the right thing. Given the choice between hiring a highly-educated intelligent person who only *sometimes* does what's right for the organization or hiring someone with moderate education and intelligence who *always* does what's right for everyone involved, which would you choose? Most would choose the one with the better track record, which proves the ability to apply knowledge to correctness. However, it's harder to find wise people than it is knowledgeable ones.

That's because wisdom is more difficult to develop than knowledge. It grows as we learn from the mistakes we make through taking risks. Jeff Foxworthy puts it this way: "Wisdom equals knowledge plus scars." People who achieve their dreams step out of their comfort zone. They try the new by overtaking fear. If you believe in God, there is no uncertainty, because he has control over all things and he will always accomplish his good purpose. If you don't believe in God, simply understanding your emotions guards against the anxiety felt upon taking risks, by helping you understand that anxiety is irrelevant to your decision.

Said another way, if you decide to take a risk, you will have already (subconsciously or otherwise) thought through your most fearful emotions and the rest is simply easier. People who expect to fail don't take risks. People who expect to learn or succeed when risk taking succeed in doing so. It's a conviction that the experience is worth the potential downside because each experience is learning, and leads to progress.

There is a positive payoff to risk-taking, but only if it is not reckless. People that are selective about the risks they take can reduce the uncertainty by taking calculated risks when the upside outweighs the downside. Poker players use this strategy. There are 1,326 possible combinations of cards a poker opponent might be holding, so the good players try to narrow the possible range to between 5-15, allowing them to make a better decision by reducing uncertainty. Playing out a risk in your mind assesses all of the variables, imagining all that could possibly go wrong when making a decision, preparing for their consequences, as well as calculating what can go right.

Here's how you develop wisdom by taking a risk: When you see a problem in your life or someone else's, ask yourself why something went wrong. Figure it out. The answer will bring you greater wisdom. Then use that newfound understanding to make a more calculated risk toward something greater. A successful life is comprised of a series of course corrections that add up to making more improved decisions.

If we can sublimate our ego and emotions during our decision-making process to figure out the right thing to do, and then proceed with what must be done, we live more according to our values and wisdom. See the big picture so that you can place yourself in the correct position relative to everything around you. Remain teachable and humble so that you can maintain an outward focus in learning more than the sum of your understanding. Ask yourself what have I learned that would make me do things differently? Then apply that newfound wisdom to action. You are building a foundation of wisdom, and that develops an attitude of wisdom.

ATTITUDE
(fuels satisfaction)
Manage left and
right hemisphere
thinking

The PACE Formula®

G.R.O.W.

GRATITUDE—Focus on Growth,
Be Thankful, Remain Hopeful
RENEWAL—Visualize, Reframe,
Act (like it is)
OVERCOMING—Truly Forgive,
Bounce Forward, Dispel a Scarcity
Attitude
WISDOM—Be a Risk-Taker
and Truth-Seeker

The Power
ᵗᵒ Thrive!

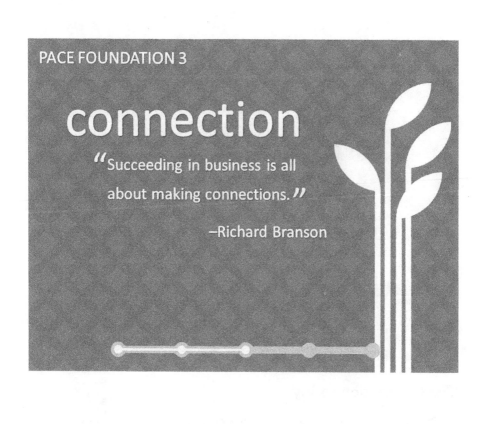

PACE FOUNDATION 3

connection

"Succeeding in business is all
about making connections."

–Richard Branson

CHAPTER 4: CONNECTION—TO FIND JOY

Thrive Drive is to...

L.E.A.R.N.

CONNECTION HAPPENS THROUGH A COMMITMENT
TO LEARN ABOUT THE OTHER PERSON

The Connection to Joy

COMMUNICATION IS ALL ABOUT CONNECTION. And connection is all about relationship. And with connection we find joy. The gist of 50 years of happiness research is that the quality and quantity of a person's social connections—family relationships, friendships, closeness to coworkers, etc.—is so intertwined to a sense of joy and well-being that the two can practically be equated. People with close friendships and family are less likely to experience sadness, loneliness, low self-esteem, and problems with eating and sleeping.

The rationale tells us that connections create psychological security so that we can grow and learn. When we feel genuinely connected in relationships, we can focus on what's inherently important, such a making something or someone better, even if that "someone" is you. That feeling of togetherness fuels the motivation for being a better person—for being a PACEsetter.

PACEsetters excel at connecting with people through exceptional communication abilities. Some call this charisma, but the skills for communicating with big impact can be practiced by anyone. Connection starts with developing trust. Many fail to connect because they fail to understand that their word—e.g. what they say—is the only expression that can bond one person to another. We can talk forever about who we are and what we are going to do, but if we fail to follow our words with action, we are considered untrustworthy. We must be consistent with our word by doing what we say we are going to do. Being faithful to our word is living with integrity. Integrity, like a river, must continually flow out of us if we are to gain the trust of others.

Transparency Causes Connection

That "PACEsetter flow" of integrity that causes connection requires being transparent. Indeed, people respect those brave enough to fess-up, and it makes them feel more comfortable in partnering with us. PACEsetters are courageous enough to admit their own faults and mistakes, and as they do, they impart the same level of courage to others, which makes others feel like the PACEsetter can be trusted and also has their best interests at heart. Transparent confession is a sign of confidence and humility that is catchy to everyone around us.

This scares a lot of people—but the truth is that for any effective communication to take place, one has to be honest and transparent in all communications for the level of trust to keep flowing. Two things happen when we give voice to failings. It lessens the power over us by releasing those secrets that fester within the destructive privacy of our mind, and it resets our thinking to a beginning point of being honest again; thus, opening the pathway for change and growth.

That old saying that confession is good for the soul is true. It represents an adjustment to realign what we know to be right with what is right, so in a sense it is chiropractic for the soul. Having released the heavy burden of representing a false persona can mitigate any negative consequences that may result from a misrepresentation. Eventually, someone will accept you for who you are, and not for why you think others should accept you.

Should the "river of integrity" stop flowing, we become stagnant, and whatever is blocking its flow (e.g., insecurity, defensiveness, lies, etc.) must be confessed and eliminated to return its onward flow. Integrity, transparency and compassion in communication are critical...without them, relationships fall victim to hurtful manipulation. With them, true connectedness takes place.

True connectedness, when it happens, displays common outcomes:

- Mutual trust
- Genuine caring
- Security
- Self-confidence
- Joy

The Firsthand Rule

This true story illustrates an essential technique for maintaining the flow of integrity. It began when one of my team leaders approached me about her direct report (Lisa) who she felt dressed inappropriately for work. Lisa often wore skimpy shorts with low-cut blouses, which her supervisor explained as a clear distraction to other workers. "Lisa is causing people to feel uncomfortable around her," Lisa's supervisor said.

"Have you told her about your concern?" I asked. "Not yet," Lisa's supervisor answered. So we discussed some appropriate conversations to increase Lisa's awareness as to how others perceive her attire, using words detailing clear boundaries as to appropriate dress in the workplace.

One week later Lisa's supervisor rapidly knocked at my office door, face flushed, hands clenched. "Lisa is claiming harassment," she said. "She walked out of the meeting and went straight to Human Resources." After reviewing the conversation with Lisa, I could not uncover any inappropriate language from the supervisor. What she said seemed perfectly in order.

Except one critical mistake had happened. Lisa's supervisor spoke to me *before* speaking to Lisa. There was no going back once this breach occurred. Lisa no longer trusted her supervisor once she discovered I was the first person approached. So instead of beginning the corrective conversation privately, the entire organization spent far too much time to safeguard itself against any legal repercussions.

This story supports a rule of integrity in communication that always precedes healthy connection: for any disagreement or problem, always approach the person with whom you have a problem *first*. We call this "The Firsthand Rule." When PACEsetters begin discussing a problem related to someone's behavior, whether personally or professionally, they halt any further interaction until the perceived offender has been approached first.

The flow of integrity runs through firsthand communication. In Lisa's case, her supervisor could have begun their discussion like this: "Lisa, there's an issue I'd like to discuss with you that can help you succeed in this company, and I want you to know that I am approaching you first about it before talking with anyone else because I am fully committed to your success." Keeping the first challenging conversation private opens the way for a positive second chance.

Prodigious Effect of Relationship

One of the most confirmed findings to emerge from research into joyfulness is that we are social creatures. Relationships create psychological space and safety so that we can explore and learn. When we feel safe and supported, we don't have to limit ourselves to survival tasks like responding to danger or finding our means for staying alive. We are able to explore our world, which creates resources for periods of stress and adversity.

Connecting through effective communication gives us a sense of belonging, and helps us understand ourselves while feeling a part of something greater than ourselves. Researchers have found that persons with strong social connections experience less stress, fewer mental and physical health problems, and faster recovery from illness. When communication leads to a type of harmonious connection, we feel more joyful and satisfied.

Social connections also can encourage and support us in healthy lifestyle habits, such as exercise, faith and moderation. Studies have surfaced that people are more joyful when they are with other people than when they are alone—and the "rise" is the same for introverts and extroverts. They also found that joyful people are more generous, pleasant, and sociable. So making strong connections makes us feel more joyful, and when we are joyful we are more enjoyable to be around, creating an "upward momentum" of joyfulness.

Psychologist James H. Fowler studied the data of 5,000 people over 20 years and found that happiness and satisfaction benefits other people through three degrees of connection, and that the effects last for a year. He says, "We found a statistical relationship not just between your happiness and your friends' happiness, but between your happiness and your friends' friends' friends' happiness." The positive effects from connecting with others are lasting and prodigious.

Scientists have observed what they call "hedonic adaption": Our tendency to quickly adapt to our changing circumstances based on the ability to build relationship regardless of the situation. This is why people who win contests, for example, eventually find themselves at the same level of happiness and satisfaction they experienced before winning based on their relationships. Strong relationships tend to stabilize emotions, just as weak relationships create instability, regardless of temporary peaks. So the key to happiness is more about connection and less about the situation in which we find ourselves.

The Difference between Joy and Happiness

Indeed, situations tend to change, as do our emotions, but it is the condition of our core, or heart, that provides stability. In the purest sense, joy is not an emotion, as is happiness. Joy is not based just on something pleasant happening, but is an attitude of the heart created through relationships that center us. During periods of joyfulness, physiological and biochemical changes take place that infuse within us a sense of well-being, transforming negative outlooks on life. Joy, found primarily in connection, motivates people to work more efficiently.

According to a study by the University of Iowa researchers, a sense of attachment and belonging to a group of co-workers serves as a better motivator for many employees than money or any other incentive. If someone chooses money or status over sincere connection with people, chances are they will always strive for more. When we build a solid relational foundation, we are joyful doing what we do, we are in the moment. Joy centers us in the present with an abundant attitude toward work and life, which tends to attract more abundance in life. Numerous studies and life experiences have proven that people who enjoy what they do tend to be more productive. Learning to be content in whatever situation you find yourself calls for an indwelling joy that stems from close connection.

CONNECTION—TO FIND JOY

The gist of 50 years of happiness research is that the quality and quantity of a person's social connections is so intertwined with a sense of joy and well-being that the two can practically be equated.

Joy is not an emotion, as is happiness. Joy is not based just on something pleasant happening, but is an attitude of the heart created through relationships that center us.

Ego-Free Joy

Close connection, though, requires a productive form of communication that engages closeness, and PACEsetters in particular consistently practice certain skills that lead to the highest form of connection. These effective relaters view communication as the construction of a mutually beneficial relationship primarily focused on the other person. An ineffective communicator disconnects relationship through an exclusively self-serving agenda that disregards the interests of the other person. An egocentric approach to communication disconnects, whereas another's focus approach connects.

So does that mean we need to sacrifice our personal interests? Quite the contrary. By focusing our attention on another person's interests, we actually open the other person's receptivity to our wants. I once conducted a study of this effect by staging discussions between two groups of paired people. There were a total of 72 individuals. The first group of paired individuals was instructed to communicate their interests first, and then check-in for their partner's response. The second group was instructed to listen first, by asking questions of their partner to learn more about them and their wants. All individuals were given one specific objective to gain from their paired partner—a second conversation after the session at a Starbucks of their choosing. We then measured whether each person gained the specific objective—a second meeting on personal time.

The group that expressed their agenda first gained 26% of their objectives for a tea, coffee, or juice at Starbucks. The group that focused exclusively on their partner and the other person's agenda gained 94% of their objective for the same type of meeting. The only difference between the two groups was that one listened for over 90% of the ten minute discussion before expressing their want/objective, whereas members of the other less successful group focused on themselves (e.g., their agenda, their lives, their likes/dislikes) for 90% of the conversation before asking the other person for a personal meeting after the session. In other words, the successful groups listened with an others focus without sharing anything about themselves until the final minute of conversation. They simply learned about the other person.

The Coffee Experiment

- **72 Paired Individuals**
- **Objective: Gain 2nd meeting**
- **Group that focused on the other's agenda succeeded 96% of time**

**Can you listen absent judging
and absent an agenda?**

Learning about someone else initiates progressive degrees of rapport, by subconsciously communicating to the other person that he or she is important enough to be understood. The L.E.A.R.N. model of communication connects people toward a constructive dialog, beginning with what we call "Unselfish Listening" (Figure 4.1).

UNSELFISH LISTENING

The L.E.A.R.N. model of connection for PACEsetters always begins with *Unselfish Listening*. Convincing someone is 90% listening to the other person's wants, and 10% talking about personal wants. Great listeners tend to be great communicators because they connect with others and they understand how to respond appropriately, but few listen well. As Stephen Covey said, "Most people do not listen with the intent to understand; they listen with the intent to reply." This explains why many people feel misunderstood.

To understand others

UNSELFISH LISTENING

Unselfish listening is more than just asking questions. It's the mental discipline of placing our needs on the shelf for the vast majority of any conversation. Our objective shouldn't surface until the other person feels understood.

LISTEN
E
A
R
N

"Most people do not listen with the intent to understand; they listen with the intent to reply."
"Stephen Covey

(Figure 4.1 - The L.E.A.R.N. model of connection)

Have you ever felt that when you were talking with someone it was like talking into thin air—they just weren't plugged in? People generally remember less than half of what they hear, according to researchers. We can improve our success using Unselfish Listening, which involves an attentive (focused) effort to understand the entire communication from the speaker, not just their words. It also tells the other person that they are being heard. PACEsetters excel at this.

Unselfish Listening is more than just asking questions. It's the mental discipline of placing our needs on the shelf for the vast majority of any conversation so that we can be attentive and appropriately responsive to the other person. Sure, we will always remain aware of our objective (our want or wants), but that objective doesn't surface to the other person until the other person senses that he or she is understood. Sometimes our objective will not surface at all during the first conversation, and that's OK if we can gain a commitment for a next discussion. Effective communication builds relationship. And if someone feels that the other person is treasuring that "someone's" wants, trust develops. When trust develops, our personal objectives can be met.

Trust-building listening is not just hearing and understanding information being expressed but also empathizing with the speakers' feelings about their subject. Strong eye contact and genuinely sympathetic acknowledgements (like nodding and smiling) make the speaker feel understood, and that establishes a strong connection between us. By saying something like, "I understand how that would make you feel," the speaker is made to feel as if we truly understand them, and gives him/her an opportunity to confirm or amend our interpretation. Even saying something like, "I heard what you said," makes the other person feel listened to.

REFLECTION

Reflection is paraphrasing and restating both the feelings and words of the speaker to sincerely reflect the meaning of what the speaker has conveyed through:

- **Mirroring which involves repeating almost exactly what the speaker says.**
- **Paraphrasing which shows not only that you are listening, but that you are attempting to understand what the speaker is saying.**

The Power of Reflection

Taken a step further, when we repeat what the other person said in our own words, that person feels even more understood. This is called a *reflective response*. Say, a person expresses in a frustrated tone: "I keep saying that people need to pick-up after themselves but no one ever listens!" A reflective response might be: "I get it. I heard you say that no one takes responsibility for picking up their own mess—and that frustrates you." Not only does that reflective response make the person feel understood, by essentially echoing (or rephrasing) what the person said in the hearer's own words (*not* just verbatim), it begins to deflate the speaker's anger from feeling unheard or unappreciated. The speaker thinks, "Oh, you really did get what I said." When people feel listened to, they become more connected to the person who confirmed what they said.

Show That You're Listening

As humans we connect with those we like. Dale Carnegie once said the best way to be likable is to be interested in the other person. People respond favorably to those who are humble, positive, and who express interest in them. That's why PACEsetters connect most effectively with people by making the other person feel that the PACEsetter *wants* to know about them.

When someone brings up a topic or situation, don't just move on to the next subject. Ask follow-up questions such as, "So how did that make you feel?" or "How did you react to that?" or "Tell me more."

The majority of us spend 75 percent of our waking time communicating, and only 40-50 percent of that time listening. Being likable is all about "being present" with the other person by understanding the "why" of what someone says. "Why is that important to you" or "Why did that affect you so?" are questions that lead to deeper understandings.

The human mind can understand almost three times faster than we can speak, according to research by the University of Missouri. So people are actually listening to only about 25 percent of what we are saying. The other 75 percent is focused on whatever else pops into their mind at any given moment. However, when we demonstrate a genuine desire to know more about the other person, we increase the other person's listening to more than 70 percent. So how do we appear interested in the other person?

Show that you're listening by using appropriate facial expressions and encouraging the other speaker with words like "uh huh" and "please continue." Never interrupt the other person with questions or a response, and try to keep an open mind without judging their comments. Your general attitude should be respectful and sympathetic as you genuinely attempt to understand the other person's perspective. You should be honest and straightforward, but always in a manner in which you would like to be treated.

Maintain an open posture (arms uncrossed, open stance, sitting forward) to set the other person at ease and convey interest. An important way of demonstrating honesty is by matching your words and tone to your body language. For example, we shouldn't laugh if we are saying something serious. Standing tall with your shoulders back, good eye contact, and a firm but not hurtful handshake will convey confidence—an important quality during first meetings and interviews.

EMPATHIZE

LISTEN
EMPATHIZE
A
R
N

"If you judge people, you have no time to love them."

~Mother Theresa

EMPATHIZE

Renowned educator Stephen Covey once said, "When you listen with empathy to another person, you give that person psychological air." Ask the majority of counselors and even psychologists to identify the most common reason for frustration between people and you will discover none bigger than the inability to feel empathy in a relationship. Empathy heals. It removes distance between people. Connection using empathy displaces a "Me-Attitude" with a "We-Attitude."

Empathy is the ability to accurately place yourself in someone's "skin"—to understand the other person's feelings and perceptions from their point of view. It is unlike sympathy, which is only being affected by the other person's feelings and perceptions. For example, if a leader shows sympathy toward their follower's sadness, the leader would feel sad as well; whereas, the empathic leader would truly understand why that person feels sad.

How to Develop Empathy

So how do you develop empathy? First, you need to imagine yourself in the other person's place. Immerse yourself in their environment and feel their emotions, especially their pains. Ask them how they feel, and why to confirm your understanding. Put aside your personal agenda and just listen to them without judging. Relate their feelings to similar situations in your own life that elicited the same type of emotions. You need to be careful not to become an enabler of the other person. In other words, you must use good emotional intelligence to clarify your own personhood to make sure you don't become overly entangled with the other person, which can cause you to take his or her feelings too personally.

You will need to be able to distinguish between different emotions from a somewhat objective point of view, so that you can deal with your own emotions and bias—get in touch with yourself before touching others. One of the biggest challenges in communicating empathy is when you don't feel it toward another person, because of some bad experience or anger toward them. It takes time and practice to remove these barriers by recognizing the other person's right to be heard. Some of the hardest people to love are the most damaged. Your responsibility in developing your empathy skills is to identify the why of someone's feelings without the need to determine whether their feelings or even their negative behaviors are justified.

Third Person Empathy

One of the most innovative techniques (besides unselfish listening) for developing empathy requires a forced third person perspective, which is the discipline of imagining how the other person feels and thinks. Try this by putting yourself in an actual third person. Practice (internally) taking whatever view point the other person holds. Don't go with your default reaction immediately. Start with the other's perspective on a situation or problem, and work your way back.

Good debaters use this technique when debating a case that opposes their own view. You can practice this "shift in viewpoint" by taking one of your firmly held beliefs, find someone with a similar point of view, and start debating the opposite of that point of view. It's an exercise that forces you onto both sides of a debate to help open your mind to the realities of how people with different points of views see their world.

I hope you will give it a try, even for a short while, and I hope it improves your life and the lives of those around you even if just a little. The trick is to identify with the other person's experiences. When someone begins to share, focus on their feelings and situations that you've experienced in the past that are similar. This will deepen your emotional insight into the other person's plight.

For those with opposing views, begin to practice emotionally detaching—not allowing the other person's negative behavior to determine your mood or choices. In time, you will gain a greater sense of identity and separateness that will offer you the advantage of perspective. If that's too difficult, imagine the person as an innocent victim. Put him or her in a vulnerable position where they've experienced rejection, and use a situation where that person might or has suffered to help you visualize them through softer lenses—perhaps because of the behavior(s) that caused you to feel negatively toward that person.

Third Person (Forced) Empathy

- Pick a strong viewpoint (e.g., a H.S. degree is important; high taxes are bad; people shouldn't lie; cleanliness is important; gaining weight can harm health)
- Try to reason the other point of view
- Find a friend to argue your "counter point of view"
- Can you force empathy by overcoming prejudices? If so, that's mindset reset to develop empathy

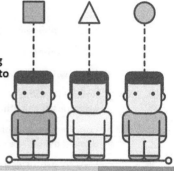

Sometimes an "unlovable" person appears difficult because they are going through a rough time. My wife, Renee, has great empathic/non-judgmental skills. While working at a company her supervisor, Barb, turned into a grouch, making work miserable for everyone in the department. Instead of judging Barb as a "bad boss," Renee took the high road of confronting Barb with empathy. She walked into her boss's office and said, "Barb, I've noticed that you haven't been particularly happy recently, and I just want you to know that I'm here to help if you need a listening ear." Immediately, Barb responded by sharing with Renee that Barb caught her husband having an affair. After that meeting, Barb's attitude turned more positive—because she finally felt understood, believing that she had a friend.

10 WAYS TO INSTILL EMPATHY

- Imagine yourself in the other person's environment and feel their emotions.
- Ask the other person how she/he feels and why.
- Listen without judging.
- Relate situations in your own life that elicited the same emotions as the other person.
- Consider the possibility that the other person may be damaged if he/she has offended you.
- Imagine a difficult person as a child in order to lower your defenses by seeing their vulnerability.
- Talk to people outside your social circle to cultivate curiosity about them.
- Challenge prejudices about people by forcing yourself to interact more frequently with them.
- Walk in the person's shoes for awhile by placing yourself in the same situation or environment.
- Remain vulnerable to the other person by sharing your similar challenges.

Often when we consider the person in the vulnerable light, our defenses tend to lessen, and we begin developing the ability to connect.

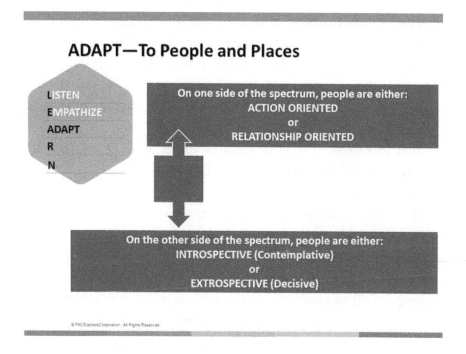

ADAPT—To People and Places

LISTEN
EMPATHIZE
ADAPT
R
N

On one side of the spectrum, people are either:
ACTION ORIENTED
or
RELATIONSHIP ORIENTED

On the other side of the spectrum, people are either:
INTROSPECTIVE (Contemplative)
or
EXTROSPECTIVE (Decisive)

© PACEsettersCorporation. All Rights Reserved.

ADAPT

Failure typically occurs as a result of the failure to adapt, and success is mostly the result of successful adaptation. The popular line of thought is to be different. While that holds true for many advances like innovation, sometimes it's best to be like others. In Harvey Mackay's blockbuster selling book, *Swim with the Sharks without Being Eaten Alive*, the key to surviving with the sharks is to become like one of them. If a shark recognizes a fish or some other food source, it will eat it. But, sharks do not eat other sharks.

Being willing to adapt your behavior increases your ability to build connection with other people, and it allows you to conform to situations when appropriate. Few actually practice adaptability, though. Perhaps that's because, as research shows, people view themselves as more versatile than they truly are. In order to develop the skill of adaptability, you must first practice empathy, tolerance and respect for the other person. Empathy is the most important contributor to adaptability, which is essentially feeling how the other person feels, or "walking in their shoes."

Strong empathy for another person usually leads to greater respect for them, and a higher tolerance for their faults. If we feel the need to compete with someone else, or if we will only accept our way, then be prepared to be attacked by the sharks. If you are attacked or rejected, don't give-up. Being adaptable requires that you bounce back from rejection to suggest alternative ways in which to work together. If a situation calls for you to be outgoing when you are an introvert, fake it until you make it.

Remember that people will positively respond to those who maintain a positive attitude in finding ways to accommodate their style and agenda. People respond favorably to those who can offer a collaborative approach in attending to *their* needs. Telltale signs are always given off by people to alert us to their mood as to whether they are receptive, bored or irritated, like foot tapping or checking the time. So the adaptable person must be perceptive in reading these signals, and to adjust their response accordingly.

The ability to self-correct behavior is a key need to develop adaptability. If something isn't working, change course. "It's not all about me," says the adaptable person, 'it's about *us*." Understand the other person's behavioral style, and their mind-body style in order to reflect your behaviors to match their preferred style. For example, when dealing with an authoritative person, you'll want to show respect and speak concisely in support of their efforts—and *this will open you to stronger connectedness.*

Here's How to Adapt to a Person's Behavioral Style

Most know the Golden Rule from Matthew 7:12 of the Bible: "Do unto others as you would have them do unto you." The *Social Interaction Rule (SIR)* states: *Treat people in the manner with which they feel most receptive.* People respond differently depending on their behavioral style.

Essentially two categories describe the vast majority of people: 1) They are either *action-oriented or relationship-oriented*, and 2) They are either *introspective (contemplative)* or *extrospective* (decisive).

The combinations of each type generally determine a person's behavioral style. An Extrospective/Relationship-oriented person is called a *Socializer*. An Extrospective/Action-oriented person is called a *Director*. An Introspective/Relationship-oriented person is called a Relater. An Introspective/Action-oriented person is called an *Analyzer*.

> *Socializers* enjoy being the life of the party and are motivated by social interaction, so the SIR is to involve them in social activities and conversation, often telling stories. *Directors* want action and tend to believe their way is the only way, so the SIR is to be forthright with them with little or no banter (cut to the point). *Relaters* want everyone to get along and they tend to be the caretakers, so the SIR is to avoid conflict with them and to ask them questions about family, friends, their team, etc. *Analyzers* enjoy solving problems and tend to be numbers oriented, so the SIR is to present them with statistics, information, proof—they thrive on reasoning and calculations.

You can determine a person's type by their mannerisms, social interactions, and accouterments.

> *Socializers* appreciate meetings, group activities, and drawing attention to themselves. Their primary tendency leads to enthusiasm, often telling stories and entertaining others in order to engage them. *Directors* are proud to display their awards and achievements. Their primary tendency leads to action, often interrupting others to make sure their point is heard to get things done. *Relaters* tend to include family and team pictures in their office. Their primary tendency leads to consensus, often checking-in with others to make sure they feel included. *Analyzers* thrive through processes, such as figuring

out a problem or validating theories. Their primary tendency leads to correctness, often challenging assumptions to make sure they are accurate and validated.

When interacting with each type, the key to engaging them is to reflect those behaviors that fit within their comfort zone. Adaptability requires the ability to adjust our own behaviors to accommodate the various behavioral styles. Don't assume your likes are their likes—one size does not fit all.

When with a Socializer, be gregarious and attentive; with a Director be straightforward and decisive; be considerate and caring with a Relater; and speak or act logically and factually with an Analyzer. Each style responds to interactions differently.

The key to adaptability is to mirror others' common behaviors, and to respond accordingly.

Figure 4.1 details these behaviors for each style.

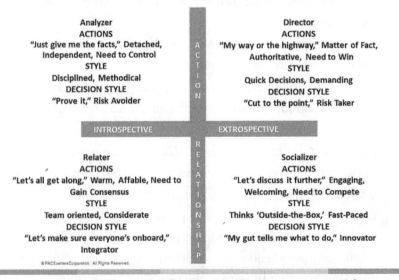

Primary Characteristics of BEHAVIORAL STYLES

Analyzer	Director
ACTIONS	ACTIONS
"Just give me the facts," Detached, Independent, Need to Control	"My way or the highway," Matter of Fact, Authoritative, Need to Win
STYLE	STYLE
Disciplined, Methodical	Quick Decisions, Demanding
DECISION STYLE	DECISION STYLE
"Prove it," Risk Avoider	"Cut to the point," Risk Taker

INTROSPECTIVE — EXTROSPECTIVE

ACTION / RELATIONSHIP

Relater	Socializer
ACTIONS	ACTIONS
"Let's all get along," Warm, Affable, Need to Gain Consensus	"Let's discuss it further," Engaging, Welcoming, Need to Compete
STYLE	STYLE
Team oriented, Considerate	Thinks 'Outside-the-Box,' Fast-Paced
DECISION STYLE	DECISION STYLE
"Let's make sure everyone's onboard," Integrator	"My gut tells me what to do," Innovator

(Figure 4.1 - Model for the Social Interaction Rule)

After You Identify a Person's Behavioral Style, Use Versatility

Versatility is the most important discipline of adaptability. Versatility allows us to adjust our behavioral style to that of someone with a different style, such as a Relater dispensing with "small talk" when speaking with a *Director*, and instead communicating crisply and forthrightly in short order. Or a *Socializer* taming down her enthusiasm with an *Analyzer* to convey the facts and figures that Analyzer needs to make a decision. A versatile *Director* will take time to listen and ask about a *Relater's* family, setting the Relater at ease, and an *Analyzer* will defer his need for confirmation to simply engage a *Socializer* with equal enthusiasm for what the Socializer is sharing, by mirroring the Socializer's open gestures. Whatever behaviors are preferred by a particular behavioral style, even if they seem unnatural, the versatile communicator uses those types of behaviors in order to connect.

ADAPTING EXPRESSIONS

- Self-confidence
- Empathy
- Optimism
- Respect
- Humility

"You can have everything in life, if you will just help other people get what they want."

~Zig Ziglar

To align our style with a different style or a differing agenda requires versatility acquired through the *four connecting expressions* of *self-confidence, empathy, optimism, respect* and *humility*. Humility defers our egocentric wants in order to accept differing opinions and practices. In turn, humility gains the respect and attention of diverse people.

Versatility attracts people to your point of view through the four connecting expressions, and if any are lacking, connectedness suffers. For example, we know that optimism attracts people and feeds their enthusiasm. The same happens when we can defer any bias or prejudice against someone to show them the respect that should be afforded to any human being we encounter. Attempting to understand someone, and to learn about their wants and needs builds respect.

The four *disconnecting expressions* that thwart versatility are all egocentric: *inflexibility* (not budging), *negativism, arrogance* and *impatience.* Usually those who practice these disconnectors fall into the trap of mental laziness.

Versatility practitioners, PACEsetters, are some of the most attentive people on earth. As a practiced discipline they notice the environment as well as the subtle movements, words and posture of others. This enables them to identify problems and solve them most effectively—they are like the detectives on TV that you see who are able to solve every crime. Coupled with a can-do attitude, these students of people and life demonstrate the tenacity to get things done. They can readily correct themselves through an openness to feedback, and because of their humility, they are not restricted by the need to be right all of the time. Instead, the versatile person can say, "I think this isn't working, so let's try something different."

RELATE

Being Vulnerable & Genuine

Esteem is the confidence of connection. Shame is the fear of disconnection. Shame says, "I'm not good enough." Confidence says, "I can share my flaws with you." For connection to occur we need to be vulnerable. When people are vulnerable with each other they express to each other that they are worthy of love and belonging. They exhibit a sense of courage in common, because they demonstrate the courage to be imperfect by expressing compassion for each other. Connection is the result of authenticity, which conveys humility—traits of a PACEsetter.

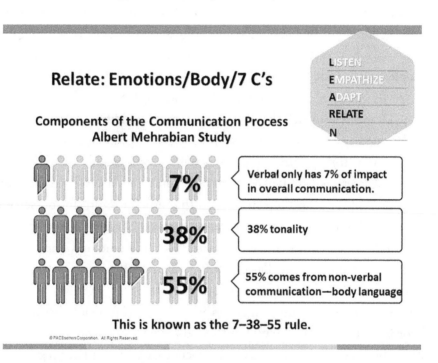

Dale Carnegie, wrote an overnight success considered even today as one of the all-time best for its teachings on dealing with people—it's entitled, *How to Win Friends and Influence People*. He wrote about how to make people like you, and ways to win people over to your thinking. But, his pervasive theme is that none of the lessons will work if the intent is manipulation. The word "genuine" appears throughout his writings as the foundation for winning over people.

The takeaway is that only with honesty and authenticity will we be able to influence people over the long haul. Most people are pretty adept at detecting if someone is genuine or if they are "fake"—meaning that they are behaving unnaturally. Unfortunately most phony people don't realize that others can recognize their fake behavior. *So the key is to get real.* When someone asks you for your opinion on a subject, be honest about the way you feel, and avoid telling her something that you think she wants to hear. Be willing to share your faults, your flaws and your mistakes.

Just imagine that the person will know whether you're telling the truth or not—so why not be transparent? We all need to accept who we are—so know yourself and be as authentic and as vulnerable with others as possible. Insecurity causes us to be fake, so learn to accept yourself and people will accept you—and if they don't, so what? So-called friends gained through deceit are not really true friends at all.

"To err is human," the saying goes, but in addition to forgiveness being "divine," admitting our mistakes and flaws, even laughing at them, is absolutely *supernatural!* Fitting in with people should never be the goal. PACEsetters often need to stand alone. Instead, we should just accept people as who they are and do the same in return for ourselves. Mean what you say, and say what you mean. Trying to guess what somebody wants to hear is a winless game. Compliments and smiles given in sincerity are great, but flattery only will turn off people. Better than compliments is trying to help the other person.

Genuine people are caring, and when we make people happy, the favor is always returned with a feel-good response. Don't try to appease others by accepting invitations or projects that you will later regret. It's OK to politely turn down an invitation to the opera if that's not your thing. It's OK to admit you're not perfect. Just be yourself. Everyone else is taken.

Using Connecting Emotions

Emotional connection builds relationship. Relating to another person starts by connecting to the other person's feelings, and recognizing their emotional response. There are six connecting emotions that open a person's receptivity, and six corresponding disconnecting emotions.

Use the connecting emotions when speaking to another and avoid the disconnecting emotions. Relationship is built on emotional connection. Remember that emotional moments can be opportunities for teaching so don't respond to an upsetting emotional reaction with a disconnecting emotion—keep your connection going. Then listen to the other person. Keep your eyes focused on theirs, lean forward, let them know that you've heard what they have said by acknowledging their sentiment, not just their words.

Avoid judging the person's emotions. If you maintain emotional connectedness, you will have the opportunity to relate to a disagreeable person only after their emotions have calmed, and they have acknowledged back to you that they are receptive to what you are saying. Only after the other person is feeling understood should you proceed to the solutions part of your conversation.

Too often when others relate their brokenness to us we immediately jump into the fix-it mode. That opportunity will arise when the other person is ready to receive it, and not just when we are ready to suggest it. Encourage emotional expression, but set limits on what behavior is appropriate; and, don't expect instant openness. Our ability to relate happens as we demonstrate a genuine interest in the other person using sincere emotional connection.

Connecting and Disconnecting Emotions

Connecting	Disconnecting
Love	Mistrust
Empathy	Inflexibility
Compassion	Negativity
Composure	Impatience
Kindness	Arrogance

Smile

Those smiles can spread sunshine on a rainy day, yet most people do not freely give them, unless they are PACEsetters. Recent research reveals that small gestures like a smile can make people feel more connected. That simple gesture of kindness can make even a stranger feel more connected to the one who is smiling immediately after those face cheeks spread, according to a study reported at the annual meeting of the *Society for the Study of Motivation*. Highly charismatic people do this routinely—it's been documented that they even use more muscles in their face. Genuine smiles cause wrinkles around the eyes. Forced ones center primarily around the mouth.

A sincere smile is always the best strategy to build and establish rapport. The smile maintains attention, helps bolster trust, and reassures the other person of your sincerity. *The key is being the first to smile, not waiting for others.* A smile establishes the person who gives it as being well-mannered, immediately. A smile can brighten the mood, improve the outlook of a relationship, and leads others to make positive choices using sound and good judgment. That's the power of a smile.

When we encounter someone, we intuitively ask ourselves whether that person is a "friend or foe," and the answer to that question determines whether we want to cooperate with that person or not. Arguably, smiling leads others to think that we are "friends" and they should therefore cooperate with us.

Nice People Get Ahead

But being viewed as dominant can only get you so far. According to research by Amir Erez, who earned his Ph.D. at Cornell University, a leader's positive mood and expressions do have a positive impact on his/her followers. Leaders who were rated most charismatic tended to smile and laugh more.

Consequently, the researcher found that leaders who were rated as more charismatic (they smiled and laughed more) had followers who were happier as well compared to followers with lower "charisma." Erez hypothesized that people follow leaders like John F. Kennedy and Ronald Reagan because "they make us feel happy and happiness is like a drug." Consequently, they want more of it and continue following the leader as long as the charisma keeps working.

So does a smile and friendliness correlate with success? Well, for the PACEsetter the answer appears to be yes, because they expect others to perform at high levels and they set high standards, and their friendliness fosters an environment where people are treated with respect, and have more fun while getting work done. Furthermore, PACEsetters more frequently recognize people, making those people feel more motivated and energized by how well appreciated they are by the PACEsetter—who, frequently smiles, laughs and engages them.

Richard Branson, founder of the Virgin Group, which comprises more than 400 companies, related in an interview that his success was largely determined by his ability to practice the attributes of being pleasant. "Actually," he said, "it is counterproductive to be ruthless. People tend to come back and do more business if they feel they have done well with you. That attitude has helped me over the years to attract and keep good partners and staff. My ability to listen to other people and accept it when their suggestions are better than mine has been useful during my 40 years in business."

Speaking of Virgin's success, Branson continued: "As I've mentioned… back in the `60s, our friendly approach helped us to sign the Rolling Stones to Virgin Records. We often joked around as we worked together, and so Mick Jagger and the rest of the band saw us as being like themselves, rather than just stuffy coin counters in suits and ties."

He goes on to say about the Virgin culture: "At Virgin, we all know that our smiles make a difference. When you get onto a Virgin plane, it's the smiles from our staff that make you feel good—that touch of heartfelt service that says 'We give a damn.'"

The benefits of friendliness were confirmed by a study co-authored by Timothy Ketelaar, associate professor of psychology at

New Mexico State University, with a caveat. Ketelaar explained his findings in a statement: "Smiles can put you in a positive light by signaling that you're friendly and trustworthy, and that you aren't a threat to others. But higher-status individuals often want to appear in charge and as a threat, and they lose some of that power by smiling." The researchers argue that less dominant human beings have relied on smiles to appease stronger, more hostile individuals for as long as we have been able to cause those little wrinkles around the eyes.

But strength in the form of dominance runs counter to the PACEsetter model. For the PACEsetter, strength is shared and utilized for the collective benefit of all concerned, such that strength in character supersedes strength in position in terms of importance. So "getting ahead" refers to *the team* getting ahead, and not any one individual. That's analogous to the Navy SEAL Creed: "My loyalty to Country and Team is beyond reproach," which is summed-up in one overriding principle: We either succeed together or we fail together—there are no individual heroes and no one gets left behind. This dedication to team accounts for the Seal's unparalleled success in accomplishing their extraordinarily challenging missions.

One probably would not acquaint Navy Seal soldiers with smiling, but smiling is actually one of the most effective ways for disarming hostilities in any situation, and soldiers use their smiles to make the innocent natives in battle zones feel more at ease. The amazing thing about a smile is that when you give it to someone, it causes him or her to reciprocate with a return smile, even when you're both faking it.

Professor Ulf Dimb at Uppsala University, Sweden, conducted a study that proved how our unconscious mind exerts direct control of our facial muscles. In an experiment of 120 volunteers, Dimb used equipment to measure electrical signals from muscle fibers. When coached to try controlling their facial expressions, the twitching of the volunteers' facial muscles mirrored the expressions they were seeing in pictures, even when they were trying not to. Apparently "mirror neurons" in the brain cause us to mirror the facial expressions of others, and smiling positively influences other people's attitudes and how they respond to us. And this produces an environment conducive for success by opening constructive possibilities.

Being Nice Causes Connection

Studies overall prove that most encounters will be more positive, relationships will last longer, outcomes will be more successful, and connectedness will significantly increase when people make an effort to be both nice and giving. Countries with the highest levels of giving per capita, with cultures that support one another (like the Okinawans), have the strongest social connections as well as higher rates of happiness and greater life expectancy.

Evidence has also been mounting that both smiles and laughter enhance the immune system, open customers to salespeople's offerings, attracts people to each other, and smiles even extend longevity! If you take notice of PACEsetters over a long period, you'll notice they smile a lot.

Another study, reported by Lindsay Abrams at *the Atlantic,* supports that smiling and just being nice is good regardless of the situation. Researchers found that smiling—even when it's forced—can ease stress and lower heart rates, even in the midst of multitasking. The conclusion? "When a situation has you feeling stressed or flustered, even the most forced of smiles can genuinely decrease your stress and make you happier."

This equates to simply showing that you are nice, because nothing can turn someone around like an act of charity and kindness. Being nice to someone you dislike doesn't mean you're disingenuous. It means you are confident enough to tolerate your dislike towards them.

The proposal that we need to smile even when we don't feel like isn't so much about others. It's about smiling for you and how it changes your physical state. It's about turning around the pressures in life to realize that your perspective can override circumstances with something as simple as some humor and a smile. Then as we lighten the mood for ourselves, we invariably lighten it for others as well. PACEsetters smile a lot because it provides multiple benefits—it usually elicits a return smile, sets a positive tone, establishes instant trust, disarms otherwise antagonistic persons, relieves stress, and fosters instant rapport. Besides all that, who wouldn't rather be around nice people?

Using Body Language and Verbal Signals to Relate

We know that facial expressions, words, and emotions can serve to either disconnect or connect with others, but several studies have now confirmed that the "hidden" communication of body language serves as one of the most powerful connectors of all. About 55% of how people perceive you is through body language, 38% by your voice, and only 7% by your words. Research suggests that between 60-70% of meaning in human communication is derived from nonverbal behavior.

A simple smile or a hug can actually speak more effectively than any words if conveyed sincerely. Mirroring someone's movement is known as "the chameleon effect" used in persuasion. Sincerity is the key, and so to understand the differences between appearing honest and insincere are important.

Police and forensic psychologists are trained in how to identify deception techniques that can be useful for anyone using body language and verbal cues. People who lie typically use expressions that are stiff and contained, with few hand movements except to scratch behind the ear or touching the nose. Insincere persons keep their movements tight to their body.

An important way of demonstrating honesty is by matching your words and tone to your body language. For example, don't chuckle if you are saying something serious. The honest and well-received person relaxes her face and opens her posture to directly face the person with whom she is connecting. She maintains good eye contact, unlike the insincere or deceptive person.

Honest gestures and emotions are usually consistent for healthy relaters, whereas disconnecting relaters use delayed emotional responses that stop abruptly. For example, the person who causes mistrust may say, "That's funny" after hearing a joke, and then laugh well after hearing it. The dishonest person's expressions and movements will not match their verbal utterances, like smiling after saying "It's a gloomy day outside."

When someone is faking it, their expressions are confined to the mouth as opposed to using full-face movements (i.e., eyes, jaw and forehead do not move). The person who connects using honesty smiles such that crow's-feet (wrinkles around the eyes) appear. Persons who are confident are overt; those who feel guilty become defensive, and may turn their body or head away from the other person as a form of avoidance. Facing your torso toward the other person's torso connects you with the other person. Dishonest or disconnecting people may place themselves behind tables, or move cups or other objects between the other person as a subconscious obstacle—they try to hide. Honest connectors tend to remove obstacles between themselves and the person with whom they are relating.

In conversation, *dis*connectors often will repeat your own words back verbatim, such as when you say, "Did you have a satisfying lunch across the street?" They will respond, "Yes, I had a satisfying lunch across the street." These are indicators that someone may not be telling the truth. Statements using contractions, like "I don't think so," are perceived as being more truthful than "I do not think so." Disconnectors avoid direct statements but might also over-speak, adding unnecessary details. They do not like pauses. They may leave out pronouns and speak with a monotone, talking softly and mumbling at times using improper grammar in a jumbled manner. Changing the subject connotes dishonesty to the other person, by oftentimes confusing the honest (connecting) person who wants to keep on topic.

PACEsetters possess an exceptional ability to connect emotionally by using mirroring to reflect the behaviors of the other person. Relaxed posture is met with relaxed posture, and so forth. They match the other person's gestures and mannerisms to establish rapport, allowing them to lead that person through a subconscious reaction. As a connector to other people, a PACEsetter, for example, after mirroring the other person's behavior, might lead that person by initiating a handshake of equal hand-pressure (no "bone-crusher" or "dead fish" grips), sitting or standing up tall, leaning forward, smiling, widening their stance, maintaining eye contact, and lowering his or her voice. These gestures demonstrate confidence.

Body Language That Connects

Smile Showing a warm smile is like inviting someone to spend time with you.

Use Affirmations Signal our openness through nodding and affirming vocal sounds.

Lean forward Leaning forward indicates engagement, but don't lean too far.

Use open (unlocked) posture Unlock your posture to communicate openness.

Touch Provide a warm handshake, a pat on the back, or hug if appropriate.

Maintain Eye Contact Making eye contact shows respect and attention.

Certain affirming body gestures connect people, like nodding, a softened gaze, and wearing your emotions on your face. Connectors may provide a solid touch to the other person's forearm or face their palms up, both gestures indicating a sign of rapport. Before using any touching gestures, however, it's best to assess the behavioral and cultural styles of the other person. Those gestures that build rapport probably would work well with the Relater. In some cultures touching is not acceptable.

According to research at Harvard and Columbia Business schools, holding those palms apart so that they face each other, such as with holding a basketball, forming the hands as a steeple, or standing with legs and arms stretched wide open, stimulate testosterone, the hormone linked to power and dominance, which evokes passion and authority, and that may connect well with a Driver. The Driver may in turn face her palms down to exhibit power.

There are some universally perceived negative gestures that tend to disconnect, like wrinkling the nose (a sign of disgust) or pulling one's lip corner in and back on one side of the face (a sign of contempt). One or two index fingers pointing outward can act as a disconnecting gesture by telling the other person that you don't like what he or she is doing or saying.

Establishing an effective connection with someone should always be demonstrated with respect. According to research, at least 50% of our joy comes from doing something for others—in other words, caring. When we genuinely care for someone, our body language will usually follow with the same attitude.

The 7 C's of Connection

Completeness

Correctness

Conciseness

Courtesy

Clarity

Consideration

Concreteness

Practicing the 7 Cs of Connection

Consider all of the ways in which you communicate with others. You talk on the phone, send emails, text, participate in meetings, make presentations, type reports … each day communication represents you and your intentions. Our lives are full of communicating with people.

So, how can you make each communication an effective one? You can follow the well-established Cs of communicating with impact.

PACEsetters follow the 7 Cs of connection when speaking or writing:

1. **Completeness**—They provide the what, where, how, and when of what they express, including answering any questions that might arise from their message. In written communication, being correct means proper use of grammar, punctuation and spelling. Correctness in oral communication means the right use of words, expressions, and pauses.

2. **Correctness**—PACEsetters use the right form of expression, such as professional language in the workplace, as well as using the appropriate mode of communication (e.g., visual aids, email). Correctness in business writing includes proper grammar, spelling, punctuation, and format. For spelling, punctuation, and grammar, you should use the *spelling and grammar* check under your *Tools* bar. For important documents, ask someone to proof read your work.

3. **Conciseness**—By ensuring that their message is clearly understood by avoiding wordy expressions, staying on purpose, and not repeating yourself, PACEsetters convey confidence. Anyone who wants their communications to be taken seriously by busy people, makes them brief. They say what they need to say, and say no more (while maintaining goodwill, of course).

4. **Courtesy**—PACEsetters respect the feelings, expectations, and customs of the other person or group, while also expressing appreciation. For example, instead of a store manager at closing time abruptly telling a customer that "The store is closed," the PACEsetter might say, "Thank you for shopping with us and I simply wish to let you know we are closing now, but we'll be open tomorrow." Their message is positive-building goodwill and focused upon the listener or reader. They're careful about customs for different cultures, knowing the person's name, gender specific language, and proper use of titles.

5. **Clarity**—Emphasize the specific topic or goal, rather than saying too much at one time. Check your communication to see if you are using any unnecessary sentences or (filler) words such as "for instance," "sort of," and "basically." Use familiar words and avoid technical terms or business jargon.

6. **Consideration**—Being considerate implies a level of understanding or empathy for others by displacing a "Me-Attitude" with a "We-Attitude." PACEsetters put the other person first. Remaining sensitive to the audience's background, expectations, and views is key in order to avoid offending them. They keep the spotlight on the other person's interests, and speak in the language and customs of the person with whom they are communicating.

7. **Concreteness**—PACEsetters give their audience a solid picture of what they are communicating, by providing an appropriate level of detail (but not too much) with pinpoint focus using vivid facts. A bad example of using concreteness would be saying, "I am going to make you

effective today." There's no imagery or detail in this sentence. A good example might be: "How much time do you spend duplicating your efforts? Today we're going to change that! By doing the job right the first time, you'll save time and enjoy your work much more." Note how the passion and details work.

NEGOTIATE

Some may view negotiation as a form of manipulation—it is not. In its purest sense negotiation is about getting to a point of transparent connection, where the needs of each other are interdependently served through collaboration, and where together each person is stronger than either would be apart.

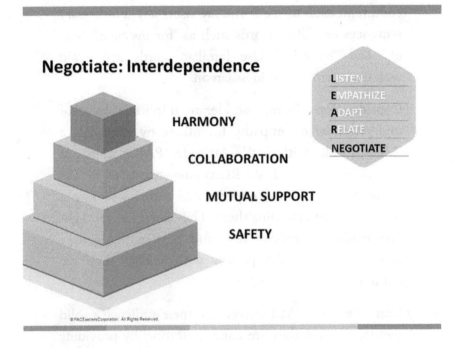

In 1943, Abraham Maslow created a well-known hierarchy of needs, which he displayed as a pyramid. Our basest needs to maintain life (e.g., food, water, etc.), according to Maslow, needed to be met first before moving up the pyramid to higher needs. The next need, for safety (e.g., security, family support, health), would be sought only after meeting the basic needs for existence. Third, the need for belonging and being loved served as the driving force once these others were established. And, then second from the pinnacle or top was the need for self-esteem, confidence, achievement, and the respect for and from others. The top need in the pyramid was for morality, creativity and spontaneity. At the height of healthy relationships, and at the top of Maslow's pyramid, people are elevated to the point of making principled decisions, they tend to think more innovatively, and they feel free to openly express themselves.

Connectedness reflects a similar pattern of needs to those determined by Maslow. In relationships, we must first feel safe and secure with the other person. After that is established, our need is to feel supported by the other person, so that we feel that our interests are being protected. Next up the pyramid is to produce an outcome that can best be achieved together, rather than apart using collaboration. And, finally at the top, our need is met through a fully merged or integrated nature of wants so that the "you and me" of a relationship become simply, "us." Negotiating to this pinnacle of relationship is a little like a dating relationship, which start with feeling safe, then moves to an awareness of being protected, then becomes collaborative (e.g., working together), and is finally consummated with a sense of union, or harmony (see Figure 4.2).

Negotiation by definition is a discussion aimed at reaching agreement, but the highest level of human interaction leads not to just agreement but to a singleness of purpose and power. When two or more disparate chords of interaction join together, the power of each melds into a harmonic power than no one note can achieve as separate.

Safety

Similar to Maslow's Pyramid, the Connection Pyramid starts with creating a safe environment. When people feel like they can trust the other person, they feel safe. Trust can be established through transparency, boundaries, patience, friendliness, and reliability.

Negotiate: Safety

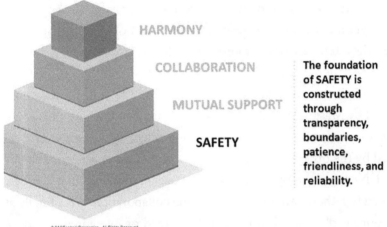

The foundation of SAFETY is constructed through transparency, boundaries, patience, friendliness, and reliability.

(Figure 4.2 - The Connection Pyramid of Negotiation)

Here's how to develop these five characteristics in a relationship:

1. Build **transparency** *through vulnerability.* People appreciate when we show our humanity. Saying "I'm not really sure" or "I goofed up" opens the other person to trust. Confessions give us a fresh start, a new beginning. And then asking something like "Would you be able to help me with this?" opens the door to the next step of mutual supportiveness.

2. *Establish* **boundaries** *or non-negotiables for moving forward.* Right from the start boundaries must be established in order to create rules for the relationship. Saying something like, "I need time after 6 p.m. for family and social time," lessens hidden resentment in the future.

Asking the other person about their boundaries is imperative as well.

3. *Practice* **patience** *by stepping away from a heated conversation or practicing the skills of reflection and acknowledge in order to diffuse conflict.* Once hostility occurs in an emerging relationship, trust is damaged. If this happens, apologize and use your empathy skills to show that you want to understand the other person.

4. *Demonstrate* **friendliness** *with a smile and caring directness.* Something as simple as a smile relaxes the other person and usually elicits a similarly positive response. People tend to process messages better if spoken with kindness and directness. They know exactly what you mean, and can clarify their processing with you based on the facts, not conjecture, as long as the message is conveyed with genuine caring for the other person's success.

5. *Practice* **reliability.** *This means that once a responsibility has been accepted, the accountable person must remain committed to its satisfactory completion—no ifs, ands, or buts about it—you're obligated at that point.* So be careful in what you say "Yes" to—it's better to decline something than to not do it well. Once a responsibility is accepted, you'll need to define the requirements to be met. Ill-defined expectations and tasks that cannot be objectively measured can lead to an unfair evaluation of the work completed by the person who is expecting it. You might think you've done a wonderful job, but if it isn't what the other person expected, from their perspective you didn't satisfactorily complete the work.

Safety in Relationships

- **TRANSPARENCY**–Confessions give us a fresh start, and opens the other person to trust.
- **ESTABLISHING BOUNDARIES**–Established upfront, boundaries lessen hidden resentments.
- **PATIENCE**–The power of reflection diffuses conflict in order to avoid hostility.
- **FRIENDLINESS**–A smile and caring correctness relaxes the other person with kindness.
- **RELIABILITY**–Once a responsibility is accepted, no ifs, ands, or buts about it–we're obligated.

Mutual Support through Equal Power

Negotiate: Mutual Support

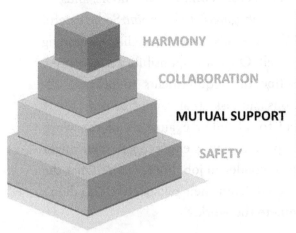

HARMONY

COLLABORATION

MUTUAL SUPPORT

SAFETY

The foundation of MUTUAL SUPPORT is constructed through interdependent responsibility, mutual vulnerability, and mutual respect as well as unselfishness.

Research shows that equal power helps create relationship success. Though people often express a commitment to equality in a relationship, cultural models of mutual support demonstrate a tendency for those in a relationship to seek personal control. Power imbalances are destructive to most relationships, primarily because of a person's perceived need to be right all of the time. Here are the three steps to ensuring mutual support through equal power sharing:

1. **Interdependent Responsibility.** Each person in the relationship fails or succeeds together. Their success as well as their positions toward any endeavor becomes interdependent. Failure shared decreases failure. Success shared multiplies success. Always view the other person's success as your own.

2. **Mutual Vulnerability.** Only one person sharing his or her vulnerability will not suffice. Being vulnerable together is the single most important aspect of building connectedness. Without mutual vulnerability, the relationship regresses back to the need for safety.

3. **Mutual respect and unselfishness.** Mutual respect and unselfishness are the two biggest reasons for lasting connectedness. Partners can't get too mired in their own selfish wants. This insight into lasting connectedness was borne from a study of 120 couples with marriages in excess of 30 years. Those who wanted a 50/50 split in getting their way didn't succeed as well as those who would settle for 40/60, with each agreeing to offer the most to the other. This only works if both sides agree to do more for the other.

In my research of 20 leaders within a San Diego-based company, each felt they shared their power equally with their work partners. However, in meetings several of these people demonstrated otherwise. For example, some showed up to meetings late. Showing up on time indicated compliance, not power. Those who showed up consistently late for meetings actually had the power, because they dictated when the meetings started. Some opted not to participate in meetings all together, sending out a non-verbal message that the other participants were not worth their time. They were not a priority. But no one wanted to admit that is the message they were sending. These kinds of power plays made others feel unsupported, which result in an unhealthy company culture.

Mutual Support in Relationship

- **INTERDEPENDENT RESPONSIBILITY**—Interdependence means that each person in the relationship fails or succeeds together
- **MUTUAL VULNERABILITY**—Only one person sharing his or vulnerability creates disconnection; however, being vulnerable together fosters a transparent and therefore trusting relationship
- **MUTUAL RESPECT AND UNSELFISHNESS**—Be prepared to give more, and find someone equally willing to do the same.

Power is dynamic, changing from situation to situation. PACEsetters in leadership positions ensure that no one on the team holds all of the power, and they often do this by rotating responsibilities so that no one person holds the power all of the time. For most, this has been found to be challenging, since shared responsibility runs contrary to many high achievers. They can perceive accommodation as a loss of power. Showing any kind of weakness was disagreeable to most in the leadership group studied, such as accepting a project that appeared demeaning, or allowing the other person to choose an alternate path. This type of "power leading" proved ineffective over the long term by demotivating teams.

On the flip side, PACEsetter leaders are a complicated and effective mix of intense professional will and exceptional personal humility. They create superb results but shun adulation, and are never boastful. Most would describe them as modest. An example of such a leader who epitomized humility is Mark Lortz, who founded a hugely successful company called Therasense (which was eventually sold to Abbott Laboratories). Therasense topped the Deloitte Technology Fast 500, a ranking of the fastest growing technologies in North America, by demonstrating a 296,080% growth rate over five years. Lortz defined himself as a team player first and a CEO second. As a PACEsetter leader, he was a man of the people, practicing management by inclusion. Shunning all manner of praise, Lortz is quoted as saying, "You shouldn't boast about anything you've done; you ought to give credit to others when credit is due."

Clearly these accomplished PACEsetter leaders don't espouse the meaning of humility as "meek." Quite the opposite, it is a source of their strength. Practicing humility improves relationships across all levels, it prevents power struggles, it encourages more openness and paradoxically, it empowers teams more than any single person can do. But the notion of being self-effacing is one that we struggle with in our competitive culture, causing many to brag of their achievements or to play office politics. The outcome is a drain in the team's power, or energy. Just saying these eight empowering words could save expensive team building retreats: "I would like us to consider *your* idea." Ahh...shared power feels good.

Distributing Power through Negotiation

Another key to overcoming power struggles was found in eliminating the tendency toward gaining the upper hand, or position, through a negotiated resolution. In the book *Getting to Yes*, which was based on the work of the Harvard Negotiation Project, authors Roger Fisher and William Ury suggested that to effectively negotiate, we need to separate the people from the problem by focusing on *interests*, not positions. Once position becomes secondary, or even tertiary to mutual interests, the influence of power diminishes.

They wrote that we need to define objective standards as the criteria for making decisions. When someone wants you to take on another project when you're already maxed, you need to remain assertive by saying "no" through effective negotiation, but leave the door open to the other person's wants. Perhaps, for example, you could negotiate a lighter workload—which would get you to "yes," or redefine your role and responsibilities as an opportunity to move forward. You have plenty of options, but just saying "no" creates an imbalance of power. So the key is to say "no" to the task, but "yes" to the person at the same time.

Begin by explaining your reason for saying "no" so that you are clear as to whether just the timing is wrong, or whether there are other prohibitive factors. If someone understands your justification, they're more likely to agree with it, or at least they are less apt to become confrontational. Shared power begins through a negotiated settlement for satisfying mutual wants. Whether a response is yes or no, the negotiation process focuses on how to get the task or project done versus the positions needed to do so.

Next, think through different ways for the other person's wants to be met. Consider other resources and areas of flexibility by searching for common interests to achieve the primary end-goal. Gaining the other person's trust is central to any negotiation process. You do that through genuinely trying to understand their needs, and assuring them that you respect them enough to want to work through a solution that will get them to where they want to be. You could say something like, "I'm sorry, I know you need to get this done and I want to help you, while at the same time I'm committed to a project this week and don't have the time to do a good job for you right now, but I have a couple of other ideas. Jane is anxious to develop her skills in this area—would you like me to show the project scope to her so that she can take this on?" Or say, "I can do this in about two weeks if you like."

Looking for that proverbial win-win establishes equal power sharing. Just saying no, or ignoring the wants of someone else shifts the power to your side, but distances the other person sense of mutual support. Jockeying for position, or even regarding positions more important to the task than what it will take to achieve the desired outcome, creates an imbalance of power. To achieve true collaboration, power must be equally shared through an outcome based on working equally with each other.

Collaboration

Once power and responsibility are equally shared, communication can be elevated to the next level of interaction on the Connection Pyramid. The highest form of empowerment is collaboration, which is working together to create something larger than any individual contributor could ever devise on their own. The needs of the team or relationship always come first. Collaboration is working together to achieve a larger collective goal. It is a repetitive process where two or more people or organizations work together to realize common goals. Good collaborators don't look at a piece of pie and try to distribute the pieces evenly—they try to create a bigger pie so that their group can consume more of it.

Collaboration goes beyond just cooperation…it is more than the sharing of common objectives but a unified determination to reach an identical goal by sharing resources, knowledge, learning and building consensus. Collaboration moves persons from a "you and me" perspective to an "us" perspective. The key is to make it an intentional way of interaction.

Collaboration across Boundaries

Collaboration across boundaries is the most important element in establishing effective communications, although only 7% of the senior executives surveyed in a poll considered that they do it effectively. Boundaries exist everywhere in life, and similar statistics apply for people in teams, in one-on-one situations, across different countries, integrated businesses (mergers) and even within different communities.

Negotiate: Collaboration

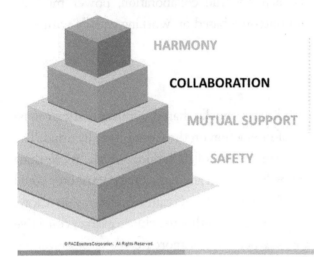

HARMONY

COLLABORATION

MUTUAL SUPPORT

SAFETY

Once power and responsibility are equally shared, an opportunity arises to attain a collaborative relationship.

© PACEsettersCorporation. All Rights Reserved.

Navigating across boundaries requires that we venture beyond our own confines, and that we adapt to new environments by identifying common connections and mutual interests between different people and groups. Showing respect for people is the most foundational principle for navigating across boundaries, and the second is a willingness to compromise and cooperate with each other.

To do so, we need to discontinue our bias and expectations, place our agenda aside, and just listen to the other person or group. Sharing with an open mind is the key success factor in collaboration, learning from others, and valuing others' opinions and ideas. Self-focused communication will undermine any attempt to traverse across boundaries, so an open, honest and consistent dialog between members must happen through a commitment by each person to own the communication process. Moving forward together means progress; jockeying for position means regression—there's no standing still.

Here's how:

Collaboration in Relationships

- Share intentions and visions.
- Respect all concerned.
- Share information freely *(no hoarding of knowledge)*
- Compromise when appropriate
- Define success as benefitting all
- Celebrate successes
- Give credit and recognition generously
- Maintain a solutions focus
- Embrace and initiate change *(answer the WIIFT and explain why it is necessary)*
- Limit tangential activities *(focus on the target)*
- Accept conflict as normal, however avoid emotional fights that don't lead to consensus
- Mitigate failures with a forward *approach—what was learned, what can we do better?*
- Challenge preconceived notions
- Achieve consensus *(which drives compliance)*

Collaborative communication leads to a harmonious relationship whether corporately or individually. Disney-Pixar represents a good example of a corporate merger where the two groups navigated through their own operating channels to emerge as a collaboration made in cartoon heaven. Conversely, the merger of Daimler/Chrysler ($37B) failed because of a corporate culture clash—many thought the high-end Daimler group swaggered in and attempted to tell the Chrysler group what to do. This created an imbalance of power, which prevented collaboration. Had these two automobile groups humbly asked more questions of each other in trying to balance the parts in the relationship to the whole, they may have succeeded. Instead, they lost the main idea and could not keep focus on the big picture.

There are many examples of successful pairs who have effectively collaborated with each other. Steve Jobs and Steve Wozniak used collaboration to create Apple, Inc.; Herbert Fisher and Zelma Fisher, born in 1905 and 1907, respectively, were married in 1924 in North Carolina. The marriage ended only after Herbert died in 2011, after 86 years, nine months, and 16 days—because they functioned collaboratively with each other to overcome many trials, through the proven process of expecting to give more in the relationship than each one expected of the other.

My favorite story involves an employee I supervised (I'll call her Lisa), who was in a constant power struggle with another employee in my company, Craig. Give Lisa a glass half-full and she would have said it was in fact three-quarters empty. However, I believed that Lisa had great potential, so I treated her as the person she ought to be, and gave her a big project with one caveat: She needed to work collaboratively with Craig. After much coaching, the two produced something much bigger than either would have created on his or her own. That is the secret of collaboration.

Harmony

Collaborative communication typically creates something better than any of the affected individuals would have accomplished on their own. Once collaboration occurs, there is an even more powerful level of interaction that can happen: Harmony. A harmonious relationship involves two or more people who neither harbor nor express any negativity toward each other. Both sides look out for one another and remain optimistic despite any obstacles.

Negotiate: Harmony

HARMONY

COLLABORATION

MUTUAL SUPPORT

SAFETY

Whereas collaboration is creating something greater together than the individual can create separately, harmony is a complete abandonment of selfish needs in favor of being one with each other.

So how does one reach this pinnacle of connectedness? Of course being empowering, supportive, encouraging (e.g., praises outnumber criticisms by at least four to one), non-judgmental, accepting, sincere, honest, loving, forgiving, respectful, grateful and understanding—but there's one very essential quality that allows collaborative people to cross over the threshold into harmony. People who develop harmony *expect* the other person(s) to ultimately do the right thing. They have *faith* in each other. Positive expectations produce harmony, and to believe in someone's ultimate goodness and abilities without qualification produces a harmonious level of communication that will prevail against even the most disappointing of circumstances.

Optimistically trusting in the essential goodness and success of others synchronizes our personal expectations with another. After all, who do we trust more than ourselves? God? Yes, but humanly speaking, despite occasional bouts of self-doubt, most of us live believing in our ability to prevail. When you first learned to drive, did you expect to be able to drive someday? You probably didn't give up despite some self-doubts and maybe even a test failure or two...or three. You succeeded in gaining your driver's license because you were confident in your ability to get your license, in part because you witnessed others—even some with lesser abilities—getting their driver's license. You could not fail because failure was simply irrelevant. Seeing another person in a similar light, as having no chance to ultimately fail us, creates a boundless ability to connect at all times, by maintaining a belief in that person's rightness, which frees us to believe in them.

Harmony in Relationships

People who develop harmony expect the other person(s) to ultimately do the right thing. They have faith in each other. Positive expectations produce harmony, and to believe in someone's goodness and abilities without qualification produces a harmonious level of communication that will prevail against even the most disappointing of circumstances.

Optimistically trusting in the essential goodness and success in others synchronizes our personal expectations with each other.

When ultimate success is believed, we invariably achieve success. Sometimes our paradigm of success may change, but success is in the future—regardless. Seeing someone else in a similar light produces the same outcome. In fact, when we believe in others, they believe in us. Ultimately, they cannot fail us. In the end, they will do what's best. Try visualizing a harmonious relationship, seeing the other as invincible just as you are destined toward success, both blessed in abilities, protected as the same, and continually improving. Then as a habit start affirming one another, which builds mutual confidence in each other so that in a sense, the prophetic belief in someone's abilities works out in reality.

Music, of course, is all about harmony. Without it, disparate vibrations simply become noise. The same principle applies to people— harmonious relationships sing while contentious ones clang. Great musicians play until their fingers or breath moves instinctively, and then they keep on playing until the melody and they become as one. Until they're lost in the music. Until they become the notes and rhythm, the chords and harmony. It takes hours of practice, but some have explained that it is all worth it in the end because they "become the music"—they lose themselves in the music. And the music takes away all worry, all the heartache, the pain, the desperation and the doubts. Harmony results from getting lost in something that started outside and somehow blended itself on our fabric.

Harmony in relationships, whether as two people or as a hundred people, results when the music of conversation—affirming words— connecting words—blends with others so that you start talking the same talk, start believing the same outcomes, start thinking of your destinies as immutably intertwined. So much so that you are virtually one—a heartfelt harmony.

CONNECTION
(fuels joy)
Be transparent, genuine, and unselfish

The PACE Formula®

L.E.A.R.N.

LISTEN—(Unselfishly), Care, Reflect, Acknowledge

EMPHATHIZE—Create a We-Attitude, Confirm, Use 3rd Person Empathy

ADAPT—Know Behavioral Styles, Use Versatility

RELATE—Be Vulnerable and Genuine, Smile, Reflect Body Language, Practice the "7 C's"

NEGOTIATE—Create Safety, Share Power, Collaborate, Achieve Harmony

The Power
to Thrive!

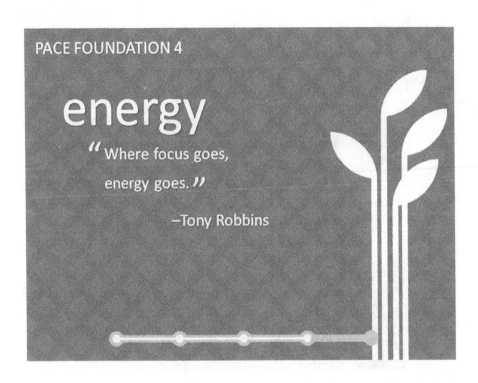

PACE FOUNDATION 4

energy

" Where focus goes, energy goes. "

—Tony Robbins

CHAPTER 5: ENERGY—TO FIND VITALITY

Thrive Drive is to...

F.R.E.E.

THE ENERGY TO THRIVE IS SOURCED THROUGH FREEING
OURSELVES OF ENERGY DRAINS, COUPLED WITH FREEING
OURSELVES TO ADOPT MORE EFFICIENT PRACTICES

ENERGY

EACH OF US HAS 24 hours in a day, no more, no less. So how do PACEsetters achieve more in those hours? They're able to manage competing demands even while the world seems to be spinning at the exhausting pace. Maintaining high energy demands that people manage themselves and their environment. PACEsetters have discovered, paradoxically, that the best way to get more done can be to do less, better. A growing body of multidisciplinary research shows that faith, rest, exercising, and good eating habits boosts productivity—and with it, health.

ENERGY—to find Vitality

PACEsetters have discovered, paradoxically, that the best way to get more done can be to do less, better.

'Working harder and longer' is the ethos of the Information Age, and it is grounded in a misguided assumption—that our resources are infinite.

Time is the limited resource which must be allocated to achieve more. Although none of us can increase our hours in our day, the answer is that we can increase our energy.

"Working harder and longer." This, the ethos of the Information Age, is grounded in a misguided assumption—that our resources are infinite. Time is the limited resource which must be allocated to achieve more. When demands increase, we tend to use more time to get things done. However, time is fixed, and for many of us it is evaporating like mist on a hot day. The irony is that we're investing increasing hours and burning ourselves out attempting to find more time for the things important to us so that we can enjoy life.

Although none of us can increase our hours in our day, the answer is that we can increase our energy. Research tells us how to do it. Scientists understand energy as the capacity to maintain equilibrium and to do work. Just as with time, energy is finite, but unlike time, it is renewable. Investing effort toward a healthy mindset and resting more is counterintuitive for most of us. This approach runs contrary to current work cultures that insist hard, often exhaustive work produces more. Many cultures eschew ethereal matters such as "spiritual renewal," and downtime is generally viewed as unproductive. According to the Bureau of Labor Statistics, an average day for people who work includes 2.5 hours spent on leisure and sports, 7.6 hours sleeping, 1.2 hours caring for others, 1.1 hours eating and drinking, 1.1 hours doing household activities, and almost 9 hours working on the job.

More than half of these people work during their vacations, and almost a third do not even take time out for lunch. In most workplaces, recognition and rewards accrue to workers who stay extra hours and push themselves the most. That doesn't necessarily mean they're the most productive. In fact, PACEsetters in our study almost always prioritized the needs of their loved ones over work, and they even worked fewer hours than many of their counterparts. However, the average trend for most is toward longer hours.

Spending more hours at work can compromise time for relationships, faith, health and sleep; and a deficiency in these areas invariably takes a substantial toll on performance and motivation, while faith, rest and healthy living were shown to increase performance. A team of Baylor University researchers found that entrepreneurial people pray more than non-entrepreneurs, and they have more faith in answered prayers. A second paper shows that workplaces encouraging faith tend to have employees that are more committed to their jobs. In a published study of nearly 400 employees, researchers found that sleep deprivation—defined as less than six hours each night — was one of the best predictors of on-the-job burnout. A recent Harvard study estimated that sleep deprivation costs American companies $63.2 billion a year in lost productivity.

On the health side, workers who ate healthful meals and exercised on a regular basis had better job performance and lower absenteeism, according to research from the Health Enhancement Research Organization (HERO), Brigham Young University and the Center for Health Research at *Healthways.*

Employees who eat healthy all day long were 25% more likely to have higher job performance, the study found, while those who eat five or more servings of fruit and vegetables at least four times a week were 20% more likely to be more productive.

Without faith, rest and healthy living, energy cannot be sustained. With it, we can achieve more, do more, and feel better doing it. Dr. Charles Garfield, an associate professor at the University of California's medical school, found that "peak performers" knew how to relax, could leave their work at the office, prized close friends and family life, and spent a healthy amount of time with their children and spouses." Numerous other studies testify to the long-term benefits of healthy living as the best way to create and sustain the energy and motivation to live a successful and satisfying life.

During the course of my career, I've had the privilege of working with many very skilled management experts. Time and again, I hear psychologists and performance experts say, "The most important factor for success and high achievement is a high energy level." From some experts' point of view, energy contributes the most to overall satisfaction and success — more than personality, intelligence, advanced degrees, or social skills. Although I cannot prove that one's energy level is absolutely *the* most important factor for career success, I am convinced it serves as one of the top four reasons for the success of people we tend to admire, and it begins with faith.

FAITH

The F.R.E.E. model to develop vitality starts with Faith (see Figure 5.1). Faith is an expression of hope for a better future. More than just a hope, it's more like a belief. It's a belief rooted in the soul. Faith imparts energy to action. It imparts a sense of doing what is right that intensifies our purpose.

To focus on the 10%

FAITH IMPARTS ENERGY TO ACTION

FAITH	
R	
E	
E	

The F.R.E.E. model to develop vitality starts with Faith. Faith is an expression of hope for a better future. More than just a hope, it's more like a belief. Faith instantly reaches the subconscious mind by producing an autosuggestion that we will achieve that for which we ask, if followed with the plans for achieving that which we desire.

The key to harnessing the power of faith is to conserve our faith-based energy for those times when reason alone will not suffice.

(Figure 5.1 - The F.R.E.E. model of Vitality)

We practice faith as the evidence of things not seen. No one knows what the future holds, yet people continue to look forward to tomorrow. No one can see the billions of stars in the sky, but we know they are out there. Faith speaks of something greater than ourselves or our awareness. The more we plug ourselves in a power greater than our limitations, the more energy we will gain. Finding a higher power is the basis for energy—whether it is from natural resources or from a spiritual one. Power is imparted from an energy source of greater capacity to receivers in need of that energy to function. Faith energizes, and serves as a conduit of power. It finds itself as an expression of hope that reaches beyond rationalization to complete trust in potency.

If you're feeling downtrodden or drained, faith may be the solution. Faith helps us overcome our feelings of inadequacy. It also aids in driving us toward success. Faith in ourselves speaks of the inevitability of triumph, sometimes because of setbacks, and not just instead of them, because with faith each step brings us closer to the goal. Belief in a higher power has been demonstrated to boost that success even more. Maybe this is because people of faith desire to merit God's wholehearted love, in the same way that children of loving parents tend to want to please their parents, or they make an effort to live up to their parents' confidence in their abilities. Regardless, faith instantly reaches the subconscious mind by producing an autosuggestion that we will achieve that for which we ask, if followed with the plans for achieving that which we desire. So in a sense faith serves as the impetus that gives life and action to the stimulus of thought.

Faith gives us an inherited value beyond our own perceived abilities. We can have faith and hope in a bigger plan for our life. Belief in the unseen or unknown produces a heartfelt assurance and a resolute conviction that we have what we desire and hope for despite personal failures. Hope arises simply by believing that there is someone or something greater than our limited comprehension helping us, desiring our well-being, and caring for us all of the time.

Faith also allows us to launch beyond our artificial boundaries. As success trainer and PACEsetter Brian Tracy once said, "You need courage to launch in faith with no guarantees of success." Tracy also cited another wise advisor who once wrote, "If every obstacle must first be overcome, nothing will ever get done." Mary Bethune, turn of the century civil rights leader who started a private school for African-American students, said, "Without faith, nothing is possible. With it, nothing is impossible." Indeed, a strong case can be made that virtually every significant entrepreneurial success begins with faith and is energized through faith.

The key to harnessing the power of faith is to conserve our faith-based energy for those times when reason alone will not suffice. Energy is channeled by what we give our attention to. All conscious development (e.g., seeking the truth) and sacred practices (e.g., prayer, worship, devotion) are useful for cultivating energy and directing it toward a higher source of power. Tapping into that energy allows us to extend ourselves beyond our means, and it releases the ability to do more than what appears possible.

PACEsetter Helen Keller, the renowned blind and deaf author and lecturer, explained it this way: "I know that faith made my life possible and that of many others like me...Reason hardly warranted Anne Sullivan's attempt to transform a little half-human, half-animal, deaf-blind child into a complete human being. Neither science nor philosophy had set such a goal, but faith, the eye of love did. I did not know I had a soul. Then the God in a wise heart drew me out of nothingness with cords of human love and the life belt of language, and lo, I found myself. In my doubly shadowed world faith gives me a reason for trying to draw harmony out of a marred instrument. Faith is not a cushion for me to fall back upon; it is my working *energy*" (excerpts from *Let Us Have Faith,* 1940, pp. 9-11).

Napoleon Hill, one of the great writers on success, said this, "Faith is woven into every principle of the philosophy of achievement; faith is the essence of every great achievement, no matter what its nature or purpose. Neglecting your faith while carrying out your definite major purpose would be like trying to study astronomy without referring to the stars...The power of faith is inexhaustible. It is the ultimate renewable resource, a reflection of the Creator's desire that we use it in every way possible."

Evidence of Faith in Restoring Energy

At my research company TenorCorp, we sought the strongest evidence of faith that produced energy to succeed. No better example surfaced than an organization that specializes in resurrecting the lives of people deadened by the effects of alcohol and drugs. Perhaps the most successful and one of the longest lasting recovery program of all-time, Alcoholics Anonymous (AA), now has 1,800 groups with more than 90,000 members and an influence well beyond its membership. AA is a spiritual movement, a faith cure for alcoholism. Many in AA follow "Step Three" (belief in a "higher power") to find that they have been trying to live without God, and they then discover how to live with God. That gives a different approach to hope. Or, as one expressed it, "My mind has grasped new hope in a world I'd always wished for."

It's a leap of faith to be able to believe that there is a God personal to oneself, but surrender to the Higher Power is not difficult for most alcoholics and drug addicts, because for years they have surrendered to a lower power. Alcohol and drugs have a power, an intoxicating power. They provide an escape, a high and a cessation from fear and worry. In time, however, there is the craving, hangovers, loss of memory and sickness. In devotion to this fiendish habit, alcoholics and drug addicts will surrender reason, money, health, loved ones, and their career. To surrender to the higher power means no greater a demand than the surrender they have made to alcohol or drugs.

Some of the bravest PACEsetters I've known came from AA and organizations like them, including my Aunt Mildred Deutschmann, who was sober for more than 60 years until her death at 93. She served as a role model to many and credited her faith for the strength to persevere.

Teen Challenge, a residential service with more than 1,000 programs in almost 100 countries, serves those struggling with life-controlling addictions. Independent reports confirm that Teen Challenge has one of the highest success recovery rates of any such program in the world. A carefully controlled empirical study of Teen Challenge at Northwestern University in 1999 found this program to be more effective than any of its counterparts. In a study of 154 former residents whose lives were completely transformed for good, when asked to name what helped most, the faith-based aspects of the program were mentioned most frequently. These graduates testified of a faith beyond themselves that filled them with the energy they needed to carry on.

This representative of Teen Challenge boldly displays the power of faith that has made his recovery organization the most successful in the world.

Given that those with the least power found faith as their reason for succeeding, shouldn't those who with less controlling influences also find encouragement from the power of faith? The lesson that faith can give us the energy to prevail over almost any obstacle should fuel us forward no matter what happens, as long as we think we can prevail.

In Whom or What Should We Place our Faith?

In whom or what we place this faith tells us a lot about ourselves, and our level of vitality in life. If all that we hold most important rests upon other people, then the disappointment in those people's failings will lessen our faith. And since people by their less-than-perfect nature do fail, then faith must be based on a greater hope for goodness.

The same applies to faith in ourselves. We are not perfect, but the healthy individual continues to develop and grow. Without faith in ourselves we would consider ourselves as finished, without hope to grow into our ideal, and without faith in others we would consider them as permanently flawed without the hope that they could grow into someone worthy of our faith.

Faith in human beings is based not on their perfection but in human potential. However, our faith in a higher power believes in someone or something perfect. Most of us would agree in a higher power, even me as a former 23 year-old agnostic (afterward, I became a believer). Once I opened myself to the possibility of God, I started seeking the truth as to who God is, and then I asked for my higher power to show-up—and later...*zap*—I was filled with power! Before my faith conversion, I had thousands of questions such as "Why would a loving God permit suffering?" After it, I only knew that all of my questions had been answered in the form of perfect love. I call this post-transformation time of my life my second-half "renaissance" period. The best part of my life was launched post-faith, whereas my faithless nature before this period only served to reinforce my doubts. Faith gave me the confidence to see the unseen.

Most of us desire a personal relationship with God. That's because, according to some scientists, our brains are wired to believe in a deity. MRI's have demonstrated that certain areas of the brain light up when people pray or think about God. Perhaps that's because we gain satisfaction from faith in a perfect Creator who knows all and can do all. Believing in a higher power infuses us with the energy to persist even when people disappoint.

Faith Breeds Hope

Whether you are a believer or not, suffice it to say that faith can lead to a more vital life because of the assurances that it provides. A respected study conducted among 4,000 elder persons (those 65 years and over) asked respondents about their health problems and whether they prayed, meditated or read the Bible. According to a Garnett News Service article, researchers discovered that those seniors who said they rarely or never prayed ran about a 50% greater risk of dying during a six-year study compared with seniors who prayed at least once month. While this study is not in and of itself conclusive, other studies confirm that faith and prayer lead to more satisfaction.

Some would say that when Jesus said, "Seek the kingdom of Heaven within," he was pointing to our conscious ability to see things as we believe them, which is faith. To the skeptic, this may seem like self-hypnosis. The programmed mind thinks that unless something can be seen, as in being tangible, it cannot exist. If so, then things like love, which is not tangible, cannot be believed. And without love, one cannot begin to seek the overall meaning of life. In one of his books, Russian novelist Dostoyevsky depicts a conversation between two of his characters discussing hell. "Hell," says one of them "must be the inability to love." Amen to that!

In support of our need to keep believing and therefore to practice love, we must reach beyond the bounds of mere reason. By believing we open ourselves to greater possibilities, and an ideal beyond the limits of our own potentiality. Perfection realized and knowable through faith opens the door to possibilities beyond our imagination. It invigorates us with the notion that an entity or belief far greater than any limitation has things in control, and that feels good. Knowing that the power of love exists beyond our ability to comprehend its fullness makes even the worst situations miniscule in comparison to love's infinite ability to make it right. And that gives us energy to continue forward with hope, and the success that invariably comes with being hopeful.

The bottom line is that you can do it, and you will do it, if only you believe! Or as J.M. Barrie wrote in the story of Peter Pan, "The moment you doubt whether you can fly, you cease for ever to be able to do it."

The Three Parts of Humankind and Their Three Needs

When writing this book I struggled with the thought of expressing something too esoteric, especially when discussing faith. However, my understanding of the PACEsetter brought me to the conclusion that success often taps into the unknown, or the "little understood." Indeed, success often links the known with the unknown, just as it believes in the impossible. A PACEsetter factors in varied sources and ideas, which often leads to breakthrough. So I decided to embark on a search for the less commonly understood parts of what gives us energy, or life. Said another way, "What makes us tick?" And more importantly, "how can we tick longer and better?"

Let's begin with the most esoteric nature of humankind. The definition of the soul and spirit varies. Some define the soul as the spirit, and some define the soul as the human psyche or mind. For the sake of argument, let's define each of us in three parts: body, soul (psyche), and spirit. The body is our housing unit, our flesh, blood and bones. The psyche is our arbiter of truth, our "moral compass," or what some term as our conscience. The spirit is our part that defies most definitions, but its reality is evidenced through Near Death Experiences (NDE's), where scientists have studied unconscious people with similar experiences like seeing a brilliant light, a tunnel, rushing sounds, peace and painlessness. The unconscious brain usually does not recall clear, lucid memories—so NDE research tends to validate humankinds' "non-material" component.

To study what gives us energy requires factoring in components in addition to our physiological composition, such as the alignment of our spiritual needs with our physical and psyche's needs. We know for a fact that the body is nourished through food, water (and air), and stimulation. The soul/psyche (conscience) seems to be satisfied by doing the right thing (what is morally correct). One could say that the three basic "food groups" for the psyche are moral correctness, helping others, and doing good, which usually makes us feel good.

The spirit, the ethereal part of us, would be fed through faith. Faith connects us to the spiritual realm (see Figure 5.2), or at least it allows us to believe in more than our eyes and conscience can understand. This in turn causes hope for life after death, and for many PACEsetters, belief in the spirit feeds their faith.

Energy Needs for Our Three Parts

(Figure 5.2 - Energy Needs for the Three Parts of Us)

To achieve total satisfaction in life, the needs of our three parts must be met. Deprivation in food, water (and air) can lead to physical sickness. Selfishness and moral corruption can lead toward dissatisfaction over the long term. Corruption of the psyche can "sicken" us, as in that nagging feeling that we are doing something wrong—a "troubled conscience." Most PACEsetters will admit that feeling spiritually deprived—a lack of faith—leaves them feeling incomplete, or at least less hopeful about the future. Hopelessness might be considered as a spiritual form of sickness.

So in order to be truly successful, we need to address the needs for our three parts, by taking care of our bodies, leading a disciplined life of doing what's right, and practicing our faith.

Adopting an Eternal Focus (Hope for the Future)

Believing in the spirit changes our attitudinal paradigm because it creates another facet to our already complex nature. It changes our perspective when we think from the vantage of what mystic philosopher Pierre Teilhard de Chardin wrote about in *The Phenomenon of Man* (1955): "We are not human beings having a spiritual experience; we are spiritual beings having a human experience." Take the following true story as an example.

For years, Harvard instructor and practicing surgeon, and Duke University trained neurologist and PACEsetter Dr. Eben Alexander had dismissed near-death revelations of heaven and God as mere reactions of the brain's hard wiring. But then in 2008 he contracted bacterial meningitis, a deadly infection that shutdown his neocortex (the part of the brain that "makes us human") and sent him into a deep coma. He described his ensuing near-death-experience (NDE) as being ushered into a place both "pitch black" and "brimming with light" coming from an "orb" that interprets for an all-loving God.

His book, *Proof of Heaven*, recounts those experiences, which he wrote knowing his story might jeopardize his professional reputation, particularly amongst skeptics, like he used to be. Dr. Alexander says that science cannot explain his experience since he says his brain "wasn't working at all." His book rose instantly to No. 1 on The New York Time's bestseller list. "Our spirit is not dependent on the brain or body," he says. "It is eternal, and no one has one sentence worth of hard evidence that it isn't."

Whether you believe Dr. Alexander's NDE as real or not, the fact is our bodies are only temporary and very brief in the scope of all-time. So from an ever-lasting perspective are we made for eternity? If "yes," why do we almost never use our eternal focus? If we did, we would more easily dismiss the relatively miniscule hardships we face as fleeting moments. We would be asking ourselves questions like, "Why am I worrying about the small stuff?" "What do I really need while I am here to serve my purpose and prepare me for the next life?" We wouldn't just wait for some traumatic experience such as lying in a hospital bed with IV tubes hanging out of our body to think about what's next.

We might better examine where our focus lies relative to our loved ones, time, money, our heart, recreation, etc. to judge whether they are used for creating temporal satisfaction or to improve our vision for a life beyond this one. Living for eternity places a whole new paradigm for how we live our lives in this world. It's exciting because an eternal focus isn't concerned with dying—only living. The writer and Christian philosopher C.S. Lewis once said, "All that is not eternal is eternally out of date." You don't need to be religious to start thinking from an eternal focus. You just need to start preparing for the possibility that this life may not be all there is to your existence. Ask: "Why am I here, and where am I going—forever?" The answer may just give you the energy for striving after your ideal.

What If You Lived Forever?

- Eliminate 3 Things That Are Unnecessary
- What 3 Needs Will Serve Your "Forever Purpose"?
- Focus on These 3 Things Now That You Will Never Die
- Why Are You Here?
- Where Are You Going—Forever?

> - *What things will you do that you've not done before*
> - *What/Who will be in your life when you are the person you want to be?*
> - *How is your faith different when you know that you will live forever?*

REST: THE 90/10 FOCUS PRINCIPLE

FAITH
REST
E
E

The 'law of achievement' states that rest must always follow activity. Life should not be about traveling on the fast track or slow track, rather traveling on the narrow path toward one single destination at a time. Most of us are aware of the Pareto principle (also known as the 80–20 rule). The 90/10 Focus Principle goes 10 percentage points further because of the growing number of time invaders that creep in our lives. PACEsetters reveal that their success is 10% of what happens to them, and 90% of how they react to it.

REST

A body at rest must focus, and as it does, the intensity of its purpose is heightened. As social psychologist Michael Ray has discovered, "In some magical way, by slowing down you become more efficient, productive, and energetic...focusing without distraction directly on the task in front of you." He means focus, as in not being distracted by the frenzy of life.

We now understand that jumping from task to task (e.g., multi-tasking) runs counterproductive to efficiency. By intentionally blocking distractions, we can better focus on the essentials. And one of the most effective ways to do that is to unclutter ourselves from unproductive tasks and redundant communications, as in the daily bombardment of emails, text messages and audio-visual stimulation.

By focusing on the essentials, we conserve our energy and release whatever impedes our ability to concentrate on what's most important. Much of the success of PACEsetters can be found in their ability to focus on the major issues in life.

A psychologist, former science journalist at The New York Times and author of the bestselling book *Emotional Intelligence*, Daniel Goleman cites numerous case studies in his book, *Focus: The Hidden Driver of Excellence*, of how our ability to block out the mass of digital distractions is diminished by the "cognitive exhaustion" they cause. Mindlessness—when your thoughts are always wandering—is potentially "the single biggest waster of attention in the workplace," he says.

Developing its opposite—focused purpose—by training the brain to pay complete attention to the current moment is critical. Focused purpose allows us to concentrate on what is important and not be distracted by the noise around us. Involuntary, or "bottom-up," unintentional neural processes cause the mind to drift and, in particular, to be distracted by visual stimuli. The antidote is to cull out the distractions that tend to dull our sense of purpose, by creating a "wall of purposefulness" that ardently repels against all non-productive influences.

Ironically, it's rest that brings us to a state of heightened purpose. Rest, as in allowing the engine of our purpose to simply run mindfully without allowing distractions to shut it down. Consider how a batter hits the ball (with super-focus) or how a racecar driver wins the race (hyper-focus), and how the PACEsetter leads (with honed purpose). They rest in their purpose, refreshed, dedicated, and mindful of what needs to be accomplished.

The 90/10 Focus Principle

The "law of achievement" states that rest must always follow activity, and by focusing, we can achieve more while working less. But instead of working to live, most live to work. In the past, our society reflected greater commitment to friends and family, less dependence on drugs and alcohol, and more civility to strangers. Whereas once upon a time a person could expect to retire with the same company, now the illusion of security fades further into the past. A 40-hour workweek, once considered the norm, now seems like a joke to most workers. The fast track of success has produced more stress, more addiction to money and power, anxiety about unemployment, frenetic lifestyles, and greater social inequality.

Life should not be about traveling on the fast track or the slow track but rather traveling on the narrow path toward one single destination at a time. Further, each thing we do should be fueled by something we can get passionate about, because passion breeds energy. Spreading ourselves too thin dilutes our passion just as spreading a color too thin dilutes its vividness.

Studies now have disproven the effectiveness of multi-tasking. We cannot do it all, because to try is to lose focus, and losing focus leads to scattered thinking and inefficiency. Most of us have heard of the Pareto principle (also known as the 80–20 rule), which states that for many events roughly 80% of the effects come from 20% of the causes. The *Focus Principle* goes 10 percentage points further because of the growing number of time invaders that creep in our lives—saying that roughly 90% of results stem from only 10% of focused effort. Essentially, the best way to achieve more is to do less.

Indeed, 10% of the real estate agents control 90% of the inventory. About 90% of a publisher's revenue is generated from 10% of the titles it publishes. Roughly 10% of total Internet marketers make 90% of the money online. The Center for Economic and Policy Research concluded that 10% of the households in America have 90% of the stocks, bonds, trust funds, and business equity. Betfair.com, the world's leading gambling exchange, states that 90% of the money staked comes from 10% of its clients. Only 10% of the average meeting time is spent on the 10% of actions taken as a result—the rest, 90%, is spent on idle chit-chat or non-productive discussion. About 10% of industry costs are spent on roughly 90% of point of sales. Peter Drucker once said that 10% of events account for 90% of results.

The Focus (90/10) Principle says that a small percentage of efforts results in the vast majority of results. If we ask successful people, many would reveal that their success is 10% of what happens to them, and 90% of how they react to it. Like each of us, they have 24 hours in day, but what separates the top producers is that they spend those hours only on the top 10% of what's most important. By resting more and doing less, we can actually produce more. With some practice, focusing on the greatest return on energy (spent) can produce a more thriving lifestyle.

Imagine that you want to get in great physical condition. You could either (A) exercise for 30-40 minutes of jogging for five days per week, or (B) run three to five 30-second sprints, followed by one minute recovery bouts and performed just three days per week. The first (A) exercise requires almost 200 minutes a week; the second (B) requires about six minutes a week. Exercise (B) causes better endurance even though it uses a fraction of the oxygen uptake. Like exercise for our bodies, focused efforts on each activity, with peak effort, matter more than long protracted efforts expending several times the energy in time and exhaustion.

Here are the five stages of the 90/10 Focus Principle:

The 5 Stages of The 90/10 Focus Principle

❑ Establish your desired outcome (e.g., your big impact)
❑ Focus on the most direct route to your desired
   outcome (e.g., the least time and effort)
❑ Eliminate everything but the essentials for getting to
   your outcome
   a. pack lightly
   b. choose to work only with those who give you
      energy; in other words, they are not 'high
      maintenance'
   c. ask yourself: "Can we succeed without this?"
❑ Do it
❑ Eliminate distractions by asking yourself: "Is what I'm
   doing essential for getting me to where I'm going?"

I've started three successful companies, been a leader for more than 20 organizations, including as an executive for some of the largest companies in the world, and I have won many awards—but I've failed at least as many times as I've succeeded. I'm a firm believer that a good "batting average" is above 30% by rejecting most of what life throws at you. As I've grown in my abilities, asking this simple question has significantly reduced my failure rate, "Can we succeed without this?"

By eliminating almost 90% of the niceties and focusing only on the necessities, my businesses have grown more successfully. But, what's more important is that I now do only the things I enjoy doing. If I'm asked to do something, and it doesn't create within me some enthusiasm, I usually say "No." Now I rest a lot more, and do almost 10 times more of the things that give me satisfaction. And since practicing the 90/10 principle, I've lost 50 pounds and can exercise like I did in my thirties with as much energy as I had in my youth.

I've learned that focus and rest translate into maximal effectiveness. Focus increases confidence and boosts our power. Time management isn't the answer, because it's the busyness of life that gets in the way of our productivity. Slowing down and doing fewer things is the answer. Instead of a to-do list, try making a *not* to-do list. Do less and think more. Reflect on what really matters to you. We've become overstimulated with technology coming at us in all directions. Reclaim your life.

Choose Your 10%

You have found yourself in a mission critical situation. You are limited to 3 items. Choose which 3 are most important to you.

How do you prioritize what's most important in any situation?

Get the Monkey Off Your Back

Dump the Monkey

Adopting other people's problem is one of the biggest time wasters of all-time. One of the top best-selling articles published by the Harvard Business Review entitled *Managing Management Time: Who's Got the Monkey*, authored by Bill Oncken Jr. and Don Wass, addresses this common energy drain.

Have you ever felt like someone or some people keep dumping stuff on you? Do you feel at times like you're doing the work of others instead of doing what *you* need to accomplish? Adopting other people's problems is one of the biggest time wasters of all-time. One of Harvard Business Review's best-selling reprints ever was a December 1974 publication entitled, *Management Time: Who's Got the Monkey?* It helps to answer the question as to why managers are typically running out of time while their subordinates are typically running out of work. The answer lies with how managers tend to assume the burden of figuring out their subordinates' problems for them.

So for example, if John can't figure out how to operate an accounting system, the manager feels obligated to teach John how to use the system, or to figure out a way in which John can learn it. In that scenario, which one carries the monkey on his back, John or his manager? Of course, the manager assumes the monkey that John placed on his back by trying to solve John's problem for him. If the manager simply told John he would have to come-up with a solution on his own using the resources available to him, the manager would have kept the monkey on John's back, and that would eliminate one more time-drain that the manager could use for something else.

Monkeys are the distractions where someone else gives extra work or additional tasks to you. They prevent you from completing your important goals. We take the monkey as soon as we accept someone else's responsibility, and it can come in the form of a lost file, a frustrated customer, or a simple request for help from a friend. The first lesson about how to prevent the monkey from leaping on you back is to just say "No."

Tactful Assertiveness—How PACEsetters Do It

If you are a people pleaser who always wants to take care of others, you should practice being more assertive. Those who fail to be tactfully assertive often find themselves losing control, and losing valuable time and joy. When someone asks you to do something, rather than just doing it, ask them to explain more about the task and what's involved, and then challenge them to come up with a solution on their own as an opportunity for growth. If the monkey is from your manager, you can try to explain what you're already working on and to postpone the deadline for completion in order to do what's top on your list of priorities. Don't give-in. Use tactful assertiveness.

Tactful assertiveness means adroitly and justly expressing your feelings, opinions, and needs in order to strengthen relationships, reduce stress, and obtain an effective resolution. Assertiveness should not be confused with aggressiveness, which is being self-centered, arrogant and inconsiderate. Instead, a polite but assertive refusal to accept unfair or excessive requests from others will prevent you from becoming overwhelmed and frustrated.

Being nice is one thing, but when you suppress your needs "to not cause trouble," you may be allowing a greedy or dominant person to take advantage of you, which only serves to reinforce negative, self-centered behaviors. People who take advantage are placing the monkey on your back. This places you in a stressful frame of mind.

Researchers suggest several approaches that will help you achieve a healthful state of tactful assertiveness. The first step is to realize when you've been overly passive (compliant), and to recognize your rights as an individual. If you can't say "no" to someone who asks you for a favor, you have trouble disagreeing during a meeting, or your spouse or children are controlling your life, you need to assert yourself.

Begin speaking to the other person by telling them very factually what they've done to upset you. Avoid general accusations such as, "You never listen to me" by using specifics like, "When I asked you to clean your room before 10 o'clock, you instead watched TV." Make the other person aware of the consequence of their neglect, such as saying, "Because your room wasn't cleaned, we will not be able to go to the game this afternoon." This places the onus, or monkey, squarely back on the child to clean his or her room instead of you just jumping in and doing it. PACEsetter parents do this routinely.

Be open about how the offense made you feel, but don't get emotional. Just make eye contact, be firm but in a pleasant tone, stand or sit-up straight and focus positively on the changes that can be made to help both of you reach your goals. Start your sentences with "I" instead of "You" so that your statements don't come across as attacking. Saying "I was affected by..." shows honesty and accountability, and avoids blame. Don't assume you know all the answers, so make sure to ask questions to gain a complete understanding. The goal is to reach a mutually beneficial win-win so that the responsibility isn't just thrown onto your back.

Getting the monkey off your back requires being assertive, which may not feel easy at first. But if tasks keep piling up at the risk of jeopardizing your most important responsibilities, you'll end up taking the blame for things not getting done. The key is not just prioritizing your schedule, but to schedule your priorities with yourself and others. Do what's mission critical on any project or responsibility by stopping the monkey from jumping on your back, and you'll find that you're less stressed and more rested.

Tactful Assertiveness: 6 Ways

- Realize the you've been overly passive (compliant) by asking yourself if the request creates low self-esteem, fear, anxiousness, or feelings of guilt—all signs of being exploited.
- Recognize your rights as an individual.
- Tell the other person very factually what he or she has done to cause you any of the symptoms of exploitation
  NOTE: Avoid general accusations such as, "You never listen to me," by using specifics like, "I asked you to clean your room before 10 but instead you watched TV."
- Be open about how the offense made you feel, but don't get emotional.
- Start your sentences with "I" instead of "You" *(saying "I" shows honesty and accountability).*
- Ask questions to gain a complete understanding *(How can we make this better going forward?)*

Take a Break

When we strive, our mind begins to race. The stress of trying something new, like starting a new job, mentally exhausts a person by consuming more energy than normal. Rest restores this energy. It even automates parts of the thought process by allowing the mind to think through different scenarios a person might encounter while allowing for the creative thought process to uncover different solutions. Resting makes us more clear-headed and successful.

Now research tells us to heed our inner alarm clock and take a break or rest. Even brief intermissions can significantly improve one's ability to focus on a task for longer periods of time. Scientists say that after a certain period of time your cognition decreases and your performance begins to decline. Some researchers explain that this "vigilance decrement," as they term it, results from a drop in one's "attentional resources," said University of Illinois psychology professor Dr. Alejandro Lieras, who led the recent study.

He describes the brain's tendency to stop registering a sight, feeling, or sound if a stimulus remains constant over time. For example, over time most people lose awareness of the soft music playing in the background of a store. Lieras says that the body becomes "habituated" to stimuli, such as looking at a fixed object in one's peripheral vision until that object completely disappears from view. "Constant stimulation is registered by our brains as unimportant, to the point that the brain erases it from our awareness," Lieras said.

The study by Lieras and his team point to the need for people to overcome that guilt feeling from taking a break to detach from their work and to reinvigorate their internal resources. So if your mind starts wandering, take a walk or do some other movement; don't just go from one sedentary position to another. Of course, don't take it to the extreme because too many breaks can cause procrastination. So the next time your boss says you have to work through break time, tell him about these latest studies, or better yet, invite her/him to go for a walk with you.

Dedicate Time for Recreation

Jack and Jose think about recreation differently. Their skills sets, experience and abilities are roughly the same. However, Jack, the archetypal workaholic, hasn't taken a vacation in more than three years and rarely takes time out to recreate, whereas Jose takes regular vacations and remains active in sports and other forms of recreation. Which one is the more productive of the two? The answer is Jose— he's the PACEsetter.

In addition to helping you lead a more interesting life, recreation is important because of the many health, social, work and educational benefits it can provide. Even the word itself (re-create) implies that something in our normal routine needs to be replenished. The most basic recreation can release the pent-up energy that is needed for us to perform at maximum capacity. You may be surprised. For example, some people will tell you that watching TV is wasted time, or that it destroys brain cells, but guess what? Your brain cells need to rest in order to maintain health, and if TV reduces stress and creates a more positive environment, especially if you can share some laughter with others, you will reinvigorate your brain.

Relaxation is important for health. Our bodies tend toward sickness if we go non-stop all of the time. The father of modern advertising and marketing pioneer, John Wannamaker, said, "People who cannot find time for recreation (will)... sooner or later find time for illness." We know that sleep regenerates the mind, but even sitting still and consciously taking a time-out can do roughly the same. Try lying in bed for a few minutes. Just listening to the pleasant sounds outside can actually reduce your blood pressure by calming your mind.

Once you get outside, segment out some time during the day or week to participate in some kind of group activity—a sport, a chess club, a movie or theater production—these have several benefits. The relationships you build from these group activities will develop a non-stress community with which you can build your social networks and talk about more relaxing topics. Just getting outside, even if it's for a few minutes in the sun will get you out of the inside air that contains disgusting pollutants from insect pieces to airborne germs. The sun's vitamin D will boost your immune system.

Think of recreation as mental refreshment that can take many forms from reading, just lying on a couch, exercising, or taking a long cruise or camping. You need to get out of your normal life—even God rested on the seventh day!

Focus on the Present

It's hard to maintain our focus in a world with demands that constantly vie for our time. Focusing on the 10% of what's most vital to us requires a rigid discipline moment by moment. Staying focused on the present forces attention onto the situations and people who truly matter. Not only will living in the present have a dramatic effect on our emotional well-being, but the detrimental effects of stress on our body are lessoned as well.

It also makes you more effective. Being still, knowing that we can only influence current matters with an ever-present attitude slows us down, allowing us to get things done one opportunity at a time. Prioritizing our life first with that which is found in our midst eliminates distractions that can impede our ability to relate effectively and get things done. Getting sidetracked usually involves looking too far ahead or too far behind. Living the minutia of life with intentional purpose and accepting the past as settled stills us in the moment.

As your attention narrows, your awareness will merge with the action you are performing, and you will gain a sense of personal power over it so that anything you do in the moment will seem almost effortless. Deeply breathe in and exhale to center you in the moment. Accept your emotions, your situation, and your thoughts without any need to reconcile them. Stop confusing your world with useless conjecture and self-defeating worry.

Overthinking and self-evaluation are two of your greatest impediments. Keep life simple by focusing your thoughts and actions only on what's significant. Consider something fresh within your familiar surrounding with what some call a "beginner's mind"—a new sight, sound or smell with no need to judge any of it. Slow down to savor the moment. Appreciate life as it is instead of looking to tomorrow or dwelling on the past, and peace as well as increased efficiency will follow.

PACEsetters have well-honed coping strategies that they employ under stressful circumstances to keep them centered in the moment. This lowers their distractions regardless of what's happening in their environment, ensuring that the interruptions they experience are intermittent and not prolonged, which also coincidentally lowers stress.

They do this by eliminating "What if?" statements that increase stress, which, according to a Yale study, causes degeneration in the area of the brain responsible for self-control. When scattered thinking occurs, the mind races in several directions, and the more time one spends worrying about different possibilities, the less time that person can focus on taking action on the here and now. Centered PACEsetters know that asking "What if?" will only divert their ability to be productive for what's in their midst. Instead, they take-in situations without immediately judging them, and then process what's available through an unfiltered sense of stilled purpose. And this allows them to respond instantly to the situation at hand.

They know that "now" is the only time they can control. They have a "gift" for looking people in the eye, listening to what is being said, enjoying a pleasant experience, or pondering an issue before acting. They rarely seem rushed, and they get more done than most. PACEsetters take full advantage of each moment given to them. PACEsetters don't manage time; they use it in the present.

As a PACEsetter, your life centers all around now, and now has always been about your life. If you're not living in the present you're relinquishing your life. Now is your most precious possession, don't waste it on anything else.

Focusing on the 10%

PACEsetters have well-honed coping strategies to keep them centered in the moment. They do this by eliminating "What if" statements that increase stress, which according to a Yale study causes degeneration in the area of the brain responsible for self-control. When scattered thinking occurs, the mind races in several directions. PACEsetters take-in situations without immediately judging them, and then process what's available through an unfiltered sense of stilled purpose. And this allows them to respond instantly to the situation at hand.

At the University of Massachusetts, a study headed by Dr. Richard J. Davidson measured the brain effects of those who practiced getting still versus those who did not over a 56 day period. An MRI of both groups showed that those who stilled themselves daily actually shrunk their amygdala, a small mass of gray matter deep inside the cerebral hemisphere that drives disturbing emotions like stress.

Getting Still

At the University of Massachusetts, a study headed by Dr. Richard J. Davidson measured the brain effects of those who practiced meditation versus those who did not over a 56-day period. An MRI of both groups showed that those who mediated daily actually shrunk their amygdala, a small mass of gray matter deep inside the cerebral hemisphere that drives disturbing emotions like stress.

Another study by Professor Elizabeth Blackburn, a Nobel Prize winner in Physiology or Medicine, discovered another positive effect on the brain when people meditated. She found that regular meditators over a period of time experience more telomerase activity, an enzymatic process that preserves the length of telomeres across cell divisions in stem cells. It is thought to play a role in the proliferation and therefore immortality of cells. When telomeres drop below a critical length, the cell can no longer divide properly and eventually dies.

The study by Dr. Blackburn is the first to link positive well-being and longevity to higher telomerase as a direct result of meditation. Meditation is a restful awareness response that occurs from breathing deeply and slowly in personal silence accompanied with a mindful state of essentially "decluttering" the brain. It's been shown to increase normal blood flow and prevent blood clotting, just by stilling oneself. Some meditate by repetitively humming to themselves sounds like "ohm" or listening to the sounds of nature (i.e., the ocean waves, the wind blowing, rain), or by using a prayer language.

Simply changing what we think doesn't produce that positive meditative state. Rather, positive meditation pauses the mind. Try it by getting alone, inhale deeply through your nostrils while at the same time relaxing your belly muscles. Feel as though the belly is filling with air. Fill up the middle of your chest. Feel your chest and rib cage expand. Hold the breath for a moment, then begin to exhale as slowly as possible. As the air is slowly let out, relax your chest and rib cage. Begin to pull your belly in to force out the remaining breath. Close your eyes and concentrate on your breathing. Relax your face and mind. Let everything go. Hum or pray quietly while doing this for about 10 minutes in the morning and for about 10 minutes after you return from work.

EXERCISE

Negative and Positive Energy

Feeling fatigued right now? Maybe you need to exercise more. Our energy level goes down as toxins (or waste) accumulate in the body, causing fatigue. During rest and exercise, energy is restored, and the toxic buildup is decreased. Everyone uses mental activity while we're awake, which serves to tense our muscles. Physical activity, on the other hand, usually leaves the muscles relaxed. A sedentary life produces tenseness that can cause stress, creating an imbalance in our bodies. The same can be said of many achievement-oriented Type A people, who produce the negative type of energy that results from being tensed. This Type A can develop a deceptive high from getting lots of work done, that invariably leads to fatigue and the negative feelings that go with it.

Exercise

FAITH

REST

EXERCISE

E

Our energy level decreases as toxins accumulate in the body, causing fatigue. During rest and exercise, energy is restored and toxic buildup decreases. Everyone uses mental activity while we're awake, which tenses our muscles. Physical activity on the other hand, usually leaves the muscles relaxed.

Many achievement-oriented people produce a negative type of energy that results from being tensed. This can develop a deceptive high from getting lots of work done, that invariably leads to fatigue, loss of focus, and the negative feelings that go with it. Exercise helps flip that negative to positive energy.

Exercise helps flip that negative to positive energy. And whereas PACEsetters may not always be the fittest (though some are), they do maintain a positive energy through exercise. The benefits of exercise are testified by experts such as those at the Mayo Clinic, who state that exercise helps our bodies resist illness, besides improving our mental alertness and mood by producing a productive form of energy that balances mental energy with the energy derived from exercise, which lowers the body's overall tension. The result is a longer lasting form of energy that's produced through an effective exercise regimen.

Walking and other types of moderate exercise can help reduce stress and elevate our mood, especially if done in a calm and inspiring location. Researchers at the University of Georgia found that sedentary, otherwise healthy adults who exercised for as little as 20 minutes with low to moderate aerobic exercise, three days a week for six consecutive weeks, reported feeling less fatigued and more energized.

Exercise releases endorphins that make you feel relaxed and happier. It also increases the blood cell's ability to carry more oxygen and nutrients to muscle tissues through the production of adenosine triphosphate, a coenzyme often called the "molecular unit of currency" of intracellular energy transfer. After only 10 minutes of walking, your body temperature will increase, thus triggering this response that can happen by just taking a quick walk before an important meeting or a jog before going to work. You don't have to be a triathlete to enjoy the benefits of increased energy through moderate physical activity.

However, intense workouts, like running for 50 minutes, temporarily reduce the body's energy level. According to the U.S. Department of Health and Human Services exercise guidelines, healthy adults need to engage in 2.5 hours of weekly moderate-intensity exercise, such as brisk walking or gardening. For more physical fit adults, 75 minutes of vigorous physical activity, such as speed-walking, jogging, swimming, cycling, and hiking uphill can offer similar benefits in half the time.

Experts also recommend that adults lift weights twice a week. Behavioral therapist and personal trainer Therese Pasqualoni, PhD, says that when exercising for energy, "You should always aim to exercise in your low to moderate training heart rate range. This will prevent you from depleting your body, and help you avoid feeling fatigued, which would otherwise prevent you from getting the maximum energy benefits."

Of course, some people's definition of "moderate" may be vary, so these experts agree that you should judge how much exercise you can do before becoming fatigued, depending on how well your body is conditioned. While most experts agree that moderate exercise is the key to increasing energy, even if you push your limit too much, your final result may still be less fatigue.

Some research shows that although intense exercise can tire a person, it also reduces tension, so that after about an hour or so after the muscles start to recover, that person might realize a surge of energy but without the tension. The key is to eat a little fruit about 30 minutes or so before a workout, which serves as a type of energy that can be utilized as nutrients within the bloodstream, producing more energy before and after the workout. It's also important to drink lots of water before, during, and after the workout to help reduce fatigue.

Dealing with Fatigue

Fatigue alerts us to the need for rest. It is usually not a good idea to ignore this signal or to try to counteract it with drugs. The "coffee break" is anything but restful. Coffee and cigarettes provide an artificial stimulation, but without any recuperation, as happens with exercise. The underlying cause of fatigue is still there. As fatigue increases, efficiency and performance decrease. As a rule, plan to go to bed early (before 10 p.m.). It has been estimated that every hour of sleep before midnight is worth two after midnight. Studies have shown 7-9 hours of sleep per night to be most healthful. Nine or more hours have been associated with decreased health and six or less with the poorest health.

The first prerequisite for a good night's sleep is daily exercise. Activity always precedes rest. Remember, too little activity creates an imbalance between physical and mental activity. Too much brain work and not enough physical work cause the muscles to be in a state of tension (However, too much exercise too near bedtime can keep you awake.). Tension lessens the depth and soundness of sleep. The quality of sleep depends on the ability to relax. Avoid starting new activities late in the day. Allow yourself time to wind down. Avoid stimulants such as television, sugars, and rich, spicy food at night before going to bed. Large evening meals can interfere with sleep. If needed, some studies show that a 10-15 minute nap before lunch can be worth about 45-60 minutes of nighttime sleep.

Manage your stress levels by remaining positive and by not feeling defeated if you do something unhealthful—just get back on track. Healthy habits usually start to set in after about 20 days of practice. It's important to start a routine now so that exercising and rest become a normal way of living.

Health and wellness begins with an earnest commitment that should rank at the top of anyone's goals. It begins with a nutritious diet of three to five servings of vegetables each day, and two to four servings of fruit. According to HealthReserve.com both children and adults should eat two to three servings of dairy products and five to seven ounces of meats or beans, with at least one to two servings of fish per week. Avoid fatty foods, sweets, foods high in calories and carbohydrates that can cause heart problems, diabetes, and arthritis.

Exercise at least three to four times a week for at least 20-30 minutes per session—depending on the intensity of the workout. High intensity workouts (i.e., aerobic exercise) can be done on alternating days. The Mayo Clinic states that exercise helps your body resist illness, besides improving your mental alertness and mood. Drinking alcohol in moderation (i.e., no more than one to two glasses of wine a day) is fine, but excessive consumption can lead to diseases like hepatitis. One of the main causes of sickness are vices like smoking, drugs, and excessive alcohol, which can harm the kidneys, lungs, brain, heart, and other organs.

EATING FOR ENERGY

Foods That Give Energy

My wife and I had lunch with a PACEsetter the other day, our friend, Sheila Harden, who's been battling cancer for about 10 years, and despite the hardships, has helped numerous people as a speech therapist, radio blogger, mentor, counselor, philanthropist, investor and real estate manager for properties she owns across the nation. During our lunch, Sheila shared that her cancer is in remission through natural remedies and a healthful diet minus gluten, sugars, and most carbohydrates. And by the way, her energy as a single mom and world traveler surpasses that of people 40 years her junior. The right diet works—it can even heal. But not many are willing to dedicate themselves to a healthy eating regimen, and their energy level shows it.

Eating (foods that cause energy)

FAITH
REST
EXERCISE
EATING

Certain foods increase energy, and others decrease energy. For example, foods high in fat and calories can cause fatigue, since they require more energy to digest. Fruits and vegetables will help you maintain energy levels.

A study published in the journal Neurology found that 50% of people with chronic fatigue syndrome were deficient in folate which led to increased systemic inflammation. Less inflammation means less stress, and that translates into less fatigue.

What we eat certainly makes us feel better, or worse—it depends. Research suggests that certain foods affect mood—for better or worse. Diet can produce chemical and physiological responses within the brain that alter our behavior and emotions. "Most people understand the link between what they eat and their physical health," says registered dietitian Elizabeth Somer, author of the 2010 book *Eat Your*

Way to Happiness. "But the link between what you eat and your mood, your energy, how you sleep, and how well you think is much more immediate. What you eat or don't eat for breakfast will have at least a subtle effect by mid-afternoon, and what you're eating all day will have a huge impact today and down the road."

What about yours truly? Do you ever find yourself dozing off after lunch or going for a coffee to get you through the day? How much sleep you got the night before may not be the only reason for your lethargy. The variety and the portions of food you eat factor into your energy level at any given time. For example, foods high in fat and calories can cause fatigue, since they require more energy to digest. You can make a choice to stay alert even for those boring things by making wiser choices about the foods you eat to fuel your body.

Fruits and vegetables will help you maintain energy levels. Certain vegetables, like spinach, contain all the protein and carbohydrates you need to sustain you through the day. Spinach is an excellent source of iron, an important mineral for producing energy in the body. Spinach is also an excellent source of B-vitamin folate, an essential nutrient that plays an important role in reducing homocysteine levels—elevated levels of this non-protein amino acid has been linked to cardiovascular disease. A study published in the journal *Neurology* found that 50% of people with chronic fatigue syndrome were deficient in folate and consequently had higher levels of homocysteine. This causes increased systemic inflammation and elevates the risk of heart disease. In spinach, folate is contained in more than a dozen different anti-inflammatory flavonoid compounds. Less inflammation means less stress, and that translates into less fatigue. Eat a spinach salad for lunch, and most likely you won't feel that energy drain in the afternoon.

Another study from Emory University and the Centers for Disease Control and Prevention confirmed that people suffering from fatigue often have elevated inflammation levels. Like spinach, broccoli contains potent anti-inflammatory and antioxidant compounds called glucosinolates, which have also been shown to fight cancer growth. Its cruciferous cousins are Brussels sprouts, kale, cabbage, mustard greens, kohlrabi, bok choy, and watercress. Better to eat these raw, steamed or lighted stir-fried, as these vegetables lose up to 30% of their nutrient value after being boiled for five minutes, and some are less than half after only 10 minutes.

Fruits such as blueberries, bananas, apples and oranges serve as excellent sources of energy. Fruit offers a significant dose of glucose, which your body can easily metabolize into energy. Most fruits can be digested in under half an hour, which makes them a quick, nutritious way to get a burst of energy.

As to brain function, mental tasks and cognitive performance, blueberries may be the best choice available. A study published in the *Annals of Neurology* suggests that antioxidant-rich blueberries can reduce cognitive decline in older adults by up to 2.5 years. The blue in blueberries are polyphenol pigments called anthocyanins, which are anti-inflammatory and antioxidant. Anthocyanins are associated with increased neural signaling in the brain, especially around the areas that affect memory function. Blueberries also contain resveratrol, the compound that caused red wine to be considered healthful.

Proteins

Proteins form an important foundation for energy production. Acids in the stomach catalyze the hydrolysis reaction of protein. Then the amino acids that are formed by the hydrolysis of protein can be used to make new protein, or they can have amino acids removed and then the remainder of the molecule can be oxidized to provide energy.

There are different sources of protein, with meat, poultry and fish usually the first to come to mind. Of these, fish provides the best source for energy. The body uses omega-3 fats found in salmon and other cold-water fish to make anti-inflammatory compounds. Since chronic fatigue is associated with elevated markers of inflammation, eating fish and/or supplementing your diet with omega-3 fats can significantly improve energy levels. This effect was proven in a large study that looked at long-term fatigue in breast-cancer survivors. Those who consumed a healthy dose of omega-3 fats were less likely to suffer from fatigue. This benefit may also extend to some cancers.

Although it's important to consume more omega-3, it is equally important to reduce your omega-6 fat intake. Omega-6 fats are precursors to pro-inflammatory compounds, and the problem in our diet is that we eat too much of it. Omega-6s are found predominantly in industrial vegetable oils used in fast food and processed meals. The ratio between omega-3s and omega-6s is more important for your health than just trying to ensure that you're getting enough omega-3s. What's the simplest way to do this? Eat more fish and less junk. This alone may be enough to banish your energy slumps for good.

Containing the highest complete form of protein in any food (a whopping 97% of it can be absorbed by your body!), eggs provide 30% of your daily value of protein. All of the essential amino acids that your body uses to rebuild muscle can also be found in eggs. Maybe it's time to become an egghead to improve your energy levels. Ever since the discovery of cholesterol's implication in heart disease, we've been told to reduce our egg consumption, with the misunderstanding that dietary cholesterol has little effect on blood cholesterol. In fact, a number of recent clinical trials that looked at the effects of long-term egg consumption reported positively *no* negative impact on various indices of cardiovascular health and disease.

The high-quality protein in an egg is the perfect way to start the day. In a study that compared egg eaters to bagel eaters, those who ate eggs lost almost twice as much weight, had an 83% greater decrease in waist circumference and reported greater improvements in energy after only eight weeks. Egg yolks are a rich source of choline, a nutrient that we produce ourselves to some extent but need to supplement through our diets. Iowa State University researchers estimate that more than 90% of Americans are choline-deficient. Choline is critical in reducing inflammation through several pathways, including by reducing homocystein and increasing folate levels. Choline can also boost your brainpower because your body uses it to reinforce your brain. Choline is also used to make acetylcholine, a neurotransmitter that is the body's primary means of communication between our nerves and muscles. Improving brain and nervous function is a guaranteed way to combat fatigue.

Beans, another source of protein, are widely available and come in varieties to suit every taste. Adding beans to your diet can help you fight fatigue and the seemingly insurmountable obstacles that come with it. It's the nutritional content of beans that make them so effective in fighting fatigue. Although the bean comes in many different varieties, all are low in fat, contain high fiber, and give a good balance of carbohydrates and protein.

So, why is it that this combination of beans is so fantastic in combating the exhausting effects of fatigue? Fiber stabilizes the blood sugar in the body, which prevents dips in energy levels. This means that energy levels remain balanced, which is not the case if you drink stimulants like coffee and energy drinks. Both a protein and a complex carb, beans are a must for both carnivores and vegetarians.

Nuts provide another source for protein. In addition, some nuts like chestnuts, cashews and almonds—are alkaline-forming. By including them in your diet, they won't zap your energy like acid-producing foods but instead will help to regulate your protein intake. Almonds in particular are loaded with healthy monounsaturated fats, contain fiber, magnesium, protein and an entire serving of calcium in only a few nuts. Clinical trials have shown that eating almonds can help lower LDL cholesterol, fight inflammation, lower blood pressure and help with weight loss when substituted for complex carbohydrates.

Carbohydrates

Carbohydrates have received some bad press over the years, but before you eliminate all of those carbs, it's important to note that carbohydrates differ. Carbohydrates offer fuel to the body in the form of glucose, which is the most effective energy source for the brain and central nervous system. A diet rich in whole grains and complex carbohydrates is needed for energy, since low blood sugar is a very common cause of low energy levels. Brown rice can aid weight loss as a source of slow-release energy, which keeps you satisfied for longer. Rich in manganese, the mineral that helps produce energy from protein and carbs, it will help you maintain high energy all day. Oats, like other cereal grains, are valued primarily as a source of carbohydrates that provide calories for energy needs. Oats have been shown in scientific studies to favorably alter metabolism and enhance performance when ingested 45 minutes to 1 hour before exercise of moderate intensity.

A quick sugar fix like candy or soda will only help fight this fatigue for an hour or two. The best thing you can do is to avoid refined carbs. If you eat a bowl of pasta for lunch, expect an energy slump. The carbs in sweet potatoes are mostly complex carbs that are absorbed slowly so that you won't experience those sudden spikes. High in carbohydrates and loaded with beta-carotene (vitamin A) and vitamin C, sweet potatoes will help fight off midday fatigue. In 1992, the Center for Science in the Public Interest compared the nutritional value of sweet potatoes to other vegetables. Factoring in its protein, vitamins A and C, fiber, complex carbs, iron and calcium content, sweet potatoes ranked first in nutritional value.

Yogurt and Honey

Yogurt and honey are other sources of energy. Not all yogurts are created equal. Greek yogurt is particularly beneficial for healthy eating as it has up to twice the protein of other yogurts protein and less lactose, carbohydrates and salt than regular yogurt. A cup of yogurt makes a good snack or breakfast without adding a high number of calories to your daily intake. High in protein and calcium and easy to digest, yogurt has enough carbs to be a valuable source of slow-release energy. It is also rich in potassium, thiamine, riboflavin, and vitamin B12. Rich in magnesium, which is crucial for the release of energy, yogurt is great for a post-workout to help replenish your glycogen sources.

A spoonful of honey in that yogurt just adds to the energy boost. Honey is nature's equivalent of an energy drink. Low on the glycemic index, this natural sweetener acts as a time-released muscle fuel during exercise and helps replenish muscles post-workout.

Water and Coffee

Some of us drink lots of coffee but not enough water. You can tell if you fit into the "too dry" category by viewing the color of your urine. If it's not clear, you're probably not drinking enough water. Researchers at the University of Connecticut's Human Performance laboratory have found that even mild dehydration (a 1.5% loss in the body's normal water volume) alters a person's mood, energy levels, and mental functions. A healthy water intake is from 1.2 to 2 liters per day (six-eight glasses), but optimal intake varies by individual, and other factors like age, climate and physical activity have their effect. Try to make it a part of your routine so that you won't have to think about how much to drink. Drink a glass or two of water as soon as you wake up in the morning; carry a bottle of water with you anywhere you go and drink water whenever you have a craving for a sugar-based snack. This way you'll be energized and clear.

Unlike water, which just about everyone agrees is good for maintaining the good/lasting form of energy, the debate about the benefit (or detriment) of drinking coffee continues. In moderation coffee, can be a benefit, and that's good news for our coffee-crazed society. According to the *Journal of Agricultural and Food Chemistry*, a cup of brewed coffee represents a contribution of up to 1.8 grams of fiber of the recommended intake of 20-38 grams. Two cups of coffee can cut post-workout muscle pain by up to 48%, *suggests The Journal of Pain*, March 2007. A typical serving of coffee contains *more antioxidants* than typical servings of grape juice, blueberries, raspberries and oranges. Antioxidants in coffee may dampen inflammation, reducing the risk of disorders related to it, like cardiovascular disease.

There is considerable evidence that caffeine may protect against Alzheimer's disease (*from the European Journal of Neurology*). How coffee affects you depends on many factors, including your age, caffeine sensitivity, pregnancy, metabolism and diet. Overall, observations suggest a proportional benefit for caffeine: Lower doses improve performance while doses above 500 mg may worsen it. The key is moderation, which is typically 2-3 cups a day, to get the coffee health benefits but avoid the negative issues associated with too much caffeine.

Dark Chocolate

I confess to being a chocoholic. I have tried to remain fairly objective on this one, though. Chocolate is more than just a "feel good" and "taste good" food. It offers numerous benefits like boosting heart health and, according to research, the cocoa flavonols in dark chocolate may even improve brain function—no kidding! During a study in Italy, one group of participants consumed a small amount of a cocoa flavonol beverage, a second group drank a moderate amount of the same beverage, and the third group consumed the highest amount. The outcome showed that those participants who consumed the most amount of the beverage demonstrated elevated verbal memory, hand-eye coordination, and an improved ability to multi-task.

Researchers believe that the link between flavonols and improved cognitive ability is related to increased insulin absorption. Dark chocolate in particular helps the body to lower blood sugar. A similar study in Great Britain as reported in *Science Daily* reported that flavonols seem to improve blood flow to the brain for two to three hours, which then boosted cognitive alertness. These and other studies appear to indicate that cocoa flavonols may improve the brain's function for people struggling with fatigue and sleep deprivation.

But there is a caveat: The benefits of dark chocolate seem to disappear if you eat too much of the compound, probably because the cell receptors involved become overloaded. "What's surprising is that you only need small doses of the compound to generate large effects, and our data suggests that more is not better." The optimal daily dose is found in a five-gram piece of dark chocolate, which is the size of two regular postage stamps.

See the following chart (Figure 5.3) for some energy providing foods.

The Energy Foods

VEGETABLES	Spinach, Broccoli, Brussels Sprout, Kale, Cabbage, Mustard Greens, Kohlrabi, Bok Choy, Watercress
FRUIT	Kiwi, Bananas, Blueberries, Apples, Oranges
PROTEINS	Salmon (or other cold water fish), Eggs, Beans, Nuts (especially chestnuts, cashews, and almonds)
DAIRY	Greek Yogurt (with Honey)
CARBOHYDRATES	Sweet Potatoes, Oats, and Brown Rice
FLUIDS	Water, Coffee
SWEETS	Dark Chocolate

(Figure 5.3 - The Energy Foods)

ENERGY
(fuels vitality)
Do more with less,
better

The PACE Formula®

F.R.E.E.

FAITH—Establish a Faith-Focus,
Take Care of Your 3 Parts, Focus
Long-term
REST—Use 90/10 Principle, Get the
"monkey off your back," Be Tactfully
Assertive, Get Still
EXERCISE—Used Focused Exercise,
Tap Positive Energy, Negate Fatigue
EATING—(Well)—Ingest Foods that
Give Energy (use chart)

The Power
to Thrive!

CHAPTER 6: THRIVING

Thriving Factors

WHAT DOES IT MEAN TO thrive, anyway? Thriving refers to continuous development and growth. "Thrive" derives from an ancient Norse word, "thrifa," meaning to seize or grasp. "Thriving" has become a contemporary buzzword, as we often hear the question, "Are you just surviving ... or are you thriving?" The history of the word clarifies its meaning, because in this context, we can rephrase the question: are you just surviving in your life, by letting life happen to you ... or are you seizing your life, grasping opportunities, and being purposeful?

We had to find the answer for many if not most people, by asking several people what makes them thrive. Then we looked for common themes—"a happy family," "making a significant contribution in life," "raising well-adjusted children," "making others happy," "having a successful career," "finding balance in life," "loving and being loved." Most answers related to significance, loving relationships, enjoyment, satisfaction and contributions. People who rated themselves as joyful, or content, viewed the world and its challenges as opportunities. Seeing life's events as opportunities served as the standard viewpoint for these people who answered in the affirmative as to whether they considered themselves as thriving.

Their standard viewpoint was then contrasted to how they lived—whether they were financially secure, whether they had a satisfactory home, whether they felt supported by loving relationships. Again, those who expressed themselves as happy, content, and/or thriving rated their living conditions as very good or excellent. Finally we viewed their personal pleasures, such as hobbies, vacationing, dining out, or anything that gave them pleasure. Those who felt their life has meaning and fulfillment also stated that their personal pleasures were met or exceeded.

All three areas were important to the thriving individual: viewpoint, lifestyle and personal pleasures. Can you guess which one of these three was ranked most important to a thriving life? If you guessed viewpoint, you would be correct. In fact, some of the respondents who exhibited the highest level of wellbeing lived lifestyles that some might consider poor, with personal pleasures some would consider mundane.

In fact, once individuals reached a level of subsistence, at or beyond the point at which they could support themselves, advances in their lifestyle or personal pleasures did not significantly affect their level of satisfaction in life, as long as they maintained their hopeful viewpoint. How they viewed their own lives as well as life in general mattered most. And of course, those who viewed their life and conditions as full of potential rated themselves as thriving the most.

So the greatest influencers for a thriving life are proportional, based on the importance rated by those who considered themselves as "generally satisfied." By weighting the responses, one's viewpoint determines 56% of a thriving potential, lifestyle amounts to 22% of a thriving potential, and personal pleasures relate to 16% of one's thriving potential (see Figure 6.1). The remaining 6% of all factors relate to various responses that didn't seem to fit any of these categories.

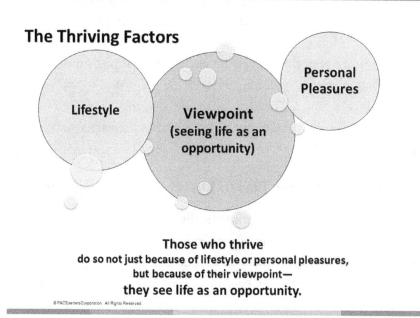

The Thriving Factors

Lifestyle

Viewpoint
(seeing life as an
opportunity)

Personal
Pleasures

Those who thrive
do so not just because of lifestyle or personal pleasures,
but because of their viewpoint—
they see life as an opportunity.

(Figure 6.1 - Factors for a Thriving Life)

How to Change Viewpoint

Being a truthseeker, always seeking to grow, and reaching beyond the ego can change one's viewpoint. Those who developed their PACE foundations, as noted by our PACEsetter sample group, discovered that their perspective turned more positive as a result. By making conscious choices to improve themselves and their environment, or by simply being more aware of themselves (self-awareness), these PACEsetters changed their outlook.

The other two life factors, lifestyle and personal pleasures, became even less important as the PACEsetters grew their positive viewpoints. The threshold for being satisfied with their lifestyle became more attainable as these PACEsetters developed the skills necessary to grow their attitude. So when people view the stressors of their life as a challenge rather than a threat, they tend to come up with more effective solutions *and* feel more motivated (rather than drained) as they tackle these circumstances. Noticing the different between needs and wants, ridding oneself of time-wasters, being content, and becoming more grateful can also increase personal pleasures.

Finding purpose, planning effectively in order to make a big impact, developing a healthy attitude, strong connections, and productive energy all contributed to a more thriving, satisfying life. These are the hallmarks of a PACEsetter.

Overcoming Negative Bias to Direct a Positive Viewpoint

We know that living more optimistically can improve almost all areas of our life. However, as humans we tend toward the negative. Suppose, for instance, that you received mostly positive comments during the day, but that one criticism can ruin your day and sticks with you months later. Psychologists call it negativity bias. Our selective memory harbors negative encounters more than positive ones because they provoke more intense reactions, which makes us more timid and less willing to take risks.

Thankfully, we can take steps to overcome our negative propensity so we can escape the disease of pessimism without having to ascribe to that worn-out axiom of believing the "glass half full." Several experts suggest that we review our past accomplishments to remind of us of how we are capable of accomplishing much. So remember what you've done well in the past to give hope for the future.

Secondly, being grateful impresses a powerful influence on your thinking. It not only makes you feel better, but it reverses your focus onto the positive. There's no need to ignore all of the problems around you, but if you can think of them as challenges or better yet opportunities, your brain will subconsciously replace the paradigm of failure, which the word "problem" evokes, and replace it with a more encouraging outlook.

Humorous Optimism

Psychologists also have found that humor and just being silly can replace negative impulses with a more childlike optimism, igniting more enthusiasm and creativity. Most people want to be around someone who makes them happy, and cheerful. Sharing some humor with colleagues and friends, knowing the boundaries of your environment, of course, reduces the stress evoked by stiff workplace attire, the sound of computer mouses clicking from workstations, or a somber looking person looking for a grief partner. Sharing funny experiences that make people laugh creates a sense of comfort and happiness in people, and that usually inspires the same for the giver in return.

Research from the University of Kent revealed that positive reframing, acceptance and humor are the most effective coping strategies for people dealing with failures. In a paper published by the international journal *Anxiety, Stress & Coping*, Dr. Joachim Stoeber and Dr. Dirk Janssen from the University's School of Psychology describe a diary study that found these three strategies to be most effective in dealing with small failures and setbacks, and helping people to keep up their spirits and feel satisfied at the end of the day.

For a long time, researchers have studied how humor helps patients relieve stress and heal. Melissa B. Wanzer, EdD, professor of communication studies at Canisius College in Buffalo, N.Y., has looked at humor's overall effect, with her research on how humor helps medical professionals cope with their stressful jobs. She also looked at how humor affects the elderly, and how it can increase connection in the workplace and in the classroom.

She wondered, how do health care providers care for terminally ill people and manage to come back to work each day? So she asked them, in high population studies. Their answer? Humor. In fact, Wanzer found humor to be beneficial in almost all areas of life. "Employees also reported higher job satisfaction when they worked for someone who was more humor-oriented and used humor effectively and appropriately." It reduces stress and produces a more engaging environment. The same can be found across all types of people and their circumstances in life. Wanzer and her colleagues recently collaborated on research that found aging adults who used humor more frequently reported greater coping efficacy, which led to greater life satisfaction. This was the third study she conducted, with three different populations, where the conclusion was the same.

So Can Someone Develop a Sense of Humor?

One depressed businessman decided to join a comedy club and discovered that his disposition changed dramatically in the process. Anyone, even the most serious person, can develop a good sense of humor. It begins by smiling more. For a lot of people it's about giving yourself permission to laugh. Nobody's watching, so laugh at yourself the next time you trip over a crack or knock over those papers. Make faces at yourself in the mirror while brushing your teeth—flap your ears, roll your eyes—until your silliness makes you chuckle.

Humor is all about adopting a lighter attitude toward life, and when we approach life more lightheartedly, the whole paradigm of what's serious and what's not will shift around you. The key is to find out what things make you laugh. Discover what TV shows, books, or comics make you laugh-out-loud and take regular doses of these provocations—treat yourself to comedy nights by renting your favorite comedic movies or go to a comedy show.

Remember those embarrassing moments or those simply hilarious times in your life that can open your mind to the more humorous aspects of life. Cartoonists and comedians work by exaggerating situations, and doing the same from our vantage point can help us to develop a humorous perspective. Even when confronted with difficult people we can use humorous techniques to diffuse inflamed circumstances. When someone incites your anger, try responding with humor instead of hostility. For example, if someone says you look overweight, say, "You'd make a great motivational speaker."

Try soliciting funny stories or experiences from friends or coworkers on a regular basis—pretty soon they'll start giving you impromptu material for jokes, and they'll want to exchange some humorous banter with you. Basically, we need to create a more humorous environment around us, which can be done as easily as posting funny cartoons or sayings at work and at home, like "You know you're getting old when the candles cost more than the cake."

Laughter can trigger a more positive awareness, as does fun play, like creating a game in which you make a habit of actively searching for the positive side in everything. Positive Awareness is simply an awareness of positive energy which is created by lightheartedness, encouraging thoughts, affirming words and reassuring statements. Trying new things can also increase positive awareness.

Affirmations over Failure

Besides a little humor now and then, positive affirmations have been found to overcome failures with a more encouraging sense of thriving. Too many pre-programmed negative expectations cause people to avoid challenges for fear of failing, and then when the inevitable challenges come their way, they consciously or subconsciously expect to fail, and to no one's surprise, they do. To change these patterns, you need to make compelling statements that success is a fact, not just a possibility, by associating your affirmation with other occasions in which you've succeeded, and discounting your failures as merely "prep time" for your certain success.

Be clear as to your goal, and then tell yourself that regardless of how many times you may need to reroute or alter your plans, you will succeed—somehow, someway—and leave no doubt that success is a foregone conclusion. Your positive affirmations should include statements like, "I deserve to be successful," "I am a high achiever," "I can control my own satisfaction in life," "I always reach my goals," "I enjoy being who I am," "I reject abuse from others," "I deserve to be successful," I am getting better each day," "I'm going to go after my challenge and prevail," "I am strong and valuable," "I am beautiful," "People respect me," "The best is yet to come," "I forgive myself and others," "I am better because of my mistakes," "I accept myself without reservation," and "I am a PACEsetter!"

If your former programmed way of thinking resists believing in these affirmations, acknowledge them as part of your past and continue affirming your inherent value with these positive affirmations. Remember to be intentional when using your affirmations, and not merely emotional in saying them. Conviction will be instilled within your psyche when you repeat your affirmations regularly as a routine part of your day. Record your affirmations in a place where you can easily retrieve them (i.e., your wallet, your computer screen) to remind yourself of them during quiet times, breaks, lunchtime, and before sleep. Use them during your goal setting and while visualizing your success—start *believing—with conviction.*

Then, if some naysayer says something negative about you, or if a discouraging thought crosses your mind, remind yourself of your affirmation(s). Next, laugh at the negative or discouraging statement, as something so outlandish, so farfetched, and so ridiculous that the mere suggestion of something contrary to your positive affirmation merits an immediate dismissal. A faith group we observed tried this exercise using God's promises as their affirming statements. One woman confessed that she felt unattractive, and remembered the psalmist's declaration—"I praise you because I am fearfully and wonderfully made; your works are wonderful, I know that full well"— and then she started laughing out loud. She later explained that this simple mockery of her false belief made her feel more beautiful. Try it, you may be surprised at how effective it can be to simply laugh-off negative statements and replace them with positive affirmations.

Here's a hard a fast rule for speaking words to yourself: Don't give yourself any counsel that you would not give to somebody you care about. For example, you would not say to a loved one, "You are a failure," or "You never get it right," or "You're ugly." And yet, people speak those words over themselves all too often, especially during times of despair. So the next time you catch yourself speaking negative self-talk, attempt to distance yourself from yourself, as if speaking to a loved one in the mirror, and start counseling yourself with words of encouragement and truth, keeping in mind that any condemnations spoken by you or to you are simply lies.

Anchor your thinking to positive absolutes and view your present state as good, if not great. Use past successes as confirmation that your future success is inevitable. Looking for the heretofore unseen good around you can also awaken you to the reasons for being optimistic by moving attention from the dark side of life. Also using more positive speech, by replacing words like "things will *never* get better," to "it will be better *tomorrow*." If you act like an optimistic person, your mind will accept that as your reality. Also, people will be attracted to your brighter outlook in life and will respond with more encouragement back to you. Our attitude toward life determines others' attitude toward us. Seeing the opportunity in everything makes everything a possibility for good.

Taking Care of Your Well-Being

Life is dynamic, and so is our state of wellness. An opportunity-based outlook can change over time. Just as our bodies can get sick, so can our state of being. So we need to attend to our well-being as diligently as we attend to our health. There are six areas that will determine our total well-being in life based on our satisfaction with each of these categories: (Note the following diagram listing these areas.)

Your Life—The Power to Thrive!

Would you like to know your state of well-being? Think of each of these categories and rate your level of satisfaction with each from one to 10, with one being the lowest level of satisfaction, and 10 being the highest level of satisfaction. Now average your level of satisfaction in all of these areas by adding your scores for each and dividing by six. How did you score?

First, one caveat: These are only general assessments, and should not be viewed as "gospel." If your average score was seven or above, then you are thriving. If you average between five and six, you are striving in life. If you scored four or below you are struggling, and perhaps you should seriously consider making some changes, and seeking help. Again, because life is dynamic, even a low score may not be cause for alarm.

Still, each of us can improve our wellbeing by focusing on those areas in life that give us the least satisfaction. By ask ourselves "Why?"

we begin the first step toward a more thriving life. What people, factors, qualities, or missing pieces must change in order to get back to a healthy level of well-being?

Eliminate those toxins that are slowly poisoning you. Don't just believe that that old adage that "Everything in moderation" is good—poison in moderation is *not* good. Some people get a charge out of others' failures. You can decide to plug into their negativism or unplug yourself from those kinds of people. Tell yourself, "I will succeed no matter what others say" and "I will not allow my aspirations to be someone's exasperation." Avoid the drain influencers whenever and wherever possible. Tell them you will not be able to spend as much time with them because of a project, a craft class—anything that will serve as a suitable replacement to your normal interactions.

If you need to add some piece in order to make life whole, then do it—whether it be attending a club or church to find new relationships, or finding a new job or position, or changing your diet, or putting together a budget or moving—you can start now. If your physical well-being is suffering, exercise just a little longer and maintain a healthy diet and you will be more satisfied with life, as confirmed by a study at the National Institutes of Health.

Also, if you scored highly in one area, don't just be content with maintaining the status quo. We should always build on our strengths and improve our weak areas. Someone who scores 10s in all five areas but only a one in one area will still need to improve the one, but the higher areas will tend to compensate for the lower ones. Still, our goal should be to increase our satisfaction to a seven or above in all areas of life.

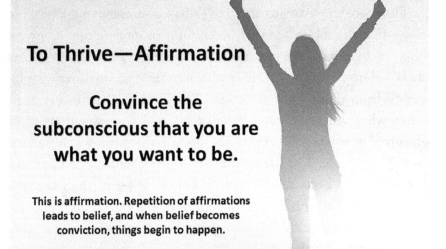

To Thrive—Affirmation

Convince the subconscious that you are what you want to be.

This is affirmation. Repetition of affirmations leads to belief, and when belief becomes conviction, things begin to happen.

In Conclusion

BEING A PACESETTER MEANS that you are in a perpetual state of intentional purpose and growth. This means that you continuously improve, learn from failures and successes, and look forward to your best achievements—as long as you build upon your PACE foundations. The four foundations are PURPOSE, ATTITUDE, CONNECTION and ENERGY. Purpose starts with a P.L.A.N. to be intentional in everything you do. It develops through the process of learning and growing. We can G.R.O.W. our attitude, L.E.A.R.N. to connect through optimal communication, and F.R.E.E. ourselves to stay energized and motivated.

After finding your intentional **purpose**, leading a life of significance, then answering the who/what/why/when/and how of a P.L.A.N. to achieve your purpose can make a big impact. *Learning* to expand your vision can lead to new possibilities. *Analyzing* the details of your plan for making a big impact will rid your purpose of misconceptions, and establish a solid foundation for moving forward. And then you know when your purpose has been fulfilled by objectively determining whether it has *satisfied the needs* of your arbiter and those of yourself.

Our **attitude** unfolds through our commitment to G.R.O.W. The process begins with developing an attitude of *gratitude*. That takes a *renewal* of the mind through the three techniques of *visualization*, *reframing*, and *acting* out something new as though it already exists. *Overcoming* the trials in life happens through the powerful tools of forgiveness, resilience, and optimism. And through life's challenges our growth manifests itself in *wisdom*— the ability to apply the knowledge we've learned productively by way of risk-taking and via seeking the truth.

Underpinning all of our actions is communication, the means by which we **connect**. Its effectiveness is completely dependent on how we L.E.A.R.N. Always, communication begins with *unselfish listening* to understand the other person. Understanding at its core requires *empathy*—being able to walk in the other person's proverbial shoes by learning their behavioral styles, and then *adapting* our style to achieve greater connectedness. We can best *relate* to each other through authenticity, using the connecting emotions, and the effective expression of body language and other signals. Finally, to maximize connectedness, we need to *negotiate* up the pyramid of connection, from guaranteeing the other person's *safety* to demonstrating *mutual support*, *collaboration*, and ultimately achieving a state of *harmony*.

The final achievement factor for the PACEsetter is **energy**, which can be optimized by setting ourselves F.R.E.E. of the drains that can sap us of our motivation. Through *faith*, we can achieve something greater than ourselves, igniting within us the fire of hope, and changing our focus to an everlasting vision of the future. One of the biggest drains on our life comes with the frenetic pace of this world, and the way to counteract this is to *rest*, using the 90/10 Rule to do more with less, focusing on the present, taking breaks and getting still. However, nothing can free us enough to stay motivated unless we *exercise* our body and *eat* right. Studies now confirm how we can increase the motivating power of energy through an exercise and diet plan that is very doable and entirely effective.

So set the PACE, and thrive in this life by addressing all of the foundations in your life that contribute to your well-being and achievement. In the process, others will admire you, just as you have admired other PACEsetters. On your mark, get set, DO IT! You are a *PACEsetter*!

Thank you for sharing this journey ...

The Power to Thrive!

Below are other books by this author which were published in collaboration with TenorCorp and PACEsetters, by the publishing company UpWord Media.

DAILY KEYS TO SUCCESS
Essentials for a Thriving Career and Life

THE 22 MOST IMPORTANT THINGS
For Creating a Thriving Career & Life

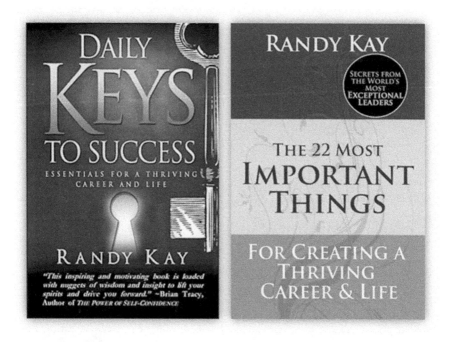

You may order your copies at www.pacesetters.training or through most major book distribution stores and websites.

ACKNOWLEDGMENTS

I AM THANKFUL FOR BEING surrounded by PACEsetters. My father was a World War II hero, and a man who escaped poverty to educate and enable his three children. My mother imparted enough love and support to her entire family to last several generations. My wife is a thriving entrepreneur, strong nurturer of our children, and an amazingly supportive friend and partner in life. Our two children, Ryan and Annie, are PACEsetters in their own right. Ryan is an uncompromising man of integrity who counsels others with wisdom, and Annie is an emerging businesswoman and defender of the underprivileged and downtrodden—she has what we call, "a heart of gold." My in-laws, Ronald and Marilyn Vanderbilt, have helped countless people by welcoming them into their home, besides welcoming me into their loving family. My adopted son, Dr. Jonathan Woolery, escaped abuse to become a healer of broken bodies as a critical care physician. And then there's our adopted family member Florencio (Reid) Bartolome, who overcame poverty and abuse in the Philippines to help others in need.

I've been privileged with many mentors, supporters, friends, and family members. During my career I've known PACEsetters who achieved new heights of success, all with the utmost integrity. A special thanks goes to all those PACEsetters who helped us with our research for this book. They came from all walks of life, and each one impressed our team by demonstrating strengths in the four PACE foundations. To my editor Rob Bignell, and the one who formatted this book, Ellie Searl—you added the finishing touches for which I am very grateful.

I am tremendously grateful for you, my readers, who give me reason to write, and to teach, and to help everyone who wishes to grow as a PACEsetter. I wish you a lifetime of achievement, satisfaction, and joy in helping others!

CREDITS

Alessandra, Tony, PhD and Michael O'Connor, PhD. *People Smart in Business.* Alessandra & Associates, Inc., 2009.

Blanchard, Ken. The Ken Blanchard Companies, Situational Leadership Workshop.

Branden, Nathaniel. *The Psychology of Self-Esteem.* New York: Jossey-Bass, 2001.

Bronson, Po and Ashley Merryman, *NurtureShock.* New York: Hatchett Book Group, 2009.

Carnegie, Dale. *How to Win Friends and Influence People.* Pocket Books, Paperback Special Anniversary Edition, 1998.

Cialdini, Robert, PhD. *Influence: The Psychology of Persuasion.* Collins Business Essentials, 2007

Carter, Sherrie Bourg. "8 Easy Organizational Tips to Increase Your Productivity at Work." Psychology Today, September 18, 2011.

Collins, Jim. *Good to Great.* New York: HarperCollins, 2001.

Csikszentmihalyi, Mihaly. *Flow: The Psychology of Optimal Experience.* Harper Perennial, 1991.

Diener, Ed and Robert Biswas-Diener, *Happiness*

Dixon, Matthew and Brent Adamson. *The Challenger Sale: Taking Control of the Customer Conversation.* Portfolio Hardcover, 2011.

ExecuRead. "Speed Reading Facts." http://www.execuread.com/facts/facts.

Ferriss, Timothy. *The 4-Hour Workweek: Escape 9-5, Live Anywhere, and Join the New Rich.* Harmony, 2009.

Frederickson, Barbara L., Ph.D., *Happiness Is Contagious Positivity*

Freeman, John. *The Tyranny of E-Mail.* New York: Scribner, 2009.

Gladwell, Malcolm. *The Tipping Point: How Little Things Can Make a Big Difference.* Bay Back Books, 2002.

Goleman, Daniel. *Emotional Intelligence: Why It Can Matter More Than IQ.* Bantam, 2006.

Hawkins, Jeff. "Voices of Innovation." Bloomberg Businessweek. http://www.businessweek.com/magazine/content/04_41/b3903463.html.

Hersey, Paul, PhD. The Situational Leader. Center for Leadership Studies, 1997.

Kahneman, Daniel. *Thinking Fast and Slow.* Farrar, Straus and Giroux, 2011.

Kantrowitz, Barbara, and Karen Springen. "What Dreams Are Made Of." Newsweek, August 9, 2004.

Kawasaki, Guy. *The Art of the Start.* Portfolio, 2004.

Kelly, Tom. *The Art of Innovation.* New York: Doubleday, 2001.

Lyubormirsky, Sonja, *The How of Happiness*

MacKay, Harvey. *Swim with the Sharks without Being Eaten Alive.* Collins Business, 2005.

Maxwell, John. *Failing Forward.* Thomas Nelson; Reprint Edition, 2007.

MindTools. "Get Started With Mind Tools." http://www.mindtools.com/pages/article/get-started.htm#.

Nightingale, Earl. *Think and Grow Rich.* Brilliance Audio, 2011.

Peck, M. Scott. *The Road Less Traveled: A New Psychology of Love, Traditional Values, and Spiritual Growth.* Touchstone, 2003.

Robbins, Anthony. *Awaken the Giant Within.* New York: Free Press, 1991.

Simmons, Annette. *The Story Factor: Inspiration, Influence, and Persuasion through the Art of Storytelling.* Basic Books, 2006.

Thomas, Kenneth and Ralph Kilmann. *Thomas-Kilmann Conflict Mode Instrument.* CPP, Inc., 2002.

Tracy, Brian. *The Power of Self-Confidence: Become Unstoppable, Irresistible, and Unafraid in Every Area of Your Life.* Wiley, 2012.

Walton, Sam. *Made in America—My Story.* Bantam Books, 1993.

Watkins, Michael. *The First 90 Days: Critical Success Strategies for New Leaders at All Levels.* Harvard Business School Press, 2003.

Ziglar, Zig. *Secrets of Closing the Sale.* Felming H. Revell, 2006.

Zook, Chris. *Beyond the Core: Expand Your Market Without Abandoning Your Roots.* Harvard Business School Press, 2004.

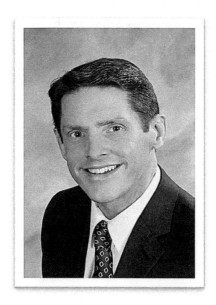

About the Author

R ANDY KAY IS A BUSINESS leader, entrepreneur, trainer, speaker, author and coach who as an executive and advisor to start-ups and several Fortune 500 companies has contributed to the success of thousands of top performers. He is also the author of *Daily Keys to Success*, a compendium of 366 success factors. His numerous promotions and attainment of the highest accolades within each of the organizations in which Kay has participated speak to his career success, while his leadership in charitable organizations and strong family life give voice to Kay's personal success.

As Chief Executive Officer of the strategic development and human resources company, TenorCorp, Kay counsels and supports market leading organizations all over the world. Formally, Kay has been a CEO of three companies, including a biotech, an executive with companies such as Johnson & Johnson, and a board member for more than 20 different organizations. He has lectured at several companies and teaching institutions such as at his alma mater, Northwestern University, as well as at several religious institutions following his ordination as a minister. Kay's writings and teaching are changing the way professionals and contributors of all kinds define and work toward success.

Find out more at www.pacesetters.training.

THANKS FOR READING *The Power to Thrive!*

CPSIA information can be obtained
at www.ICGtesting.com
Printed in the USA
BVHW041353140122
626197BV00009B/148